Cities and Stability

Cities and Stability

Urbanization, Redistribution, and Regime Survival in China

JEREMY L. WALLACE

OXFORD
UNIVERSITY PRESS

OXFORD
UNIVERSITY PRESS

Oxford University Press is a department of the University of Oxford.
It furthers the University's objective of excellence in research, scholarship,
and education by publishing worldwide.

Oxford   New York
Auckland   Cape Town   Dar es Salaam   Hong Kong   Karachi
Kuala Lumpur   Madrid   Melbourne   Mexico City   Nairobi
New Delhi   Shanghai   Taipei   Toronto

With offices in
Argentina   Austria   Brazil   Chile   Czech Republic   France   Greece
Guatemala   Hungary   Italy   Japan   Poland   Portugal   Singapore
South Korea   Switzerland   Thailand   Turkey   Ukraine   Vietnam

Oxford is a registered trademark of Oxford University Press
in the UK and certain other countries.

Published in the United States of America by
Oxford University Press
198 Madison Avenue, New York, NY 10016

© Oxford University Press 2014

Library of Congress Cataloging-in-Publication Data
Wallace, Jeremy L.
Cities and stability : urbanization, redistribution, & regime survival in China / Jeremy L. Wallace.
pages cm
Includes bibliographical references.
ISBN 978-0-19-937898-2 (hardback : alk. paper)—ISBN 978-0-19-937899-9 (pbk. : alk. paper)
1. Cities and towns—China.   2. Urbanization—China.   3. Rural-urban migration—Government
policy—China.   4. Recording and registration—Government policy—China.   I. Title.
HT147.C48W355 2014
307.760951—dc23
2013049366

"人聚于乡而治，聚于城而乱。"
顾炎武 的著作《日知录·人聚》

When the masses dwell in villages, order prevails; when the masses flock to the cities, disorder ensues.
—Gu Yanwu (1613–1682), *Record of Daily Study*

The larger the area which a constant number of inhabitants occupy, the more difficult it is to revolt; because it is impossible to take concerted action quickly or in secret, and it is always easy for the Government to get wind of plans and to cut communications: but the closer together a numerous people draws, the less can the Government usurp from the Sovereign [i.e., the people]; chiefs deliberate as securely in their chambers as the Prince does in his council, and the crowd assembles as quickly in public squares as troops do in their barracks. In this respect great distances are therefore to a tyrannical Government's advantage. With the help of the support groups [*points d'appui*] which it sets up, its force increases with distance, like that of levers. By contrast, the people's force acts only when concentrated, it evaporates and is lost as it spreads, like the effect of gunpowder scattered on the ground and which ignites only grain by grain.
—Rousseau, Social Contract, *book, 3, chapter 8*

CONTENTS

LIST OF ILLUSTRATIONS

Tables

Figures

Box

ACKNOWLEDGMENTS

Many individuals and institutions have helped me along the way of writing this book. I wish to thank them all and apologize those not named below.

This book began during my time as a PhD student at Stanford University and was supported there through grants and fellowships from Stanford's Asia-Pacific Research Center and Department of Political Science. During my first quarter at Stanford, Alberto Diaz-Cayeros helped open my eyes to the utility of following the money in politics. Jean Oi, my dissertation chair, gave me helpful comments on innumerable drafts, pushed me toward this doable and exciting project and away from others that had neither characteristic, and introduced me to field work in China. Her judgments consistently pointed me in the right direction. Jim Fearon and David Laitin made me think more deeply about my claims, both their details and broader implications. Discussions with each of them have improved the work immensely. Beatriz Magaloni served on my committee and spurred me to think more carefully about the connections between the pieces of the argument. I would also like to thank Josh Cohen, Steph Haggard, Allen Hicken, Pierre Landry, Isabela Mares, Michael McFaul, Jonathan Rodden, Scott Rozelle, Andrew Walder, and Jeremy Weinstein for helpful suggestions along the way.

I was lucky to be part of an excellent cohort of graduate students, many of whom waited patiently over the years commenting as course papers became a prospectus that evolved into chapters and so on. In particular, I want to thank Claire Adida, Sarah Anderson, Yuen Yuen Ang, Dan Butler, Matthew Carnes, Martin Dimitrov, Jesse Driscoll, Desha Girod, Nahomi Ichino, Kimuli Kasara, Alex Kuo, Charlotte Lee, Matt Levendusky, Neil Malhotra, Yotam Margalit, Kay Shimizu, and Jessica Weeks.

My field work was productive in large part due to the assistance of friends and colleagues from the United States and China. My research assistants helped me compile data, understand regional accents, and improve my understanding of China greatly. The community of graduate students in Beijing was helpful in staying connected to political science and in making connections in China. Greg Distelhorst, Chad Futrell, Jihyeon Jeong, Andrew MacDonald, and Rachel Stern were responsible for a great part of my many great times in China.

My colleagues at the Ohio State University have helped the work develop as a dissertation about regime survival and cities became increasingly relevant as China along with the rest of the world endured the Great Recession of the late 2000s and the protests in Tunis and Cairo leading to the Arab Spring in 2011. In particular, I would like to thank Tony Mughan, Marcus Kurtz, Sarah Brooks, Irfan Nooruddin, Philipp Rehm, Sara Watson, Michael Neblo, William Minozzi, and Eric MacGilvray for their comments, questions, and advice. Both Ohio State's Mershon Center and Institute for Population Research (which is supported by the National Institutes of Health under award R24HD058484) supported my work, intellectually and financially. Sean Escoffery, Joshua Wu, Xiaoyu Pu, and Ethan Rodriguez-Torrent all provided excellent research assistance.

I have finished the book while serving as a Fellow at the MacMillan Center for International and Area Studies and the Council on East Asian Studies at Yale University. I have benefitted from the thoughtful comments from colleagues at Yale and at other universities where I had the privilege of presenting pieces of the book. Special thanks to Tariq Thachil, Susan Hyde, Jason Lyall, Ellie Powell, Stathis Kalyvas, James Scott, Susan Shirk, Lei Guang, Barry Naughton, Thomas Pepinsky, Dali Yang, Melanie Manion, Lisa Blaydes, Victor Shih, and Eddy Malesky.

The editors at OUP have made every step of this process transparent and smooth. In particular, David McBride at OUP expressed interest in the contents of this book years before the manuscript arrived at his desk and provided excellent comments once it finally did.

Finally, I would like to thank Jessica Weiss, whose presence beside me on this path made the work and the years indescribably better. It is to her that I dedicate this book.

CHAPTER 1

Introduction

Jasmine Revolutions, Failed and Successful

Perceptions of the durability of nondemocratic regimes took a severe hit in 2011 with the ousting of long-time dictators in Tunisia and Egypt. Ben Ali of Tunisia was pressed out of office following protests in the streets of Tunis, the capital. A lack of economic opportunities and increasing food prices were the timber upon which an isolated incident exploded into a conflagration that brought down the regime. The spark was the self-immolation of a young unemployed university graduate, Mohamed Bouazizi, in Sidi Bouzid, a small city in the interior of the country, after local officials and police punished him for selling vegetables on the street without a permit.[1] This sacrificial act ignited demonstrations in that city that were violently put down by security officers of the regime. Ben Ali replaced the regional governor and promised massive spending to employ university graduates.[2] Despite these concessions, the protests became more deadly, and by 12 January they spread to Tunis. Ben Ali fled the country for Saudi Arabia on 14 January.[3] The Jasmine Revolution had begun.[4]

The downfall of the Mubarak regime in Egypt followed quickly thereafter. Massive demonstrations on 25 January 2011 took over numerous politically significant locales, most prominently Tahrir square in central Cairo. Inspired by the Tunisians' success, citizens frustrated with high levels of unemployment, unfair elections, crumbling infrastructure, corruption, state violence, and an aging dictator angling to replace himself with his son Gamal—who epitomized

---

[1] "Q&A: Tunisia Crisis" 2011.

[2] Voice of America 2011.

[3] Al Jazeera 2011.

[4] The name "Jasmine Revolution" comes in the tradition of naming revolutions for colors and flowers: Carnation Revolution (Portugal, 1974), Rose Revolution (Georgia, 2003), Orange Revolution (Ukraine, 2004), Tulip Revolution (Kyrgyzstan, 2005), Green Revolution (Iran, 2009), with the Jasmine flower having some political resonance in Tunisia (Frangeul 2011).

the regime's corruption—marched *en masse* and took over the central square.[5] The army refused to open fire on the crowds, which remained in Tahrir until Mubarak stepped down on 11 February.[6]

The contrast with the situation in Beijing and other Chinese cities could not have been greater. There were no massive protests expressing outrage at the rule of the Chinese Communist Party (CCP) in Beijing or in other major metropolises. Activists did attempt to use the demonstrations in North Africa to call attention to problems of governance and freedom in China, but only by using much safer methods. Concerned with being identified by the regime as "against the Party," the suggestion was made that those so moved should "stroll (*sanbu*)" through plazas in thirteen different Chinese cities on Sundays.[7] Notably, Tiananmen Square was not the chosen location for Beijing, despite—or perhaps because of—its status as the center of the last protest movement that seriously threatened the regime in 1989.[8] The regime quickly detained some activists, put into place Internet controls that reduced the ability of "netizens" to search for terms related to "strolling" and "Sunday," and curtailed the activities of reporters.[9] Within a few weeks, restrictions were lifted.

What differentiated China from Tunisia or Egypt? Why has the CCP regime endured while other seemingly durable regimes collapsed? Scholars have pointed to a number of different factors that affect regime survival—including the identity of the leader or the presence of a legislature or other political institution. Yet less attention has been paid to the influence of geography. The distribution of resources and population throughout a country has powerful effects on the survival of nondemocratic regimes.

Three Puzzles

Three puzzles lie at the heart of this book: the longevity of CCP rule, China's relative lack of slums, and China's recent moves away from "urban bias." Resolving these puzzles improves our understandings of the Chinese regime and its political economy as well as of authoritarian regimes.

In many ways, the oustings of Ben Ali and Mubarak follow a classic model of the origins of political difficulty in nondemocracies. The danger that large cities,

---

[5] Masoud 2011; Lynch 2012.

[6] Lynch 2012, 92.

[7] 博讯新闻 2011; Human Rights in China 2011.

[8] Beijing's location for strolling was the Wangfujing commercial/retail area, which then US Ambassador Jon Huntsman "happened" to be visiting at the appointed hour on Sunday, 20 February (Page 2011).

[9] Dickson 2011.

especially capitals, pose to regimes is an old story.[10] Cities bring together masses of people, improve communication links among them, and increase the ability of private grievances to accumulate and circulate. Cities are particularly prone to disruptions via barricades, transforming key nodes in the transportation network into strongholds for resistors. Governments have reshaped the geography of their capitals in response. The wide boulevards of L'Enfant's Washington, DC, Haussmann's Paris, or modern Beijing allow the military to bring its capacity for violence to bear in ways that would be impossible with the narrow twisting alleyways of the old city, negating some of the advantages cities provide to the conventionally weak side in asymmetric warfare. In addition to this practical advantage, the long open lines also symbolically reflect the power of the center.[11] Despite these innovations, the regimes of Egypt's Sadat, Sudan's Nimeiri, Kenya's Moi, Nigeria's Gowon, and Liberia's Tolbert all faced pressures during the 1970s from urban residents due to food price escalation, and arguably all save the Moi regime fell to massive protests and elite splits brought on by such protests.[12] In the winter of 2011, China, too, faced high food prices, yet a Jasmine-style revolution failed to materialize. The Chinese regime has endured not only this recent wave of regime turnovers but also outlived its European Communist brethren when they all fell from 1989 to 1991 and persisted through protests numbering in the tens of thousands every year.[13] What accounts for the CCP's durability?

Across the developing world, cities are filled with migrants hoping to grab a piece of the modern life afforded to some in the capital. The urban poor, migrant and non-migrant alike, are often shunted off into slums full of like-minded compatriots hoping to strike it rich or at least improve their lot in the big city. China has avoided the growth of such slums, especially in its largest cities. To be sure, desperately poor workers live in the megacities of China. They construct the skyscrapers and the roads, keep them clean, and cook and deliver the city's food. But many of these poor migrants are "housed"—an overly generous word given the minimal accommodations often provided—at their work sites and kept on a short leash. The giant improvised communities found at the heart of other cities in developing countries are not to be found in China.[14] Despite massive

[10] Zipf 1941, 1949; Hobsbawm 1973; Tilly 1978. It should be noted that demonstrations did not begin in Tunis but in a smaller interior city. The large protests in the capital, however, were instrumental in the regime's downfall.

[11] Mumford 1961; Scott 1998.

[12] Bates 1981. Tolbert was killed in a coup in 1980 following the 1979 Rice Riots. Gowon was ousted while out of the country following student and labor demonstrations in 1975. Sadat was killed in 1981 after the 1977 Bread Riots and general political unpopularity. Nimeiri was ousted in 1971 by a Communist coup (before coming back to power later that same year).

[13] In 2005, officials stated that 87,000 mass incidents had occurred in China. Subsequent unofficial estimates range from 180,000 to 230,000 for 2009 and 2010 (Göbel and Ong 2012, 22).

[14] Solinger 1999b; Miller 2012, 19.

urbanization, industrialization, and economic growth, why are Chinese cities not plagued by the slums present in most of the developing world?

Keeping urban residents fed well enough with cheap bread, rice, porridge, or noodles to alleviate their hunger and anger is the basic politics of authoritarian regimes and has been so for centuries. Juvenal believed the Roman masses were sated by the state's provision of "bread and circuses."[15] In the main, only those in cities are able to partake of the state's generosity in this way. Rural residents are not only left to fend for themselves but also are often the very source of funds that pay for the state's largesse to city dwellers. These policies reflect an urban bias in policy making—buying off urbanites with proceeds from rural taxes. Such bias is endemic to the developing world.[16] Yet here, too, China is anomalous. Since the turn of the millennium, the regime has reduced urban bias and directed more resources to those who remain in the countryside. Why has China shifted away from urban bias?

Understanding Cities, Spending, and Survival

The argument of this book links autocratic regime survival with urbanization and redistribution, both within China and cross-nationally. Three motivating puzzles—the CCP's longevity, China's relative lack of slums, and China's move away from urban bias—that at first appear to be unconnected can be tied together. What links these factors is geography. People's locations and proximity to each other matter politically.[17] China's relative lack of slums arises from policies that prevent people from moving to them. Political decisions can keep people in one place rather than another. Similarly, different political decisions can lead people to move elsewhere. Taxing the products of one place and spending the proceeds in another encourages migration from the former to the latter. The political importance of the location of citizens within a territory is less appreciated. Without other sizable cities to offset its weight, the street politics of a single large city can come to dominate a country's politics in ways that yield short-lived regimes. A large population, particularly in the vicinity of the center of power or industry, can mobilize or threaten to do so at a moment's notice. These mobilizations or threats create the opportunity for political crises to bring down a regime with little warning. The policies of redistribution and urbanization intimately

---

[15] Juvenal 1999. Green's translation prefers "the Games" to circuses.

[16] Lipton 1977; Bates 1981.

[17] Geographers refer to "Tobler's First Law of Geography" to make this point: "Everything is related to everything else, but near things are more related than distant things" (Tobler 1970).

shape cities, and the shape of cities can transform the politics of urban and regime instability.

Rulers of poor countries realize that economic development is critical to improve the lives of their people and to sustain their reign. In most poor countries, development is equated with industrialization. Prior to industrialization, agriculture dominates the economy. Regimes have little choice but to extract from agriculture to finance the factories that fuel the growth of an industrial sector. From there, concerns about protests often dictate keeping workers fed as cheaply as possible. Such bias makes sense in the short run. For leaders who are humble and prescient enough to see that the short run is all that they can afford to plan for, urban bias makes for compelling politics. However, such urban favoritism is self-undermining for regimes. Urban bias does not just feed the city dwellers by taxing farmers. It also encourages farmers to become city-dwellers, exacerbating the potential for, and scale of, urban unrest should events go south.

Urban residents enjoy an advantage in collective action due to their proximity to each other and the seat of government. Because urbanites pose a more immediate threat to regime stability, self-serving regimes tend to adopt redistributive policies that favor city residents to reduce grievances and the likelihood of destabilizing protests in these key locales.[18] Such policies aim to maintain regime stability by taking from those who are relatively weak—rural farmers—and transferring resources to those who are relatively strong—urban dwellers.

I argue that urban bias induces urban concentration, a second-order effect that in the long-term undermines its intended purpose of aiding regime stability. By taxing the countryside and dispersing the proceeds to urban residents, governments induce farmers to leave agriculture and move to cities where they can enjoy the benefits of urban-biased policies. Farmers respond to incentives and are not fixed in the periphery—they can vote with their feet and exit the countryside. In the long run, urban favoritism is self-defeating because it induces rural migration to urban centers, increases the burden on city resources, and magnifies the threat of urban collective action, thereby undermining its original rationale of pacifying cities by reducing urban grievances.

Taxing the countryside and spreading the spoils in cities is not neutral with respect to urbanization. The policy of urban bias is meant to stabilize cities. This may be accomplished in the short term, but over time cities will grow, particularly the largest cities as they will be targeted with benefits and so make the most attractive destination for migrants. Although urbanization promotes development, the long-run effect of urban concentration is to undermine the survival of authoritarian regimes.

---

[18] Bates 1981; Ades and Glaeser 1995.

Nondemocratic regimes mitigate the threat of urban collective action not only with subsidies but also through coercion. In addition to policing, regimes curb the growth of their largest cities to maintain an ability to rule over them. Rare but powerful, migration restrictions aim to control the size and demographic makeup of critical urban areas, whether through internal passports such as the Chinese *hukou* and Soviet *propiska* systems or aggressive slum clearance policies.[19]

The Chinese regime has managed its urbanization to reduce the chances of threats emanating from cities. Despite a long history of rural peasant revolution in China and the CCP's own rural origins, the Chinese regime feared urban instability more than similar activity in the countryside and engaged in urban bias, tilting policy toward cities to reduce urban grievances. Even from the earliest days of its rule, the CCP feared waves of rural migrants overwhelming favored cities and endeavored to keep farmers in the countryside. Pro-growth market reforms allowed farmers to relocate and operate China's factories, yet the regime continued to fear the consequences of free movement, employing fiscal as well as migration policies to shape China's urban landscape.

Early in its tenure, the CCP enacted a series of policies to restrict free migration around the country and to keep farmers at home in the countryside. The household registration (*hukou*) system emerged from the regime's concerns that massive numbers of farmers would attempt to escape agricultural taxes and join the protected urban proletariat. With migration restrictions in place, the Chinese regime was able to extract revenue from farmers by forcing them to sell their grain to the state at low prices. Due to limits on freedom of movement, farmers were unable to escape the yoke of these taxes by moving to the city. By forcing farmers to stay in villages, the regime has restrained the growth of urban slums. Under the planned economy, state bureaucrats allocated not only goods and services, but people as well. As the plan has been eclipsed by market reforms following the political rise of Deng Xiaoping, these migration restrictions have been chipped away by migrants and markets.

With market reforms, the Chinese economy grew but the state's total control of population movement crumbled. China's migration policies created a second-class status for migrants and pushed them to relocate on a temporary rather than permanent basis. While the overall economy continued to flourish, inequality skyrocketed, and the regime continued to fear unchecked urbanization. Old controls on migration were replaced with economic incentives. Rather than using the coercive power of the state to keep farmers in the hinterland, the regime adjusted economic and social policies to make remaining in the countryside more attractive economically. For example, in education, rural schools

[19] F.-L. Wang 2005.

became free while urban schools remained off limits for children of migrants. Many of the make-shift schools for migrants in larger cities were shuttered. In both practical and theoretical terms, these shifts directed resources to the countryside, a move away from urban bias.

After 50 years of policy favoritism toward cities and migration restrictions that kept farmers in the countryside, China has shifted away from urban bias and has begun subsidizing rather than taxing agriculture. This "populist" shift has been portrayed by the government as an effort to combat inequality and to assist those who have not benefited from China's recent economic growth. However, this policy change has an important geographic component, influenced by concerns about rapid and concentrated urbanization. Wen Tiejun, a prominent scholar affiliated with the CCP, has remarked that the promotion of rural subsidies and the delay of land privatization are a response to the government's fear of "Latin Americanization" (*la mei hua*), that is, the emergence of highly unequal megacities with their attendant slums, crime, and social instability.[20]

This new perspective on the politics of urban bias and autocratic stability addresses a number of key questions in the study of comparative politics, comparative political economy, and Chinese politics. Why do some autocracies last for decades and others disappear within their first years of existence? Do economic, demographic, and geographic structures affect authoritarian resilience? Why did the CCP, despite coming to power in large part due to the support of the peasants, turn its back on those same peasants less than a decade after taking power? Do regimes bias policy toward urban areas for stability reasons? Within China, do the origins of the *hukou* system—which effectively constrained migration within the country—line up with concerns over urbanization and redistribution? Is there evidence of regimes with long time horizons moving away from urban bias?

Research Design

To answer these questions, I use data from cross-national and Chinese sources. In so doing, I reassess the politics of urban-rural redistribution in nondemocratic states and show that urban-biased policies represent a Faustian bargain for authoritarian regimes. Subsidizing cities with farmer-paid taxes pacifies the urban population in the short run, but it amplifies the risk of instability in the long run by inflating the size of the largest and most politically salient cities.

The first task is to establish the argument's plausibility using cross-national data on authoritarian survival and urban bias. As the CCP regime endures,

---

[20] T. Wen 2006.

analyzing China alone would preclude confirming the argument's claims about collapse. Regimes with large cities that dominate the urban landscape fail faster than do their counterparts with less concentrated city systems. Urban bias reduces urban grievances but also induces greater concentration of the population in favored cities, solidifying regimes in the short run but undercutting them over time.

Having established that the life-cycle patterns of regimes are consistent with the argument, I delve into a careful single-country study of the CCP-led People's Republic of China to examine the argument's mechanisms. Connecting the general claims to the densely multilayered complexities of actual governance requires confronting a nation-state in more depth. Observing the effects of such changes in one case is more telling than contrasting different policies in different places yielding different outcomes.[21] This book traces the policy and political history of the CCP regime at both national and sub-national levels to inquire into the claims of the theory that cannot be adequately addressed at the cross-national level. National level narratives are paired with sub-national statistical analyses; plumbing variation over time and across Chinese localities shows how the regime managed urbanization for political ends through its *hukou* system and redistributive policy. Such analyses also serve to ground the theory in a place to ensure that the cross-national findings point to causal factors and not inconsequential correlations arising out of the noise of the thousands of data points.

Building on the insights gleaned from the particular politics of China, I then return to the cross-national arena to investigate if other regimes operate in ways similar to the CCP. If urban bias is a Faustian Bargain, then under what circumstances are regimes willing to make a deal with the devil? The Chinese regime tilted policies to the benefit of city dwellers but has gradually shifted away as its time horizons lengthened and its coffers filled. Using evidence of external economic and political pressures facing such regimes, I show that in times of crisis, regimes do revert to urban bias as a form of political triage. When times are tough, regimes support cities.

The research design moves between broad cross-national analyses and the specific details of the Chinese case, attempting to improve general theory using Chinese data rather than merely finding general arguments inadequate to account for the complex landscape of Chinese politics.

As China was the source of the anomalies that led to the development of the general argument about urban concentration, investigating China's policies and the politics behind them is a natural choice. It is a long-lived regime. Its

---

[21] The analogous situation in large-N research is the preference for fixed-effects models over between-effects models in work assessing policies that act over time.

economic development, redistributive, and urbanization policies have changed over time. Given China's large size, it is also possible to use internal variation to assess different policies and their effects. Finally, China is an important case to consider as it is both the world's most populous country and second largest economy as well as a regime that others learn from or mimic. Although the general argument focuses on threats to regime survival, understanding the politics of a regime that has successfully managed these threats is as important as analyzing those that have failed. Examining only regimes that fail when considering threats to regimes is akin to studying the emergence of civil wars and only looking at locations with civil wars rather than comparing those cases with other cases where civil wars were avoided.

The CCP is one of the world's longest lasting authoritarian regimes. Many have put forward arguments for why it has endured.[22] I argue that the regime's longevity is partly due to its management of urbanization. The CCP, despite its rhetorical emphasis on supporting the peasantry, has been extremely urban-biased in its policy making. As populations flowed into cities, inducing urbanization and concentration, the regime—rather than reap the consequences of the Faustian bargain—instituted migration restrictions as a loophole to avoid these consequences. These restrictions became shackles that prevented economic development during the reform era, and with their relaxation came China's characteristic spread out urbanization. Later, as the regime's revenues and prospects soared, it moved away from urban bias to spread development around the country and the countryside.

The language of the general argument is one of a generic regime that is attempting to respond to real and perceived threats with policy tools at its disposal and in its choice set. This is not wrong but is obviously not specific. When moving to the examination of a particular regime, more needs to be said about its nature.

The nature of the Chinese regime is in the eye of the beholder. An ideological and revolutionary party at its founding has transformed itself into a technocratic machine focused on stability. I argue that the CCP regime made a distinctive switch in its core practices during the transition from the Maoist planned era to the post-Mao Reform Era. In the former, ideological motivations were primary, while economic development dominated the latter, along with strong central attempts to depoliticize the regime's governance. At the local level, the policies and politics of China reflect a reproduction of central dictates buttressed by personal accumulation strategies through graft or other means. In particular, the central regime, pursuing its own survival, puts forward local policies to be

[22] Heilmann and Perry 2011. Among others: Yang 2001, 2004b; Shue 2002; Perry 2002, 2008; Gallagher 2005; Cai and Treisman 2006; C. K. Lee 2007.

implemented by local officials who individually have little capacity to affect the regime's survival probabilities. Yet rather than see this limited ability as a license to steal, most local leaders interpret central dictates in ways as best they can, when such actions can be taken without undermining their own personal income streams. For instance, regarding the major issue of protecting social stability and harmony, there is little that the party secretary or county head of Zouping County in Shandong province—or any county leader—can do to alter the probability of the regime collapsing. But local leaders act to attack those measurable evils that can be categorized as social instability—crime, complaints, and the like. They do so since the central regime leadership in Beijing has been effective in instituting a system that rewards promotions on the basis of adaptation of central dictates and local triumphs.

This view builds on two prominent arguments for the regime's political success. Those arguments respectively place, first, its adaptive governance strategies and, second, its flexibility in pairing at the fore a central leadership primarily concerned with legitimation and a local leadership principally concerned with wealth accumulation.[23] The country's size and socioeconomic diversity make it a laboratory. Issues will inevitably arise, and, rather than imposing stark centrally defined policies, the regime is nimble and willing to allow policies to be adapted to local circumstances. The regime often even goes further and tests potential policies in different locations before rolling them out nationwide. One can see the *hukou* system along these lines. While associated with historical examples in China, the migration restrictions of the *hukou* system are fundamentally a response to the unintended consequences of other economic policies. Proponents of this line of thinking argue that the adaptability and empiricism of the regime have allowed it to thrive. Yet the impetus for local experimentation is not always to the good of the regime. As many argue, more venal concerns often enter. The center willingly allows local party-states autonomy to pursue economically productive and personally enriching policies as long as they exist within and not in opposition to broad central dictates.

Policies regarding migration and urbanization exemplify the consistencies and conflicts between central and local interests. As further explored in chapter 4, in the late 1990s, an experimental *hukou* reform took place at the local level with some surprising results. The goal of the reform was to relax restrictions, yet in areas under provincial capitals, population growth slowed down rather than sped up. That is, in contrast to basic principal-agent model assumptions where better monitoring will lead to outcomes more closely in line with the principal's desires, in those more observed areas, the opposite occurred. Only in outlying areas did the policy have the expected effect. Provincial elites may

[23] C. K. Lee 2007; Perry 2008; Heilmann and Perry 2011.

promote economic growth but limit urban in-migration to provincial capitals to decrease the risk of social instability in their home base of operations. In prominent areas, everything is more observable, making instability in these cores more dangerous. Economic activities, on the other hand, count equally wherever in a territory they take place. Judged on both growth and stability concurrently, local leaders are more willing to stimulate growth and risk instability out of sight in peripheral areas. The differential political importance of large cities and their peripheries operates both at the national and sub-national level.

Structure of the Book

The book addresses questions about the stability of autocratic regimes, the political logic of urban bias, and China's management of urbanization. It is organized into three sections. The first section (chapters 2 and 3) presents the argument and examines it cross-nationally. To elucidate the mechanisms at work in the cross-national data, the second section of the book (chapters 4, 5, and 6) delves into an analysis of China based on quantitative and qualitative data collected during 16 months of field work. The final section (chapters 7 and 8) returns to a broad comparative perspective to address questions and assess implications from the Chinese case.

The second chapter develops the argument. I build on the insights of modern political economy on authoritarian regime survival and redistributive politics, adding a critical element to their analyses: geography. Classic works of political science disagree in their assessments of the location and nature of political danger to regimes in the developing world. Dispersed rural populations may be easier to rule but without urbanization and industrialization, development will not take place. What are the political and economic pressures that regimes face along the urban–rural axis? What is the danger in having a large capital city for a nondemocratic regime?

The third chapter examines the survival patterns of authoritarian regimes after World War II, showing how cities are dangerous. Simple attempts to buy off urbanites temporarily sustain but ultimately undermine regimes. Urban concentration and collective action are connected; where largest cities are more dominant one sees more instances of collective action. Data from 435 nondemocratic regimes in over one hundred countries confirm the *danger of concentration hypothesis*, the *induced concentration hypothesis*, and the *Faustian bargain hypothesis*. Regimes with high levels of urban concentration last on average only two-thirds as long as do regimes characterized by low levels of urban concentration. Urban bias induces more people to take up residence in the nation's largest city, confirming results from economics using different data. Finally, inducing urban concentration—the second-order effect of urban bias—dominates its countervailing direct effect of placating potential protestors when analyzed together, confirming the Faustian bargain hypothesis. Dominant cities can be stabilized by urban bias today but can grow to be overwhelming and undermine regime survival if not held in check. These findings are robust across numerous specifications, the inclusion of control variables, and for subsets of the data.

Chapters 4, 5, and 6 turn to China. The chapters present multilevel analyses, examining both national and local policy and political decisions. Building on and indebted to established literatures, I trace national level changes to account for the political factors behind the origins of China's *hukou* system, the regime's shift away from urban bias, and its response to the Great Recession. In addition, I use sub-national variation to test the implications of the argument at lower levels, since provincial leaders are incentivized, particularly by the promotion system, to reproduce national level priorities in their own domains.

The fourth chapter demonstrates that the Chinese government's policies toward rural areas are critically shaped by their implications for the shape of urbanization. The narrative focuses on the political turns that led to the development of China's *hukou* system as well as its use as a method of restricting internal migration. These internal barriers allowed the regime to escape the Faustian bargain of urban bias. Urban workers were subsidized using funds raised from the countryside, while farmers were forced to toil in their fields without the freedom to move to cities. The relaxation of the *hukou* system during the reform era illustrates the government's continuing concern about the politically destabilizing consequences of urban concentration and unchecked migration. Although the government has promoted urbanization, its policies have favored the growth of small and medium cities and restricted movement to China's first-tier cities. This pattern is also apparent at the sub-provincial level. Using new data on local experiments in the late 1990s, I show that the relaxation of *hukou* policies across ten pilot provinces led to faster population growth in peripheral areas yet had no or even negative effects in politically sensitive provincial capitals.

Since the central government's fiscal resources stabilized in the late 1990s, the Chinese regime has reduced its redistributive policy's previous urban favoritism by directing resources to the rural interior. In the fifth chapter, I describe the center's fiscal shift away from urban bias—the replacing of fees and taxes on agriculture with subsidies for farmers. Analyses of sub-national budgets and fiscal transfers show that the CCP has used fiscal policy to maintain stability and manage urbanization. Since the national level campaign to "Develop the West" began in the 1990s, the Chinese government has pursued regional development policies, assisting areas that had not benefited from the reforms. How have the center's concerns about urbanization affected local officials? How are central directives implemented by lower levels of government? Combining cross-sectional time series data on social stability, geography, budgets, and migration for the vast majority of China's nearly 3,000 county level units, I show that the location of a county—that is its proximity to relatively unstable urban areas—affects the amount of transfers that it receives from higher levels. In particular, *ceteris paribus,* counties near unstable cities receive more transfers than those where potential migrants are likely to move to stable cities. This finding corroborates the answers received in interviews, confirming that local officials are able to use the fear of migration to unstable cities as a way to argue for increased transfers from higher levels. This represents an attempt to reduce the incentives of farmers to locate to those unstable areas by improving the situation in their home counties.

The sixth chapter examines China's experience of, and response to, the Great Recession of the late 2000s. The Chinese economy and regime sailed through the swells with little apparent damage. Why did the downturn not generate the political instability that many predicted? I argue that China's success in weathering the storm was partly due to its long-term strategy of managed urbanization and migration along with an economic stimulus. These factors combined to structure, disperse, and reduce discontent generated by the Great Recession. Although the broad strokes of China's response to the crisis—a massive fiscal stimulus plan in November 2008 and massive loans to businesses—are well-established, the geographic distribution of the stimulus funds has received far less attention. The fiscal and financial stimulus packages were directed to different locales. Whereas one might expect the government to have directed all funds to coastal provinces that bore the brunt of the economic downturn, the government instead sent much of its fiscal stimulus investment to interior provinces. Why? I argue that the regime, fearing instability and unrest among newly unemployed migrant workers along the coast, sought to encourage employment in the interior. Along with continued collective ownership of land in the countryside and the *hukou* system, the fiscal stimulus facilitated stability by providing channels for those negatively affected by the crisis to return to the countryside and smaller cities in the interior, dispersing discontent. While the fiscal stimulus continued the regime's pro-rural, pro-interior development policy, at the height of the crisis, the regime also vastly expanded loans to urban industries in contrast to its general move away from urban bias. I support this argument with investment and local government bond statistics, together with personal interviews with Chinese government officials and academic advisors.

Is China's response to a potential crisis atypical? The final section of the book returns to the cross-national level of analysis account for variation in urban bias across nondemocracies. I argue that urban bias has short-term benefits but also long-term costs. At a moment of crisis when short-term incentives dominated more distant concerns, the Chinese regime did open the floodgates to urban loans in support of urban employment. Do other regimes retreat to urban bias in tough times? The seventh chapter addresses this question. I exploit external events that affect regimes' revenues and political stability to examine changes in redistributive policy. Negative economic and political shocks lead to redistributive policies that are more urban-biased, akin to political triage as governments attempt to maintain a baseline of support. For importers, global oil price increases represent a drain on resources; similarly, civil wars erupting in neighboring countries can affect political stability at home and shorten time horizons. Consistent with the general argument, when pressures mount, nondemocratic regimes direct resources to those with the greatest capacity to act collectively against the regime, namely urban residents, and increase urban bias.

The book concludes with discussion of China's political and economic future. The CCP is in the midst of shifting its bases of support away from the poor to the rich elite, transforming itself from a left-wing nondemocratic regime to a right-wing dictatorship right in front of our—and its citizens'—eyes. How will the regime change now that most of its population is urban? Do the political advantages of urban concentration for potential revolutionaries remain in an era when technology has made information dissemination instantaneous and in ways that shrink geographic distances?

2

Urban Bias

A FAUSTIAN BARGAIN

Public security officials concentrate their efforts much more in the cities, where dissident thought can have much greater impact and dissident groups can cause much greater damage than in rural areas. The thoughts of urban cadres, intellectuals, and especially those responsible for the written word are taken much more seriously than the dissident behavior of peasants far from the center of power.

—Ezra Vogel, *"Preserving Order in the Cities"*[1]

Nondemocratic regimes are often treated as a residual category, as the term itself makes clear. Countries not living under democratic rule mostly have been examined with questions of when they will democratize at the forefront. While regime type has fundamental political importance and should be studied, a core motivation for this book comes from a belief in the importance of understanding the fall of authoritarian regimes and not only of authoritarianism itself. Knowing why some authoritarian regimes, like China's, endure and others collapse is necessary to understanding their internal and external politics and requires analyzing the threats that they face.

Telling a tale of survival is difficult because survival, like other forms of success, has many fathers. When analyzing a failed regime, there is a moment of failure, and a narrative of its sources can be traced out. One can look for underlying origins of regime decay and proximate causes of collapse.[2] On the other hand, regimes that endure simply endure. The aim of this book is to isolate one of the fathers of resilience—China's management of urbanization—by highlighting the significance of urban concentration and protest in the collapse of other

[1] Vogel 1971, 80.
[2] Kalyvas 1999.

nondemocratic regimes and trace the policies and politics of the CCP leadership's control of where and how its people live and work.

While this book studies China's long-lived CCP regime, it is not solely a study of China. Political science and comparative politics spend significant intellectual effort in isolating pieces of what may amount to general laws of politics that cross cultural and linguistic borders. Iterating between China and cross-national comparisons provides some connections across disparate literatures. The experience of the CCP can help illuminate core theoretical issues in comparative politics: Where are the threats to regimes located? How are policies that attempt to address these threats implemented? How do citizens respond to policy choices?

In this chapter, I build on the ideas presented in the introduction, connecting cities, redistribution, and authoritarian regime survival. The three puzzles that motivate this project—the CCP's longevity, China's relative lack of slums, and the fiscal shift away from urban bias in contemporary China—are intimately linked. However, the political science literature tends to examine these topics in isolation. I build on insights from previous research and integrate them into a common theoretical framework attempting to bridge these divisions.

Urbanization is often found in regressions run by political scientists but is usually seen as a factor to be controlled for rather than theorized about. Since the work on urban bias in the 1980s, the classical divide between town and country has gone relatively unexamined. Eclipsing that line of scholarship, instead, are perspectives condensing political competition into a Marxist class divide between the rich and poor, yielding many insights but omitting other dimensions of politics in the developing world. In addition, political economy scholarship considers tax and spending at the core of its work, but the opacity of nondemocratic regimes makes testing redistributive theories difficult as well.

The framework I develop here demonstrates the political significance of second-order effects, the often dreaded unintended consequences of policies. The Chinese regime attempted to industrialize via a Big Push following the Soviet Model in the 1950s. As a consequence, farmers flocked to cities at an unprecedented scale. To prevent this unintended result, the regime restricted rural residents' ability to move to cities. Eventually, these constraints were relaxed because they were seen as holding back economic development. Yet the regime instituted financial incentives for farmers to remain in rural areas and continued to maintain other restrictions as insurance. Regimes respond to threats with policies that can in turn lead to subsequent threats and policy responses. This perpetual motion forces regimes to constantly try to keep their heads above water. In moments of strength, regimes are high enough above the water to gain perspective and consider the consequences of their actions in longer time scales.

Regime survival is affected by political geography, which is in part shaped by state policy. Cities are intimately connected to development and industry but also to danger for dictators. How do cities bring ruin to regimes? How do regimes respond to these threats? Why do leaders tilt policy in their favor nonetheless? How has the Chinese regime navigated these landmines? The chapter continues by answering these questions in turn. First, I detail various channels by which cities threaten nondemocratic regimes. Second, I lay out the responses that regimes use to combat these threats and argue that they can be a Faustian bargain, addressing problems today only but exacting a more serious toll in the end. Third, I describe why regimes are willing to make such a deal with the devil despite the inherent dangers. Finally, I offer an assessment of China's CCP regime and the ways that it has mitigated and avoided these dangers during its long reign.

Large Cities are Dangerous for Nondemocratic Regimes

The threats that cities pose to nondemocratic regimes manifest themselves through different channels. Large cities bring together huge numbers of people in a shared space. This makes effective collective action more likely and reduces the ability of the regime to understand, observe, and govern the population. These mechanisms connect large cities with the collapse of nondemocratic regimes. Before diving into these mechanisms, first I must clarify what I mean by the terms "nondemocratic regimes" and "large cities."

NONDEMOCRATIC REGIMES

Social scientists have spent a great deal of time and effort analyzing the differences and patterns of democratization, the change in regime type from nondemocracy to democracy.[3] As its name demonstrates, nondemocracy was a catchall that contained everything that failed to measure up to a democracy. Frustrated with the lack of progress in the study of democratization, Barbara Geddes argues that different types of nondemocratic regimes might have different politics, different ways of failing, and different likelihoods of transitioning to democracy.[4] The regime as the unit of analysis broke with the prior study which took the country-year and levels of democracy as its focus. This change allowed scholars to think about the leaders of nondemocracies and the challenges that they faced.

---

[3] The lack of a single term for a transition from democracy to nondemocracy, a reversal of democratization, points to the general sense—or indeed hope—of scholars that democratic transitions were permanent and irreversible.

[4] Geddes 1999a, b. A prior literature on the types of authoritarianism exists, with Linz (2000) at its core, but did not spark the recent conflagration.

Nondemocratic regime survival is not the same as explaining the survival of nondemocracy as the ruling technology in a territory. A king killed in a palace putsch by an ambitious colonel does not contemplate the regime type of the government after his assassination. For the dead king, the continuation of nondemocratic rule in the country provides no measure of success or comfort.[5] Take the CCP's Red army triumph over the KMT Nationalists in 1949, forcing them to flee to Taiwan. This revolution did not reflect a change in China's *regime type*, but as Chiang Kai-shek and his exiled compatriots could have told you, it certainly was a change in *regime*.[6] Regimes care greatly about the possibility of regime change and make efforts to head off threats to their continued rule. Yet, until recently, the dominant focus in political science has not been regimes and their survival but changes in regime type.[7]

The study of nondemocratic regime survival has become a growth industry in the social sciences. Competing typologies of nondemocratic regimes are said to account for variation in the duration of these regimes.[8] Nondemocratic regime types are associated not only with different durations but also different foreign policy behavior, patterns of economic growth, likelihood of democratization, and the fates of leaders after they leave office.[9] Military regimes are particularly short-lived, while single or dominant party regimes endure.[10] Others have pointed to higher levels of institutionalization, such as the presence of elections or legislatures, as abetting authoritarian rule.[11] Legislatures can both tie the dictator's hands and act as arenas of information collection and exchange, aiding economic growth and political survival.[12] This burgeoning literature has shed light on what was obscured by the focus on democratization. This literature has not yet delved into the structural threats that regimes face and their strategic response to those threats.[13] Cities and urban concentration present such a danger and one that regimes attempt to negotiate.

---

[5] Post-tenure fate is something that leaders do consider when making decisions, however (Debs and Goemans 2010).

[6] Clarifying the precise empirical delineations between what is and is not a regime change is left to the next chapter. Following Geddes et al., I define regime as "a set of formal and informal rules for choosing leaders and policies" (Geddes, Wright, and Frantz 2012).

[7] Oddly, one of the few times in comparative politics where the interaction of the masses has led the social science literature over the interactions of the elites.

[8] e.g. Geddes 1999a; Hadenius and Teorell 2007.

[9] Weeks 2008; Debs and Goemans 2010; Gandhi 2008; Wright 2008.

[10] Geddes 1999b; Hadenius and Teorell 2007; Magaloni 2006.

[11] Lust-Okar 2005, 2006; Blaydes 2010.

[12] Boix 2003; Gandhi and Przeworski 2006; Wright 2008.

[13] To use Svolik's term, this book focuses on cities and the problem of authoritarian control, although as argued below, mass and elite politics interact to affect the survival of regimes (Svolik 2012).

LARGE CITIES

Beijing and Shanghai are global megacities by any measure, but they share the Chinese urban landscape with dozens of cities with population over a million and hundreds of cities on the order of half a million. Given the difficulty of defining the term, "city" is generally avoided by statistical agencies in favor of a more measurable divide: urban versus rural.[14] Urban areas are defined as areas—demarcated either by sub-national administrative borders or geography—that have a population density greater than some threshold over a sufficiently large area.[15] Rural areas, conversely, are those pieces of land which are sparsely populated and exist under this threshold.[16]

Cities are locales of high population density. They are defined by the presence of people. The buildings, roads, streetlights, and parks that one associates with cities do not make an area truly urban. They are the mere scaffolding upon which cities are built, for people to live in proximity to each other in some safe, efficient way. The "ghost cities" of China of the late 2000s were attempts to begin urban developments with the skeleton of massive infrastructure investments and construction of buildings to house and employ millions. Yet until people moved into those buildings, used those roads, and lived in those spaces, they were not live cities but bones, prepared for growth.

The particular focus of the book is on large cities or more specifically on urban concentration. Empirically, urban concentration is the share of a country's urban population living in its largest city or cities.[17] The city system of most countries can be summarized as following a power law distribution, or Zipf's rule.[18] Usually, the largest city in a country is twice as large as the country's number two ranked city, three times the third-largest city, and so on. Zipf argued that deviations from this rule—either too concentrated or too flat of a hierarchy of cities—would yield disorder. Cities pose more threats both as they grow larger and as they dominate the urban landscape of a country. In a country with a primary city that dwarfs its compatriots, that city comes to similarly dwarf other areas in political importance as it is seen as a leading indicator of the future of

---

[14] Mumford 1961, 1.

[15] e.g. five people standing in a kitchen or even five hundred people sharing space in a church during services have extraordinarily high density, measured in people per square kilometer, but the area under examination is insufficiently large to make a city.

[16] "Suburban" or "peri-urban" and other terms are also used in different contexts to demarcate space surrounding urban areas that differ from the core in measurable ways, usually population density. Unfortunately, just as the meaning of the city has changed over time, the threshold has changed for classifying areas as rural or urban across time and place.

[17] See the next chapter for more details on measurement.

[18] Zipf 1941, 1949.

the country. A rejection of the regime by the citizens of that city signifies the vanguard of the country rejecting the regime.

The threats that cities pose to dictators are numerous, but cities are also critical for economic development, making their total abolition inconceivable. Urbanization is highly correlated with development, to such an extent that historical studies use city size to estimate the wealth of societies.[19] While simply moving an individual from a rural locale to an urban one does not transform a farmer's skills, it is associated with expanded opportunities to produce goods and services that yield much higher returns than he or she would have received in the countryside. Urbanization can be good for regimes, but overconcentration and slums can be dangerous.

The piling of people on top of people in megacities is perilous because it makes large scale protests more likely and cities more difficult to govern. These two channels by which cities endanger nondemocratic regimes are detailed below.

CITIES AND COLLECTIVE ACTION

Consider a protest. Thinking of images or video footage of protests in today's globalized media tends to conjure depictions of masses of individuals sharing a small bit of often highly symbolic physical territory, usually a square in the center of the country's largest city. These images reflect much of the reality of the dangers of cities to nondemocratic regimes. Protests and other types of collective action bring people together and can bring down regimes. There are two aspects connecting cities and collective action that matter for this discussion. First, large cities are more likely to have politically effective collective action events. Second, countries with high levels of urban concentration are prone to have the politics of the dominant city overwhelm other political forces.

Large cities are more likely to have significant incidents of collective action for reasons having to do with the math of population. This mechanism operates both from the perspective of the masses who might participate and the elite activists who might organize. The larger the urban population in a city, the smaller the proportion needed to participate for a large riot to occur. Consider the difference between a megacity and a small city. In a city of ten million, a riot of 100,000 residents requires only 1 percent of the city to participate. In a city of one million, the proportion of the population that must participate for the riot to reach the same size is an order of magnitude larger: 1 in 10 rather than 1 in 100. Larger cities are more likely to have politically salient protests, marches, and riots, as such phenomena are usually conceived in ways where the total number of people involved is the critical number not the share of the population taking part.[20] Crowd sizes are rarely given as a percentage of the area's total number of inhabitants. Demonstrations are measured as large or small based on the number of people that are present at the event. Beijing in 1989, Tehran in 2009, and Cairo in 2011 were home to massive protests that challenged authoritarian regimes and toppled Mubarak in Egypt. In all three cases, protestors present at the events made up a small share of the total population of the city.[21] In a large city, fewer people as a proportion of the population need to be there for the event to be classified as a large one.[22]

A similar situation arises when considering the creation of movements by elite activists. As the population of a city increases, the expected number of extremists or activists or talented individuals present in a given spatial territory is more likely to exceed some minimum threshold. If activists represent 0.01% of the population of a city, then in a city of 100,000 people, only 10 such activists are present on average. In a city of 1 million residents, on the other hand, one would expect 100 such activists to be present. If organization requires 20 or 50 committed activists coming together to proceed, the smaller community will have serious difficulty in cobbling together a movement when compared with the larger community. Without a cadre of like-minded compatriots with whom to share it, a radical idea is likely to wither on the vine rather than blossom into a movement. If collective action requires collections of activists coming together to create an organization to motivate collective action, then such events are more likely to be possible in a large city.

Protests in large cities are also more politically damaging. The political tide in a megacity that contains one-third of the country's urban population tends to be decisive more often than in a country with ten large cities, each of which houses only a slice of the population. A popular uprising in a first- or second-tier city sends a signal of a different order than a similar protest in a third- or fourth-tier city. This is particularly the case when, as in over 90 percent of countries, the

[20] General strikes, which might normally be expected to follow such a list of political behaviors, would not follow this general pattern. When assessing a strike, the metrics are usually the extent to which normal economic life is ground to a halt. "Totally," "essentially," "nearly," or other such adverbs are the key words to describe such an event's ability to put the country/city on pause. A negative assessment is one where such activities—the run of the mill—are unaffected. As getting compliance with larger populations is both necessary for a successful strike in a larger city and more difficult than with smaller populations, strikes are less likely to succeed for reasons very similar to those that make protests and marches more likely to succeed in large cities.

[21] See, for instance, NPR's Marketplace on Tehran on how life essentially continued as normal in other areas of the city (Ryssdal and Salehi-Isfahani 2009).

[22] There is the possibility that large cities that suffer numerous events of this type might be increasingly likely to become inured to them. They might remember the million plus marches of yesterday when considering today's smaller dust-ups. For more on how varieties in social networks affect the probability and types of collective action, see Siegel 2009.

dominant city is also the political capital of the regime. China's plethora of cities allows for even large demonstrations to take place without reflecting strongly on the regime as a whole. Thousands marching through downtown Zibo or Shenyang fails to have the resonance that the same activity would possess were it to be located in Tiananmen Square in Beijing or on the Bund in Shanghai.

Proximity to the heart of the regime implies having a greater ability to impose costs on that regime. A protest in a village or outlying city is something that elites in the capital do not have to experience through anything other than news reports or dispatches from provincial officials. A march that blocked roads in the capital, on the other hand, may well keep government officials out of their offices and stuck in snarls of traffic (as well as viscerally angry at the protesters). By increasing the share of the population that lives in the largest city, urban concentration directly increases the proximity of the population to the center of power and commerce, increasing the hazard to authoritarian survival.

How do protests and riots actually lead to regime collapse? A myriad of possibilities exist.[23] First is a direct ousting by the rioters. The protesters barge through the president's gates and force him off of his chair and install someone else on that seat of power. The Romanian Communist leader Nicolae Ceaușescu, who fled a mob invading his palace for his head in December 1989, is a contemporary example.[24]

Second is an elite split where other civilian officials remove the dictator from power. Riots make such an event more likely, as they can both generate and exacerbate splits in the leadership. The May 1998 resignation of Indonesia's Suharto following large-scale riots in the capital Jakarta and other cities and his replacement by his vice-president provides one example of this mechanism in action. The protests in Tiananmen Square in 1989, though not ending the Chinese regime, certainly increased tensions within elite circles.[25]

Third is an ousting by the military. Two varieties of military actions can lead to the end of a regime. The first, and perhaps simplest, is a military coup. This is essentially the same as an elite split, only the coup is led by the military rather than civilian personnel. In a peaceful transition in Peru in 1975, General Francisco Morales replaced General Juan Velasco as the country's leader. Preceding the coup, Lima was rocked with violent riots, strikes, and student demonstrations.[26] The second variety is when acts of defiance and protest trigger an unraveling of the regime's authority over the military. When there are large-scale protests,

---

[23] This list is not exhaustive. Regimes could end by way of becoming democratic mimicking those above but also in different ways.

[24] He successfully fled his palace on 22 December but was arrested and executed three days later, 25 December 1989.

[25] Nathan 2001; Liang Zhang, Nathan, and Link 2002; Bandelj and Solinger 2012.

[26] Hofmann 1975.

the military is more likely to be in a position to be called upon to shoot at the citizenry. If such orders are given by the regime and the chain of command falters—that is, the soldiers refuse to shoot or the officers refuse to give the orders to shoot—then this represents a collapse of authority that can quickly undo a regime by any of the other types of ousters previously discussed. The Arab Spring cases of Tunisia and Egypt fit into this broad category. Huge demonstrations in the capital were not met with the full might of the armed forces.[27]

Another channel that connects protests to regime collapse is through ousting of the regime by external forces. Riots or the suppression thereof becomes a justification for outside forces to intervene and remove the regime.[28] The NATO intervention in Libya that aided in the ousting and killing of Colonel Muammar al-Gaddafi came to pass because of the violent response of his regime to anti-government demonstrations.[29]

Obviously, these different mechanisms can work in concert. Protests exacerbate a civilian elite split that in turn induces the military to plot a coup or call for outside forces to remove the dictator. Protests might lead mid-level officials to conclude that the regime's days are numbered and begin to steal everything that they can, sealing the regime's fate in the process. In general, countries characterized by high levels of urban concentration are often plagued by different groups waging political battles through direct action—from protests and strikes to coups and assassinations.[30]

The mere possibility of politically effective collective action in large cities may undermine regimes. Even before mass riots break out, the specter of slum dwellers or formal sector workers rising up can create opportunities for fissures to develop, breaking apart a regime's political coalition.[31] Of course, regimes do not cede power when the statistical service reports that the largest city's population has grown, but regimes with large cities and capitals are beset by political difficulties that may lead to shorter reigns. Regimes may enact policies to address the grievances of potential protestors but by doing so undermine their partners in the countryside. Urban concentration can add stress that might fracture a regime, making it prone to subsequent collapse. In this way, the collective action channel can operate even absent realized protests or riots.

Finally, cities, collective action, and collapse are connected by large urban areas providing focal points where people can take their cues when assessing

---

[27] The details on whether or not orders were given and disobeyed or not given because it was obvious they would not be obeyed is important to judge the leader's culpability for potential crimes against humanity but less significant in understanding the underlying political problem.

[28] Plausible candidates include the United Nations, United States, Russia, China, and others.

[29] Lewis 2012.

[30] This is akin to what Huntington terms "praetorian" politics (Huntington 1968, 210–13). N.b. Huntington does not directly refer to the term "urban concentration."

[31] On political coalitions in dictatorships, see Pepinsky 2009.

different people's opinions about the regime.[32] The presence of such focal points might shape policy choices in favor of these focal points or make regime turnover more likely.[33] Atomized populations, whether in many different cities or in rural areas, make coordination and hence collective action against the regime less likely. In some ways, the city acts as a focal place for judgments of a regime in a manner similar to an election serving as a focal moment for regimes.[34]

The most obvious focal points are crucial spaces within cities that are fraught with political significance: such as Red Square in Moscow or Tiananmen and Zhongnanhai in Beijing. During the Tiananmen protests in 1989, Deng Xiaoping refers to Tiananmen Square as the "symbol of the People's Republic of China."[35] When the control of these locales is interrupted, the regime's façade of strength collapses.

Events within cities and at focal points are public and can inform people about the quality of the regime. Elites observe citizen behavior and interpret it, updating their beliefs about political possibilities. Similarly, individuals in cities can make observations and update their sense of the distribution of sentiments about the regime in ways that either do not occur or do not involve politically pivotal actors in the same way outside of urban areas. Regimes regulate the transmission of information to greater and lesser extent in various technological domains—printing presses, copy machines, faxes, cellular phones, Internet connections, and social media. However, if they do not push people out of cities, they cannot keep the public's eyes from seeing what is happening in front of them. Resisting a regime is difficult if one does not understand that others are similarly disaffected. Seeing a protest in a public space might make resistance easier and thus more likely to be successful.[36]

It is important to stress that the collective action channel is not completely dependent on grievances. Opportunities also play a role. Activists coming together, the political implications of large population numbers, and urban areas acting as focal points, all operate independently of grievances against the regime.

---

[32] See Patel 2013 on the importance of cities having a single focal point or square.

[33] If the presence of the focal point has no effect on governance, then one would expect this to be the case. However, presumably the dictator is aware that events in urban areas are increasingly watched, by domestic and foreign audiences, as the cities of the nation develop and so will match that with improved governance. Urban bias is endemic, after all.

[34] For a description of elections as a way to coordinate private experiences with the regime to a common audience, see Fearon 2000. Cities thus are a forum for political activities.

[35] e.g. Nathan 2001, 14. There are, of course, questions about the veracity of the documents used in the Tiananmen Papers, but that Tiananmen Square has symbolic importance is not in doubt. For instance, see Hershkovitz 1993; Hung 1991.

[36] The idea that the Internet and social media provide some of the same capabilities and political benefits to rebels as do cities—namely observability, as Chinese dissident artist Ai Weiwei put it, "Twitter is my favorite city"—is considered in the conclusion (Landreth 2012).

Yet one would expect that increases in grievances would be causally related to increases in threatening collective action events.

LEGIBILITY AND POLITICAL GEOGRAPHY

Governments wish to see their populations, to ensure their ability to govern, tax, and rule over them.[37] People's congregation into cities reduces their "legibility" for a regime, threatening its production and maintenance of order. The complexity of a city's political environment increases as it grows larger, making it more difficult to govern and discern the nature of dangers that might emanate from it. While regimes have taken pains to make cities more legible, these efforts reflect the underlying concerns that make cities dangerous because they shield private activity from the government's eye.

The legitimacy of authoritarian regimes is based at some level on an implicit contract with the population. The regime promises to produce or preserve order, and in return the population promises to not revolt. Order is the basis of the regime, chaos its enemy. Regimes often go beyond this fundamental base of support and put forward legitimation strategies relying on ideology, nationalism, performance, or other factors to cement their status as not just the providers of order but the best possible providers of order. Regimes must address many threats. However, more fundamental than even threats to order is the nature of order in the first place. The regime must have some sense of the territory and people that it is ruling to ensure the production of order over this human and geographic space. That is, the nature of order requires an understanding or at least awareness of the domain under its rule.

An unawareness or ignorance of the population or the dimensions of the territory can severely undermine a regime's ability to produce order and keep chaos at bay. Without a sense of who is there, how can any regime collect taxes? Without a sense of the borders of the territory, how could tariffs be assessed? States and regimes desire to know their population and territory for this reason. A census of the population in a city, village, empire, or nation-state can be conducted for any number of reasons but the underlying purpose is to understand the population under rule.[38] Early censuses were taken to ensure that adequate provisions were met for the possibility of a siege. That is, if the city had to close its walls and attempt to hold out against an invading army, how many mouths

---

[37] Scott 1998.

[38] The Han Dynasty conducted the world's earliest preserved census in 2 C.E. (Twitchett and Loewe 1986, 240). This appears contemporaneous to the biblical Roman Census around the time of Jesus of Nazareth's birth.

would need to be fed? This calculation requires a head count.[39] More concretely, censuses identify how many individuals are in a territory that can pay taxes and be conscripted into mandatory labor (either military service or construction of public works), and what facilities and public goods need to be provided where.

Of particular relevance here is that cities in their natural state are illegible to regimes. Governments have difficulty piercing through their complex web of social interconnections. The physical geography of cities evolved over time in ways that make them difficult for outsiders to understand. Compare the irregularity and twisting paths of Beijing's *hutongs* with the massive thoroughfares of its modern ring roads.[40] As the character of China's cities transforms from *hutongs* to highways, history is lost but so too is the some of the ability to hide from the state. The former is difficult for a regime, or frankly, any outsider to navigate, to follow, or even to comprehend when compared to the latter. As such, it gives advantages to the local over the universal. Scott analogizes cities to forests. In natural forests with their irregular lines and variety of plant and animal life, one cannot see in beyond the first few trees. Compare this natural forest with "scientific forestry," where the trunks of a single species in this new forest monoculture follow straight lines.[41] The outside observer can see all the way to the end of the row. These orderly rows of trees are legible for an outsider to understand, and the cost of acquiring information about the different trees is substantially reduced. One does not need to wade through bramble to examine any given trunk that might be of interest or count the total number of trees present. "Natural" cities are similarly impenetrable. The impenetrable character of cities comes from density and anonymity. The tangle of streets in an old city is multiplied by the various corridors of the different shaped and sized buildings that abut those streets. High modernists built cities that were dominated by imposing boulevards and mega-blocks devoid of character, vibrancy, or serendipity. This drab universality overwhelmingly pervades China's provincial cities.[42]

A classic depiction of urban anti-colonial violence—*Battle of Algiers*—makes clear some of the benefits that cities confer to violent resistors. Rebels are able to plan, execute, and escape to the Casbah due to their base's proximity to their colonial targets and the city's complexity. Insurgencies, similarly, can be taken

---

[39] Less beneficent purposes are also possible. The Kangxi Emperor (1654–1722 life; 1661–1722 reign) of the Qing Dynasty desired a census to show a growing population in China as a symbol of his era's successes (Spence 1999, 73).

[40] Scott 1998, 54. Or the winding and convoluted streets of Boston with the grids of New York City or Washington, DC. Scott uses Bruges in 1500 and Paris before Haussmann.

[41] Scott 1998, 11–22.

[42] Miller 2012, 132.

on in urban areas against governments by domestic opponents, as took place in Karachi, Pakistan, from 1978 to 1996 with the Mohajir Qaumi Movement.[43]

While cities can make hiding easier, they also increase the ability of "anonymous denunciation," greatly aiding the regime's counterinsurgency efforts.[44] This brings up a general point: by moving to the city, individuals might be increasing their political voice, but they are also increasing their proximity to the agents of the state or regime.[45] If one's goal were simply to evade the regime, then a move to the city from the periphery is likely a poor decision.[46] The agents of the state are sure to be present in large cities while they are unlikely to have complete control over the periphery. Empirically, most insurgencies take place in the periphery.[47]

Urban insurgents have a disadvantage because once a regime gains control of a city, it is unlikely to retreat. On the one hand, a regime might simply allow for de facto control by the rebel group of the peripheral territory. On the other hand, primary cities are unlikely to be obliterated by a regime, whereas rural outposts and towns known to harbor insurgents are razed with some frequency.[48] The city displays the actions of the regime. Genocide or obliteration that is not supported by the population cannot be hidden in the capital as it can when it occurs in anonymous villages in anonymous valleys.[49]

State or regime officials that encounter chaotic spaces such as marketplaces or *hutongs*, even spaces that they may know well, are more likely to lose scent of the trail in such a hub of activity. Those that they pursue have more avenues of escape and possible directions in which to flee. This works in concrete terms— a police officer chasing a pickpocket—but also in more abstract terms. Where do radicals congregate to talk about political changes and organizing against the regime? Where do officers slip off to when hatching a coup plot? These are not discussions that take place in public. Cities provide alternatives that allow individuals to meet anonymously.

[43] Staniland 2010, 1632. Or retreating into the narrow and irregular streets of Qianmen during the Tiananmen crackdown in 1989.

[44] Staniland 2010, citing Fearon and Laitin 2003.

[45] Herbst 2000, 230–31.

[46] Scott 2010.

[47] Fearon and Laitin 2003. Whether this is a strategic decision by the group (choosing a rural field of battle over an urban one due to their inherent political situation mediated by state policy) or a non-strategic one (e.g., sons of the soil fighting in their peripheral homeland) is beyond the scope of this book.

[48] Kalyvas 2006; Staniland 2010. A primary (or primate) city is a country's largest city.

[49] This distinction gets at the notion, however, that violence against interlopers that incumbent residents of cities do support can take place. Race and religious riots in cities can flare up extremely quickly (see Lhasa and Urumqi in recent years or Mumbai or other cities in India for even more devastating episodes).

People, not only spaces, can be anonymous in cities in a way that is next to impossible in less dense regions. The hubbub of a city means that keeping track of everyone that you meet or see on the street is cognitively complex to the point of impossibility. Streams of people—whether they are walking down the street, driving cars, riding in trains, or biking—are everywhere in cities, and individuals simply cannot follow everyone. The state, despite its many eyes, cannot know where everyone is every minute of every day. Post-hoc analysis may find that individual agents of the state had noticed patterns of behavior that when put together point to the identification of a plot. But overcoming the flood of other possibilities and information to perform this kind of analysis in real-time is difficult.[50] The number of people that one could physically meet in a given day is a function of the distance that one can travel and the population inside that radius. The millions of people in a large city make for near endless possible connections and networks. In rural areas, tight communication between the members of a village or a clan may be difficult for the state to penetrate, but connections between that small group and others outside of said group are relatively simple to monitor.[51]

Large urban areas can provide refuge for opposition figures in ways similar to the difficult terrain of the periphery.[52] Large, dense populations have innumerable alleyways in which to hide from a dictator, apartments that are difficult to penetrate or observe, and slums that are off the grid. Regimes in developing nations often have difficulty projecting the rule of the state into the hinterland. The illegibility of large cities brings the uncertainty of the unknown to the heart of power. Parts of cities are effectively nonstate spaces. Critically, the combination of both illegible nonstate spaces and the visibility of actions of resistance makes cities threatening to regimes.

Ungoverned territories in the country's periphery are invisible and go unnoticed by political elites and masses in the major cities, but ungoverned territories inside of a country's main cities show the limits of the strength of the regime— either in terms of governing capacity or political will—and so represent failure. The mountainous regions of Southeast Asia did not bow to the valley states

---

[50] For example, the US government in different bureaucracies had much of the information needed to put together a case that the 9/11 terrorists might be plotting to act against the United States in the days and weeks before the attacks, yet these bits of data were individual puzzle pieces that were meaningless before they were connected post-hoc and able to reveal the potential threat (National Commission on Terrorist Attacks 2004).

[51] Some see urban anonymity as freeing individuals to radical actions that they may be unlikely to take when with family or friends. Unconstrained by the opinions of the strangers that surround them, rash actions may be taken. For proponents of this view, see Branigan 2009.

[52] Fearon and Laitin 2003.

below them, nor were these valley states radically threatened by them.[53] For instance, China's coastal province of Jiangsu laid out rules for different categories of "mass incidents" that privileged events that affected urban areas, regarding them as more serious than those taking place in rural areas.[54] Even more concretely, only incidents that are noticed are counted and treated with significance; incidents that occur without capturing the attention of the public, media, or government are ignored. Considered most extreme are those events with an "impact on social stability that extends beyond the province through interactive chain reactions."[55]

Cities thus provide options for those considering moving against a dictatorial regime. Cities, as argued in the section immediately above, are also places to be seen. Acts meant to elicit support for a rebel cause can be made public and observed in a city whereas a rural locale would not be as effective. Information spreads in cities. Hiding in a city is plausible, which makes plotting easier for activists. At the same time, publicity and being noticed is possible in the city as well. The options that the city presents to those interested in rising up against a dictator make governing it a political challenge.

Finally, there is the increasing difficulty and complexity in governing a massive city. Policing and extracting resources from this tangled web can be difficult.[56] People often can see when there is an under-provision of public goods, and they can attack a regime for its callousness. Also, the over-provision of goods to some parts of the city or individuals residing within it is evidence of the inherent corruption of a regime. Over-concentration comes with substantial economic costs. Although fiercely contested, modern economic studies have shown some support for Zipf's idea of an optimal level of urban concentration—with a largest city twice the size of the second city, three times the size of the third city, and so on—at least when considered in economic, and more specifically productivity, terms.[57]

---

[53] Scott 2010.

[54] "江苏省突发公共事件总体应急预案" 2006; Soong 2006.

[55] Ibid.

[56] While difficult to police, corruption is not necessarily impossible to control even in large urban areas, as is shown by the success of Hong Kong in combatting this foe (Manion 2004).

[57] Davis and Henderson 2003; Henderson 2003. Henderson also argues this point about under-concentration. That is, he believes that there is an optimal level of urban concentration for countries to experience for economic growth purposes. China's management of urbanization has left it under-urbanized and under-concentrated in Henderson's vision (Au and Henderson 2006). It should be noted, however, that this claim about economic growth is in contrast to the World Development Report 2009, which makes a case for larger cities being part of better economic development in the short-term. Over time, the WDR points to countries de-concentrating their urban populations. The mechanisms at play here are classic economics of scale issues, but also congestion costs and the like. See also Krugman 1991.

Cities are dangerous because they are inscrutable, difficult to govern, and—as a consequence—prone to explosions of unrest. How do regimes respond to these dangers?

Regime Responses and the Faustian Bargain

Regimes are constantly attempting to strengthen their grip on power. They focus on building or maintaining repressive capacity, implementing legitimation strategies, and holding together political institutions and coalitions.[58] Authoritarian regimes address the specific dangers of cities via two types of policy responses: redistributive policy and migration restrictions.[59] Redistributive policy in favor of cities, termed urban bias, attempts to reduce the level of urban grievances and improve the living situations of urban residents. This has the political benefit of reducing the chances of collective protest or other types of dissent. A second policy channel open to autocrats is migration restrictions, which broadly refers to policies that control the location decisions of individuals directly. For instance, two kinds of migration restrictions are (1) internal passport systems such as China's *hukou* and Vietnam's *ho khao*, and (2) aggressive slum clearance policies such as Robert Mugabe's "Operation Drive out Trash," which destroyed the residences and businesses of over 700,000 in Zimbabwe's cities.[60] Both types of migration restrictions aim to control the size and demographic composition of critical urban areas.

Redistributive policy operates through incentives rather than physical force or legal restrictions, directing resources toward or away from urban areas. The conventional wisdom on redistribution and urban unrest argues that survival-oriented regimes should bias policy toward urban residents, because they are better able to destabilize the regime.[61] Urban-biased policies, which are paid for by rural extraction, should have short-term benefits for regimes in addressing both channels of danger. First, bias mollifies potential urban protestors with policy payoffs such as food and housing subsidies. Second, granting benefits to the urban population encourages individuals to present themselves to the state rather than hide from it, increasing the legibility of the city to the regime.

---

[58] On repressive capacity, see Levitsky and Way 2010; Policzer 2009; on political institutions, Gandhi 2008; Blaydes 2010; and on political coalitions, Magaloni 2006; Pepinsky 2009.

[59] Of course, repression, legitimation, and political coalitions matter for maintaining urban stability, but those are not specifically about urban problems or urban areas. They are general phenomena and have been studied elsewhere (see previous footnote).

[60] Wines 2005; Tibaijuka 2005.

[61] Bates 1981.

However, this conventional wisdom ignores a second-order effect of urban bias, which is self-undermining: inducing further urbanization and urban concentration. Subsidized food and other benefits might buy off city residents and reduce grievance levels in the short term, but over time cities will grow due to the incentives these preferential policies create. Eventually, engorged cities may become powder kegs that ignite and destroy the regime.

An implicit assumption of urban bias theory is that *people are immobile*, and so the policy of urban bias does not affect migration or urbanization. However, taxing the countryside and spreading the spoils in cities should not be neutral with respect to the population distribution within a country. Farmers faced with high levels of extraction in the countryside and observing that the funds that are being taken from them are dispersed elsewhere in the country's urban areas are likely to choose to exit the economically exploited countryside and migrate to the locale where benefits are being dispersed, namely cities.[62]

Does urban bias induce urbanization or urban concentration? Davis and Henderson argue that while government policies do matter for urbanization, they matter much more in affecting the level of urban concentration in a country:

> Political and policy variables have little or no direct effects on urbanization, only indirect effects through their effects on income and sector composition. Urban concentration is affected significantly by a wide range of political or politically determined variables, including democratization, federalism, and whether a country was a former planned economy. In addition interregional investment in transport infrastructure, both waterways and roads, work to reduce urban concentration, opening markets to hinterland cities.[63]

To return to China in the 1950s, farmers were attempting to find positions at new industrial factories, not moving to any town just to flee agricultural taxation.[64] If these modern, leading areas exploded because of the political pressures emanating from over-population, the political consequences for the regime would be dire. Such activity would tarnish the party's reputation as the organization best able to move the country forward to industrialization and would do so by pitting two constituencies that theoretically were at the heart of the political coalition—farmers and industrial workers—against each other and against the regime. This also points to the importance of different cities in different contexts.

---

[62] Some individual farmers will, of course, choose to react to this extraction not through the "exit" channel but instead through the "voice" channel, complaining and protesting about the unfair treatment that they are enduring (Hirschman 1970). See also Fitzpatrick 1999.

[63] Davis and Henderson 2003, 120.

[64] Such fleeing began in earnest during the famine caused by the Great Leap (see chapter 4).

The Chinese regime of the 1950s put industrialization at the forefront of its political agenda. If those cities that were the focal points of this movement failed or combusted, the damage would have been severe. Below the national level, local officials in the CCP hierarchy had a strong incentive to ensure that the most important cities in their jurisdictions—provincial capitals—succeeded without the sort of incidents that threatened social stability.

The political logic of urban bias would lead one to conclude that urban bias should induce urban concentration. Main cities are most likely to receive the benefits of "urban" bias, since it is the political potential of the residents of those main cities and not of all cities that represent the greatest threat to the regime. As such, those locations are the ones likely to disproportionately receive targeted benefits. If farmers are pushed out of the countryside because of the heavy relative tax burden there, then it is likely that migrants will tend to relocate to these favored dominant cities rather than to a random distribution of cities; this theoretical expectation is confirmed empirically.[65]

Over time, larger cities with more marginal migrants become increasingly expensive for the government to appease and observe. The expense increases both because there are more mouths to feed and because average wages in the city tend to decrease with the influx of migrant labor.[66] High agricultural taxes lower effective wages in the countryside, which is the shadow wage, or wage from the best alternative position for a marginal urban migrant. As the shadow wage declines, the wage in the city also tends to drop.[67] The depression of urban wages harms not only migrants themselves but also existing city residents that work outside the protected formal sector.

Urban bias, then, can be said to have the appearance of a Faustian bargain for dictators. It has advantages for regime elites concerned about placating potential protestors today, but it expands the size of large cities and essentially increases the population's power by inducing individuals to transition from locations of political weakness—the countryside—to areas of political strength—the cities.

The second way that regimes respond to the political danger of cities is migration restrictions. Broadly defined, these policies do not appease urbanites but prevent or dissuade individuals from moving to major cities and capitals—prevent them from becoming urbanites.[68] If urban bias is a Faustian bargain, then

---

[65] Ades and Glaeser 1995; Henderson 2003. Empirically, in the next chapter, for the universe of nondemocratic regimes under examination, urban bias is uncorrelated with urbanization in but is positively connected to levels of urban concentration and the size of capital cities.

[66] The expansion of the urban labor supply drives down wages. These effects are moderated the more that labor in the agricultural sector can be described as surplus (Lewis 1954, 1963).

[67] Harris and Todaro 1970.

[68] On the Soviet Union's migration restrictions, see also Fitzpatrick 1999.

migration restrictions can offer regimes a loophole to that bargain. A regime with effective migration restrictions can subsidize urbanites with rural taxes, reducing their level of grievances, but, at the same time, avoid the costs associated with excessive urban concentration.[69]

Regimes have different technologies available to them to manipulate the location decisions of their populations. Thus "migration restrictions" is a catch-all term for different kinds of policies with the similar intended effects on migrants' decisions about moving to cities.[70] China's *hukou* system exists on one end of the spectrum but is not unique nor is it the only policy lever that is used for this purpose. Cross-nationally, its dominant form is in the exclusionary policies that yield slums. Cities can be made more difficult to live in and social services can be provided to a narrow set of established city dwellers rather than extended to newcomers. The systematic under-provision of public goods to new migrants in "slum" communities is a tactic used by cities and regimes to reduce the inflow of migrants.[71] As Feler and Henderson show:

> Overall, we find evidence of strategic under-provision of public water service to the types of houses most likely to be occupied by poor migrants in Brazil's localities. This under-provision appears to function as a deterrent to further entry of poor migrants, and it can explain why Brazil's "superstar" localities, which have the wealth and scale to expand servicing, also have informal neighborhoods that lack servicing. If these localities were to provide servicing to informal neighborhoods, and implicitly grant these areas formality, they would encourage further entry of poor migrants into their jurisdictions and experience further congestion and dissipation of the amenities that make them desirable places to live.[72]

By ignoring and failing to incorporate migrant communities into the public infrastructure of the city, the lives of the populations in slums are worsened.

---

[69] There is, of course, an ethical component to what amounts to an effective restriction on the basic freedom to locate here. I offer explanations but not justifications for the policies of migration restrictions that dictators put in place. I simply attempt to improve understanding and bring light to previously murky areas of political behavior in nondemocratic contexts.

[70] For a comparison of various post-revolutionary migration policies in France, the Soviet Union, and China, making clear that such policies are not the exclusive project of non-Western countries, see Torpey 1997.

[71] Feler and Henderson (2011) show evidence of strategic under-provision of public goods to poor areas in Brazilian cities, that migrants are more likely to move into areas that have higher levels of public goods provision, and that cities compete negatively (i.e., there is a negative correlation between activities helping migrants in one city and enacting policies that exclude them in others).

[72] Feler and Henderson 2011, 254.

This reduces the attractiveness of moving to the city in question. All regimes are capable of these kinds of exclusionary policies. In direct contrast to China's institutional *hukou* system which operates using a national identity card similar to an internal passport, this policy is the absence of action and as such takes zero capacity—failing to extend public services and infrastructure is something that any regime can do.[73]

Once slums have become established, regimes can regulate and remove them to achieve political ends. Slum clearance policies can have the effect of dispersing a population that is itself restive or that exacerbates extant political tensions inside the regime. Given the existence of slums and their often illegal nature, states and regimes often take the step of demolishing them without offering compensation (in contrast to eminent domain cases). Again, just as in slum formation, slum clearance policies do not take high levels of capacity to implement.[74] Robert Mugabe's regime in Zimbabwe was able to destroy the slums in the capital and other cities and did so in part to make his opponents disappear from view, from each other and the international community. "Nonsense.... You go there now and see whether those thousands are there. Where are they? A figment of their imagination."[75] Individuals who had been living in the slums, such as Killarney in Bulawayo, are instead spread out and living in the countryside or miles away from the center of the city. If the discontented cannot locate each other, then they will find acting collectively and rising up against the regime impossible.

Migration restrictions themselves come with political costs. Exclusionary policies create slums. While these policies may also reduce the size of such communities by reducing the attractiveness of migrating to a main city, they also fundamentally create a community of individuals who have been discriminated against in the main city and represent a threat to the regime.

---

[73] Slums are related to capacity. It is the inability to fully control the market for land that allows slums to develop in the first place. The kinds of anti-population movement policies that occur in the developed world are not thought of as anti-migration or exclusionary but usually in terms of maintaining real estate values or the "desirability of a community" or even attempting to reduce use of land (ignoring that the individuals do not disappear simply because they do not relocate to one community instead of another) (Feler and Henderson 2011, 254).

[74] As slum clearance represents the use of coercive force, it could precipitate the kind of crisis mentioned above when considering the use of the military in politics (the situation may call for some level of coercive intensity between that of low intensity day-to-day policing in an authoritarian regime and high intensity attacking a group of protesters (the language on the distinctions between High and Low intensity come from Levitsky and Way) (Levitsky and Way 2010, 2012). In the end, slum clearance is a policy that affects dwellings directly (by destroying or moving them) and migrants' location decisions indirectly (as the residents of the dwellings are assumed to have already left).

[75] Wines 2005.

Why Make a Deal with the Devil?

Urban bias reduces grievances in cities but can also increase the size of the cities that the regime must confront, undermining the stabilizing purpose of the policy in the first place. Yet far from being a rare arrangement, urban bias is endemic in the developing world.[76] Given these difficulties, why is the developing world rife with urban bias? Many dictators have short time horizons. The risks and costs of urban bias accrue over years and are not as pressing as short-term threats for vulnerable regimes. Governments that might lose power within months if they increase gas prices or allow the cost of grain to appreciate are likely to discount the long-term hazard of urban favoritism. The accumulation of risk creates a combustible situation but comes with a long, slow-burning fuse.

Regimes should be more willing to bias policies toward cities—to make deals with the devil—during difficult times. When economically or politically weakened, regimes face tough choices that entail trade-offs. I argue that regimes under worsening circumstances should be more likely to bear the long-term consequences of urban bias, increasing their chances of keeping control of the country through the tumult. Regimes facing smoother waters should retreat from urban bias and try to escape from such Faustian bargains.

Tilting toward cities has other reasons—economic and political—in addition to reducing urban unrest. This section describes many of the reasons why regimes make a deal with the devil. These reasons include: (1) awareness and attention tilted toward urban areas, (2) the state's self-identification as an urban employer, (3) rural extraction is often logistically simpler and less straining on the weak tax collecting capacity of regimes, (4) the general political science finding that political actors with leverage, such as city residents, receive benefits, and (5) urban bias accords with a modernizing and industrial vision of policy.

Nondemocratic regimes undertake political actions at the whim of the dictator or dictatorial institutions. Michael Lipton argued that urban bias originates because the countryside is silent and defenseless whereas the city holds the preponderance of the country's voice and talent.[77] In dictatorships, as elsewhere, squeaky wheels get the grease. Being in the cities in question, the leadership of a regime is likely to hear the squeaks—or complaints—because of proximity. Moreover, states can better identify those statements because they are likely to be made in the language and location most directly relevant to the leadership. By comparison, the countryside is silent and invisible. As noted in Kalyvas's "Urban Bias in Research on Civil Wars," there is an "invisibility of the countryside" that I argue reflects—for a dictator—the

---

[76] Bates 1981.
[77] Lipton 1977.

countryside's political weakness.[78] While such invisibility can lead researchers of violence to miss events and bias their explanations, that same invisibility allows leaders to exploit and extract from the countryside.

Relatedly, the regime and its state apparatus is a large urban employer and as such identifies with urban employers as it faces the same or similar economic realities as they do.[79] Chief among these is the desire for cheap food. By enacting redistributive policies that align with its interest as an urban employer—such as ensuring cheap food for urban workers, which keeps wage demands under control—the regime reduces its wage bill in its dominant place of employment, that is, large cities. Under the planned economy in China, the entire price system was designed to concentrate all economic surplus in a few SOEs. Extraction from agriculture was in part a way of keeping down costs in the industrial sector.[80]

Third, the administration of agricultural taxes is simpler for regimes. Business activity in the industrial and service sectors is complicated when compared to the agricultural sector. For a state to be able to assess taxes on industrial enterprises adequately requires information on the prices different firms are selling their goods for, what their inputs cost, the labor wage, and so on. In the industrial sector, at least many inputs and outputs are observable in physical terms—how much cotton was needed, how many shirts were manufactured. In the service sector, on the other hand, observability is even lower as the transactions involve non-physical, and so difficult to see, goods. It is simpler for a state to extract from the agricultural sector. Crops are planted and harvested on a calendar as regular as the seasons. For cash crops, the state's task is made easier by the fact that not only is the production, location, and timing relatively fixed, but so is the destination for the goods—ports and borders. Rather than govern the totality of the interior space of the country, a regime with strong control of the perimeter of the territory will be able to control the markets for the goods in question. The legibility of agriculture makes it an attractive target for taxation and extraction given the relatively weak capacity of most regimes in the developing world.

These three factors for urban bias are obviously significant but are joined by two dominant logics at the disciplinary boundaries of political science and economics. Political science thinks of redistributive policy principally as a matter of power or leverage, whereas economics focuses on the efficient allocation of labor and capital and trajectories for maximizing economic growth.

The power of the purse is a major one. The taxing and spending policies of governments, when combined with the capacity to limit the legal selling of

[78] Kalyvas 2004, 165.
[79] Bates 1981.
[80] Naughton 2007.

products, makes up most of the state's ability to control the economic activity within its territory. The disciplines of political science and economics tend to focus on different aspects of redistributive policy. Political science tends to examine the threats that states face and see redistribution as a principal way in which states can respond to these threats, whether by pacifying or co-opting restive populations. Political scientists are interested primarily in the division of the pie. On the other hand, the economics literature on urban-rural redistribution concerns how countries can increase the size of the pie, that is, how they can promote economic development. What policies can be put forward to industrialize successfully? The rest of this section discusses these two views of redistributive policy.

Of course, both the division and size of the economy are important. A regime's ability to survive in the post-Industrial Revolution era depends largely on whether it can improve its economic situation in an environment where wealthier places are evidence of its failure. Such stark contrasts were less obvious prior to the Industrial Revolution, an era in which most nations had similarly high inequality with only small segments of the population escaping the terrible destitution of peasant agriculture.[81] Political economy scholars have focused on the sources and consequences of inequality at the cross-country and class level. Our examinations emphasize understanding patterns in the level of inequality between the "haves" and "have nots" rather than exploring the political geography of countries, that is where inside of territories this "having" takes place. With few exceptions, the political economy literature in political science has treated urbanization and the development of cities as something to control for in cross-national regressions with little theorizing rather than a worthy subject of study in itself.

LEVERAGE OF CITIES

During recent decades, political economy scholars of redistribution in the developing world have focused their attention on class divisions based on income. Much less work during this period considers another—and arguably the most important—political and economic division in developing countries: that between city and country.[82] The urban-rural geographical divide has implications for the political leverage of redistributive politics in developing nondemocracies. Urban areas have high population densities and proximity to political

---

[81] On the other hand, in the prior era, as agriculture was the dominant economic activity, neighboring states had an incentive to capture land to extract some of the value from its agricultural production.

[82] Huntington 1968; Lipton 1977.

and economic centers, reducing the costs and increasing the political significance of large-scale collective action.[83]

Regime type and redistribution intersect at the core of the study of political
economy in the developing world. Models of the political economy of democracies predict that the many poor will dominate voting and choose to soak the
rich few.[84] Empirical support of this canonical model is murky, with questions
about its mechanisms unanswered.[85] There are also disagreements over whether
parties favor core constituencies or marginal voters.[86] Yet, when comparing
across regime types, near consensus does prevail. Public service and public good
provision appear to be greater in democracies, whether due to the pressures of
political competition or the need to appeal to relatively broad segments of the
population.[87]

While nondemocracies may be broadly expected to provide fewer public
goods than democracies, less agreement exists on who receives the benefits of
taxation and spending under these regimes. Some argue that those with an affinity for the government are bought off because their support is the cheapest to
acquire.[88] Others suggest essentially the opposite: that dictators direct resources
to those who are discontented and able to impose costs on the regime.[89] Regimes
may be able to extract more revenue from populations with fewer exit options.[90]
Local governmental power and concerns about instability may give some areas
more bargaining leverage with the center when divvying budgetary subsidies.[91]

The distribution of political power within the population lies at the heart of
many of these arguments. Analysts agree that regimes direct funds to those with
leverage, but disagree about which populations possess the leverage.[92] I argue

---

[83] Olson 1965; Lipton 1977; Bates 1981; Ades and Glaeser 1995.

[84] Meltzer and Richard 1981.

[85] Ross 2006; Kaufman 2009.

[86] Cox and McCubbins 1986; Stokes 2005.

[87] For political competition, see, e.g., Lake and Baum 2001; for broad appeal, see, e.g., Bueno de
Mesquita et al. 2003. The bulk of findings on the question of whether democracy increases public
goods provision is positive (e.g., Avelino, Brown, and Hunter 2005; Brown and Hunter 2004; Kaufman
and Segura-Ubiergo 2001; Rudra and Haggard 2005; Stasavage 2005); Mulligan, Sala-i-Martin, and
Gil (2003) find no difference across regime types. In sub-Saharan Africa, countries with more political contestation also exhibit lower agricultural tax rates (Kasara 2007). Nondemocratic countries
fail to translate gains in economic growth into increased calorie consumption for their populations,
unlike democracies and hybrid regimes (Blaydes and Kayser 2011). See also chapter 7 for more
assessment of variation in urban-rural redistributive policy.

[88] Bueno de Mesquita et al. 2003.

[89] Fearon 2000; Oi and Zhao 2007.

[90] Kasara 2007.

[91] Shih and Qi 2007.

[92] Political leverage and policy behavior vary over time as well. Electoral authoritarian regimes
adjust spending policies to coincide with elections, as they can serve as focal points for anti-regime

that urban bias follows the core of the literature's logics for redistributive policy. Extracting from atomized, weak agricultural producers and distributing to the concentrated and proximate urban population accords with our understandings of the politics of redistribution. When agricultural production is controlled by a small number of actors, the state knows who they are and who to tax; but on the other hand, these large producers often have political power and so receive subsidies.[93]

Large urban areas are threatening to authoritarian regimes because they tend to be illegible to governments and are able to facilitate politically effective collective action near the government's political and economic heart. Urbanites have political leverage and so redistribution is aimed in their direction. Yet, urban-rural status is not as fixed as other such differencing mechanisms: ethnicity, class, religion, and so on.[94] As Bates notes, part of the point of urban bias is for "African states to transform their societies" and the ways in which "governments and their allies seek to displace the peasantry, and to supplant it with a class of persons better suited to their conception of a modern industrial order."[95] Mao certainly believed that industrialization was integral to move the people of China into a new future.[96] While that transformation is partially in the realm of ideas and self-conceptions—separating a people from the land they depended on for generations can be wrenching, much of it is essentially geographic.

ECONOMICS OF INDUSTRIALIZATION

Now if the capitalist sector produces no food, its expansion increases the demand for food, raises the price of food in terms of capitalist products, and so reduces profits. This is one of the senses in which industrialization is dependent upon agricultural improvement; it is not profitable to produce a growing volume of manufactures unless agricultural production is growing simultaneously. This is also why industrial and agrarian revolutions always go together, and why economies in which agriculture is stagnant do not show industrial development.[97]

opposition (Fearon 2000; Beissinger 2007). Spending cycles align with elections, even in nondemocratic contexts (Magaloni 2006; Pepinsky 2007; Blaydes 2010; Wright 2011). A massive literature exists on political business cycles in democracies (Nordhaus 1975; Drazen 2001). Key demographic groups can be targeted for targeted disbursements of funds (i.e., pork) in the pre-election period (Blaydes 2010). Election results are used by regimes to reward supporters and punish opponents (Diaz-Cayeros, Magaloni, and Weingast 2003; Magaloni 2006).

[93] Scott takes the position that the state prefers concentration of agricultural production as large producers are easier to tax, while Bates finds that large producers are subsidized as reward for loyalty and in recognition of their political clout (Scott 1998; Bates 1981).

[94] Components of identity rarely arrive from primordial times fixed at particular values, instead they are constructed and chosen for political reasons (e.g., Anderson 1991; Laitin 1998; Chandra 2006).

[95] Bates 1981, 7.

[96] Kau and Leung 1986.

[97] Timmer 1988, quoting Lewis 1954, 433.

Why do regimes enact urban-biased policies? The Industrial Revolution changed the world and the economic policy environment. How to encourage industrial development became a major question facing regimes. With it comes a corollary, agriculture will decline, "for decline it must," but on what terms?[98] How can a regime best promote development and/or industrialization?[99] The debate is about how urban biased to be and how to be urban biased, that is the level and methods of taxing agricultural and aiding industry. This debate in economics moves the metaphor away from urban bias as a "deal with the devil" to "negotiating terms with the devil."

The economics of urban-rural redistribution and development is an old subject, with famous debates between David Ricardo and Thomas Malthus on Britain's laws protecting corn and other grain producers from international competition in the late 1800s. One view, Malthus's, held that repealing the Corn Laws would lead to increased food imports, causing the terms of trade to turn against agriculture, subsequently depressing food prices and with them the real incomes of Lords. Faced with lower incomes, the Lords would cut their spending, thereby decreasing demand for industrial goods and slow industrial growth. Yet a compelling case could be made in the opposite direction—the repeal of the Corn Laws would aid industry—as Ricardo thought. Landlords' rents hurt rather than helped aggregate demand and decreasing the incomes of landlords by lowering the barriers to importing corn would allow more demand elsewhere.[100]

The Bolsheviks in the Soviet Union faced questions of how to reorder their society and economy in an industrial fashion after taking power. Yevgeni Preobrazhensky believed that the terms of trade should be set against the rural areas as strongly as possible for two reasons: (1) to transfer resources from agriculture to industry as the former lacks the latter's increasing returns to scale and (2) to support state ownership, which at that time was purely located in the industrial sector. The other side of the debate, headed by Nikolai Bukharin, argued in favor of "equilibrium prices," realizing that squeezing the *kulaks* would decrease food production.[101] State support of the "small peasants" might

[98] Varshney 1993, 6.

[99] For a student of Chinese politics, the question of why the industrial revolution began in the West rather than the East is always near the forefront of consideration. The political implications of large factories and the low cultural status of merchants/capitalists seem to be important here. See Wong 1997.

[100] Varshney notes that "modern treatments" (e.g., Taylor 1983; Rao 1986) find that the net effect on aggregate demand depends on how wage earners spend their money sectorally. Also of note, while the repeal of the Corn Laws still represents a free trade move, it is a selective one. Protections for the industrial sector remained in place (Varshney 1993, 1995).

[101] Varshney 1995, 16.

eventually overwhelm the kulaks, but the kulaks understood the threat and fought against these policies. Joseph Stalin sided with Preobrazhensky after the failure of Bukharin's ideas and dealt with its "intrinsic economic problem" with violence—liquidating the kulaks.[102] A similar narrative followed in China. Land reform in China in the 1950s entailed removing landlords and reallocating their land to the farmers. Yet subsequently taxes would squeeze these farmers, who were then forced into cooperatives and the disastrous collectives of the Great Leap Forward.[103]

Industrializing without causing the collapse of the agricultural sector entails navigating a narrow channel between a rock and a hard place. Taxing agriculture too much could lead to famine or force regimes to spend limited resources on food rather than increasing capital stock. Agriculture must produce, but using policy to aid farmers can be a problem for industrialization by increasing effective wages in the countryside. That in turn makes the move to an industrial locale less attractive for a farmer.[104] The proposed solution, from Lewis, was to tax successful farmers' profits in order to push farmers to produce cheap food and benefit from it—but not too much. The revenue that the state received could be funneled into industrial development. Timmer described "four phases" of agricultural transformation.[105] Rising agricultural productivity which creates a surplus; this surplus is tapped by the government (through taxes or price mechanisms affecting the terms of trade) and various linkages yield contributions to general growth; despite growth in agricultural incomes, non-agricultural incomes increase more rapidly (causing political difficulties); and finally, a fully integrated economy.[106]

Different regimes undertake the promotion of industrialization for different reasons. Industrialization can strengthen a country's economy, improve the livelihoods of the people of the country, and provide a regime with the ability to buy off potential enemies and fair-weather friends. Industrialization can

---

[102] Ibid., 17. See chapter 4 for further discussion of famines in the USSR and China.

[103] Naughton 2007; Yang 2012.

[104] Lewis 1954. That is, by making agriculture more economically advantageous, workers will be unwilling to settle for the low wages that developing industry requires for profits to grow.

[105] Timmer 1988, 279–80. Unfortunately, the place of honor that the lowly turnip had earned in previous generations of this tale is less obvious than thought, thus my reluctance to tell that particular tale.

[106] Timmer (2005) has a succinct summary here; in that version, Timmer associates the different stages with authors: (1) Mosher 1966; (2) Johnston and Mellor 1961; (3) Schultz 1978b; (4) Johnson 1997, Gardner 2002. Many late developing nations, particularly in sub-Saharan Africa, are urbanizing without developing economically in terms of GDP per capita. Although there are debates about the extent to which these nations are indeed growing economically and whether GDP statistics are capturing this development (Jerven 2010; Young 2010; Harttgen, Klasen, and Vollmer 2012).

break the political and economic back of a traditional order. Like many a deal with the devil, it can also seem as if there is no alternative. The status quo of an agrarian and artisanal economy is undercut by cheap manufactured goods or by the armies of states that had industrialized previously and were funded by the profits of industrialization. It is beyond the scope of this book to provide the full range of answers as to why and how different regimes attempted to industrialize. While China industrialized for many of the above reasons, this book will not address why it chose to do so. Rather, the interactions between how the regime pushed industrialization and how the population responded are at the heart of this narrative. The ways in which it industrialized and urbanized, and especially how it managed the flows of migration to its largest cities that resulted from its urban-biased policies is an important part of the regime's survival.

The political importance of critical cities is why regimes engage in urban bias, and the amount of bias is influenced by the overall stability of the economic and political situation in which the regime finds itself. Both a regime's resources and its time horizons should influence whether a dictatorship is able to and interested in moving away from urban bias. On both dimensions, the CCP was well-positioned. With resources and the institutional capacity to look beyond the immediate term, the Beijing regime has begun to shift its redistributive policy away from urban bias. China's apparent prescience is made possible by three decades of rapid economic growth and a centralizing 1994 tax reform that filled government coffers in Beijing.[107] The mounting stockpile of revenue from export-led industrial growth provided the central government with additional resources to shield the system from economic shocks. By the mid-2000s, Beijing abolished agricultural taxes and increased subsidies to farmers. To find if the patterns unearthed in China's experience hold more broadly, chapter 7 examines variation in levels of urban bias across dictatorships.

The next chapter establishes empirical support for observable implications of the argument laid out above. Cities are dangerous to authoritarian regimes; redistributing toward cities leads to greater levels of urban concentration; and urban bias represents a Faustian bargain for regimes, decreasing regime longevity.

---

[107] Wang 1997.

CHAPTER 3

Cities, Redistribution, and Regime Survival

The CCP's enduring rule, China's rapid economic development without the slums that plague other poor countries, and the regime's recent fiscal shift away from urban bias are all puzzling. While these puzzles all exist in China, to shed light on how China and the CCP regime fits into the broader context of dictatorships requires stepping away from the Middle Kingdom to compare this regime, its policies, and its cities with those of other nondemocratic regimes. The book's research design pairs cross-national analysis of general patterns of nondemocratic regime survival, urban concentration, and redistribution with closer attention to the ways that the Chinese regime has managed urbanization. As the CCP regime endures, the argument's claims about the danger of cities for nondemocratic regimes cannot be substantiated solely based on an analysis of China. The cross-national analysis shows as clearly as possible the plausibility of the general argument.

Hypotheses

Urban bias—a redistributive strategy that favors of large cities over the country-side—follows political and economic logics attuned to the short run. Yet urban bias changes the incentives for the rural population. Over time, they will tire under the weight of oppressive taxation and relocate to the favored cities. In part, squeezing the agricultural sector is meant to aid industrial development by extricating labor from the traditional and rural agricultural sector to the modern and urban industrial sector. This relocation to urban areas due to urban bias is not evenly distributed among the various cities of a country. Instead, large cities tend to be overrun with in-migrants. To use more formal terms, urban bias increases urban concentration—the share of the urban population within a country that lives in its largest cities—rather than causing a general increase in the level of urbanization within a territory.

Urban concentration, though, represents an increase in the size and power of the main city vis-à-vis the rest of a country's territory. Urban bias is initially intended in part to reduce the political tensions in the main city by keeping those in the capital fed and happy. However, by increasing the main city's size over the long run, urban bias exacerbates the possibility of explosive collective action—and tensions among elites regarding this possibility. As such, the second-order effect of urban bias undermines and overwhelms its direct effect.

The three principal hypotheses examined in this chapter relate to the danger of cities and concentration, the potential for urban bias to induce concentration, and the idea that urban bias is a Faustian bargain.

High levels of urban concentration or large cities should shorten authoritarian regimes. I refer to this as the *danger of concentration hypothesis*. Finding this relationship would help confirm the conventional if untested contention that large cities represent areas of danger for dictators. If no relationship between regime survival and large cities or high levels of urban concentration exists, one would reject the core base of the argument that cities are dangerous.[1]

The *induced concentration hypothesis* posits that urban bias should be associated with more people moving to large cities and to higher levels of urban concentration. If it is not urbanization that is dangerous but specifically the shape of urbanization—namely, large cities and urban concentration—then establishing urban bias's effect on internal migration patterns is crucial for estimating its effects on regime longevity.

The *Faustian bargain hypothesis* claims that while urban bias might have short-term benefits for leaders, its long-term effects—namely inducing urban concentration—are self-undermining for regimes.

The loophole to the Faustian bargain for dictators is to extract from rural areas and redistribute in urban areas while limiting population movement to large cities. I also examine the extent to which migration restrictions allow regimes to survive and are able to reduce migration and urban concentration.

I test these arguments alongside competing accounts for the variance in authoritarian regime survival. Scholars have shown that the type of authoritarian regime, the presence of formal institutions, and the level of economic development all correlate with regime duration. It is possible that urban concentration and cities are mere proxies for other variables that the literature has previously identified as having explanatory power for regime duration. To confirm the

---

[1] If that relationship were positive rather than negative, then there would be even greater cause to reject the hypothesis.

argument of the book, these alternatives must not remove the effects on survival of the structural and policy variables theorized here.

On Various Variables

Clarifying what I mean by these variables and translating them into quantifiable measures is a necessary task. Below, I present discussions of some of the complex and multifaceted constructs that enter into the statistical analyses, including nondemocracy, regime, and urban bias.

ON NONDEMOCRACY

We all know that governments are different and that it is not the same thing to be the citizen or subject of one or another country, even in matters of daily life. We also know that almost all governments do some of the same things, and sometimes we feel like the pure anarchist, for whom all states, being states, are essentially the same. This double awareness is also the point of departure of our intellectual efforts as social scientists.
—Juan Linz, *Totalitarian and Authoritarian Regimes*[2]

The term "nondemocracy" possesses the advantages of being precise and relatively apolitical at the cost of sounding academic.[3] The more common term for nondemocracy is dictatorship, which is more politically fraught (both inside and outside academia) and has traveled far from its origins as an "institutional device" in ancient Rome.[4] Other terms—totalitarian, fascist, tyrannical, etc.— similarly suffer from political baggage in ways that can reduce their analytic utility. What is a nondemocracy? It is a country where the ruler comes to power by means other than competitive elections.[5] Revolutions, *coup d'état*, dynastic succession, selection by military junta or Politburo are all common ways in which these leaders come to rule their territories.

While democracies have institutional differences, nondemocracies differ in radical ways. Often treated as a residual category—that is, all times when countries that are not ruled as democracies—nondemocracy is a catch-all term with large amounts of internal variation. Nondemocracy dominates the history of humanity. It is only recently that democracy has become the regime type for a

---

[2] Linz 2000, 49.
[3] The extent to which democracy is viewed as normatively good or a "universal value," of course, makes nondemocracy—being the antithesis of democracy—normatively bad (Sen 1999).
[4] Gandhi 2008, 3.
[5] As seen below, the operationalization here uses a definition from Przeworski et al. 2000 and Cheibub, Gandhi, and Vreeland 2010.

majority of the world's countries.[6] Historically, monarchs headed most territories.[7] A family governed and passed on the right to reign over the territory to the next generation of the family, usually by formalized lines of succession. In the twentieth century, there was an emergence of new kinds of nondemocratic rule, often termed totalitarian, that instituted control that appeared monolithic and pervasive over society.[8] Scholars debated the extent to which these new regimes were all of one kind or unique enough that, to categorize them as such, would obscure more than enlighten.[9]

Political scientists spent a great deal of time developing typologies that attempted to categorize different nondemocratic regimes into different groups in order to aid analyses of their politics and particularly to see if such variation could help explain if or when they would transition into democracies.[10] The literature that focuses on dividing the nondemocratic world into types focuses mostly on how different kinds of regimes arose, when (or if) these would democratize, and differences in the lives and experiences of leaders and citizens within different kinds of nondemocracies.

A different strand of literature viewed democracy and nondemocracy as a continuum rather than opposite sides of a coin. The extent to which a country could be said to be democratic instead of falling squarely into one camp or the other mattered. Instead of asking if Japan in 1975 was a democracy or not, the question asked how democratic Japan was in 1975 when compared with other places and times (measured against some standard of democracy). Continuous measures of regime type, such as the ones created by Polity and Freedom House, are ubiquitous and numerically dominate the quantitative study of social science, but changes in these democracy scores reflect changes in the regime's leadership only on occasion.[11]

This project calls for analysis of nondemocratic regime survival, and so uses a dichotomous concept of regime type. Yet, as stated, this universe of cases contains multitudes: regimes of very different characters with prospects that vary widely.

---

[6] Diamond (2003), using Freedom House data, puts this transition as happening in 1992.

[7] "Headed" is deliberate here instead of "ruled," since the level of control that the modern nation-state has over its territory is substantially different than that of pre-modern regimes.

[8] Friedrich and Brzezinski (1956) write of the "novel" form of autocracy that they term totalitarian, they "seek to get hold of the entire man, the human being in his totality," whereas older autocracies "were satisfied with excluding him from certain spheres and exploiting him more or less mercilessly in others."

[9] e.g., Arendt 1958; Friedrich 1954; Friedrich and Brzezinski 1956; Tucker 1961; Skilling 1966; Schapiro and Lewis 1969.

[10] Linz 1985; Linz and Stepan 1996.

[11] Dahl 1971. On different measures of democracy, see Cheibub, Gandhi, and Vreeland 2010. For a more expansive treatment, see Munck and Verkuilen 2002.

ON TYPES OF NONDEMOCRACIES

Placing these various regimes into discrete bins is a complicated but necessary task. It is necessary as these types have strong associations with the survival prospects of individual regimes. For *authoritarian regime type*, I use the codings from two different typologies.[12] The original Geddes typology consisted of four different sorts of autocratic regimes: single-party, military, personalist, and hybrids of these three. The various types of authoritarian regimes differ in their elite politics, respond differently to crises, and have been shown to differ in regime duration.[13] However, the original Geddes coding omitted monarchies and non-consolidated regimes. Wright (2008) extends the data from Geddes and includes these regimes. In an alternative typology, Cheibub and Gandhi (2004) distinguish between monarchic, civilian, and military dictatorships based on succession policy, the personal characteristics of both leaders themselves and other regime elites (its "inner sanctum").

Authoritarian regimes of different kinds vary in their duration. In particular, scholars have shown that military regimes are comparatively short-lived, as military leaders are believed to care about the military's integrity and relatively less about maintaining power than other kinds of autocrats. Single-party regimes are especially long-lived; monarchies are also seen as relatively stable. While succession battles may rage in these systems, they tend to be contained to intrigue over which party or family member will be the next ruler rather than whether a party or family member will lead the country. Tied to the regime's eponymous person, personalist regimes endure compared to military regimes but crumble with the departure of the paramount leader. Hybrid regimes, unsurprisingly, contain facets of their component regimes and exhibit varied survival rates.

Such distinctions, however, may mask complex realities within individual regimes over time. For instance, take the core case for the book, that of the long-enduring CCP regime that has ruled the People's Republic of China continuously since 1949. By any measure, there has been no other party that has ruled over China during the past 60 plus years. However, to say that the party itself ruled the country is correct but only in a limited sense. There might not be a better bin to place it in, but variation in the "Partyness" of the CCP regime certainly exists. A clear example of such variation within PRC-era China is the Maoist takeover during the Great Proletarian Cultural Revolution (1966-76), when a whole range of party elites were ousted from their high positions at Mao's whim. The purges were often carried out by masses of child and student activists—the infamous Red Guards—who were loyal to Mao and not the party. The

---

[12] Geddes 1999a, updated by Wright 2008; Cheibub and Gandhi 2004.
[13] Geddes 1999a.

personality cult around Mao gave him uncontested authority during this particular epoch. The party apparatus itself became the revolution's enemy. Party branches were attacked, and new institutions rose up to take their place.[14] In China, this might not be particularly problematic for our coding as Mao was the leader of the party before the Cultural Revolution and during it. He was not ousted in some way that gave any indication that the party's leaders (if not necessarily the party itself) was in power. Yet if the single-party type implies a level of institutionalization and limits on the powers of an individual, then segments of the Mao era push on the confines of this single-party bin.

ON REGIMES

The next step is to identify authoritarian regimes in the set of country-years that are nondemocratic. A regime is "a set of formal and informal rules for choosing leaders and policies."[15] The simplest method to distinguish regimes treats each leader change as a regime change. However, this practice inflates the number of transitions by ignoring political continuity, particularly in party or monarchical states. Yugoslavia's annual rotation of rulers following Josip Tito's death in 1980 or the Jiang Zemin to Hu Jintao transition in the PRC, I argue, is substantively different than the Chiang Kai-shek (KMT) to Mao Zedong (CCP) transition in China in 1949. To address this concern, I treat all leader transitions as regime transitions unless the new leader's entry is coded in a dataset of country leaders, Archigos, as being "regular." The dataset's codebook describes their procedures for labeling a given transition as regular or irregular as follows:

> We code transfers as regular or irregular depending on the political institutions and selection mechanisms in place. We identify whether leaders are selected into and leave political office in a manner prescribed by either explicit rules or established conventions. In a democracy, a leader may come to power through direct election or establishing a sufficient coalition of representatives in the legislature. Although leaders may not be elected or selected in particularly competitive processes, many autocracies have similar implicit or explicit rules for transfers of executive power. Leader changes that occur through designation by an outgoing leader, hereditary succession in a monarchy, and appointment by the central committee of a ruling party would all be considered regular transfers of power from one leader to another in an autocratic regime.[16]

[14] Harding 1997.
[15] Geddes, Wright, and Frantz 2012.
[16] Goemans, Gleditsch, and Chiozza 2009. Archigos 2.9 Codebook, 1-2.

Moving from all leadership changes to only irregular entries reduces the number of regimes in the data from 792 to 435.[17]

As noted above, the "partyness" of the Chinese regime was in doubt during Mao's onslaught of the party during the Cultural Revolution, but, as he stayed in power as an individual, it was the "partyness" and not the regime that was put in question. There was no change at the top that might appear to be a coup or regime change. Yet, in the 1980s, both Hu Yaobang and Zhao Ziyang were removed while the true leader of the party, Deng Xiaoping, stayed in power but did so without holding the highest state positions.[18] Again, in the case of China, one can say with some confidence that these transitions occurred within the regime and never replaced an old regime with a new one. However, in a non-party military junta, such transitions are likely to be seen as regime transitions in a way that they are not in a party regime. It also biases the findings toward a result that party regimes endure.[19]

Another challenge to understanding the nature of a political regime and regime transitions can be found in the Chinese case. The CCP's reign is almost universally divided into two epochs: the Mao era (1949–1976) and the Reform era (1978-the present). That the Party's reign is so often separated into these two periods points to the political salience of this divide. What makes these eras a possible example of a regime transition is not the involuntary shunting aside of Mao's designated successor, Hua Guofeng, by Deng Xiaoping—although, of course, one could make that case as well—but rather the change in the nature of the regime's strategy of legitimation and the core membership of its political coalition. Rather than base the regime on ideological terms, Deng put forward pragmatism and performance as the sources of legitimation for the CCP during this era.[20] "It does not matter if the cat is black or white as long as it catches mice," is a repudiation of ideology's preeminence and a far cry from the politics of Mao's China. To conflate these two periods into a single regime is justified as the vast majority of the individuals and structures from the prior era persisted, but this conflation does simplify a more complex reality. More broadly, one could slice and dice the regimes of dictators in almost innumerable ways based on changes in the individuals in power, their political strategies, and the coalitions that they form with social groups.

---

[17] From 1946 to 2004. Counting each leader change as a regime transition (similar to Escribà-Folch and Wright 2010), rather than the using the regime definition above, does not affect the results as shown in the web appendix of Wallace (2013), especially tables A5–A8.

[18] Deng's official positions at the state and party Central Military Commissions did matter. On the bases of Chinese power, see Dittmer 1978; although Dittmer incorrectly hints that Hua Guofeng's tenure is likely to persist much longer than it did. Deng is listed as China's leader by Archigos despite his lack of titles in one of only a few such exceptions to their general practice.

[19] I merely note this difficulty and potential weakness of the analysis.

[20] Perry 2008. Nationalism was also emphasized after the 1989 Tiananmen crisis.

ON ORIGINS

The study of regime survival focuses on regime death. New regimes appear automatically by definition when the *ancien régime* dies. However, the opposite end of the lifespan of regimes—a regime's birth—is rarely examined in as much depth. Yet the origins of regimes may contain information about their ability to negotiate crises and the underlying strength of the political coalitions they maintain. An urban elite menaced by rivals vying for control may cohere more strongly than one not facing such a direct threat.[21] Elite collective action may help account for regime resilience, and if distinct from threats at the moment of regime origination, this effect on variation in survival could be identifiable. However, the argument made here is that the presence of urban threats should undermine regime duration, not abet it.

The power of the party as explaining duration may also be a function of the origins of party regimes, specifically their revolutionary histories.[22] Levitsky and Way argue regimes that emerge out of violence endure, and they see the literature's emphasis on the "partyness" of regimes as misplaced. Rather, they argue that instead of parties and institutionalization driving regime durability and duration, their origins in revolution enable regime elites to be willing and able to employ an armed response to potential protests, or to use methods of high intensity coercion that can help avoid such circumstances from coming about in the first place. That is, the party regimes of Vietnam, China, and other places endure not because of their Communist Parties but because of the violent origins—the fire and brimstone that these regimes had to walk through to come to power and dominate the territories that they reign over. The debate about the relative causal power of these regime characteristics is significant, but such accounts leave significant amount of variation to be explained from structural and policy factors—including choices that regimes make after their birth—as this book demonstrates.

ON CITIES, URBAN CONCENTRATION, AND CAPITALS

The principal independent variable for the analysis of regime survival is *urban concentration*, that is, the share of the urban population in a country that lives in its largest city.[23] It is also possible to think of the political importance of urban concentration solely in terms of the capital city. While for the vast majority of cases (91.8%) the capital city is in fact the country's largest, this pattern is not

---

[21] Such experience is likely to produce strong "protection pacts" among the elite rather than weaker "provision pacts" (Slater 2010).

[22] Levitsky and Way 2010, 2012.

[23] It also serves as the dependent variable for table 3.4 to assess the *induced concentration hypothesis*.

universal.[24] Measuring the size of an urban population is not a trivial task, as it requires both a count of the population in an area and a demarcation of the territory of the city in question. This analysis uses data from the United Nations Population Division's World Urbanization Prospects 2009 Revision.[25] The measure for urban concentration takes this population estimate for the largest city as the numerator and the total urban population of the country as the denominator.[26] In addition to using the level of urban concentration in a territory, I also use the size of the largest city in a country and find similar results. This alternate measure captures not just the dominance of one locale over others but also the mechanisms related to size—such as the propensity of powerful protests and the illegibility of populations in megacities—that are posited in the theoretical chapter.

However, these two measures do not capture the full range of ideas from the previous chapter. There are a number of measurement issues that need to be considered. First is the possibility of the "edge" cases. A country with only one urban individual could be seen as having 100 percent urban concentration, or in less extreme terms, a country could have essentially no cities at all and only a small central village of some hundreds of people in one "agglomeration." However, such extreme cases do not exist in the data. The time period under examination in the cross-national survival analysis, 1950-2004, is of modern vintage and includes principally only countries with populations over one million.[27] The arguments that I make are for a modern era where industrialization has occurred frequently enough to provide strategies for countries trying to industrialize and thereby reap the economic rewards of doing so. These rewards could also lead to long-term political costs for such regimes. All countries during this time have cities on the order of tens of thousands of individuals, with the largest cities in most countries possessing hundreds of thousands to millions of residents.[28]

One could replace urban concentration with population concentration, that is, the share of the total population of the country that lives in the largest city—simply, concentration—rather than the share of the urban population that lives in the largest city—urban concentration. Using concentration, the general

---

[24] In a paper published at the *JOP*, I used the capital's share of the urban population rather than the largest city's share, as used here (Wallace 2013). The results are qualitatively identical.

[25] UN DESA 2010.

[26] More details on the variable creation are found in the online appendix of the *JOP* piece (Wallace 2013).

[27] The inclusion of micro-states, those having population under 1 million, does not affect the results (Wallace 2013).

[28] Only the smallest 5 percent of country-years in the data have largest cities with fewer than 100,000 residents.

results hold but not as strongly.[29] My argument is about the dangers that large masses of populations pose for dictatorial regimes. Concentration points to the importance of a given locale in dominating the political and economic landscape of a territory. It magnifies the importance of this locale in contrast to others. Choosing between focusing on concentration and urban concentration requires deciding on the correct set of "other" locales. I focus on urban concentration because I believe that the dominance of the largest city over other cities gives the core city's street politics sway over the country, as it is most identified with modernity. On the other hand, concentration is more a function of the country's size and its level of economic development than about the political and symbolic dominance of the city in question.

While the analysis here uses the largest city in a country as its base measure of how large cities are threatening to regimes, the street politics of capital cities, arguably, possess more symbolic importance for the regime's stability than those in the rare instances in which the largest city is not the capital. This possibility makes the decision of a number of regimes to move their capital more intriguing. Myanmar's military junta moved its capital from a sprawling metropolis, Rangoon, to Naypyitaw—a space carved out of the jungle.[30] It is interesting to note—and consistent with the broader argument that large capital cities are dangerous for autocratic regimes—that each of these cases entailed moving the capital from a larger city to a smaller one.[31]

ON URBAN BIAS

The argument identifies both redistributive policy and migration restrictions as channels that regimes use to manage urbanization and urban concentration. Cross-national measures of policies associated with these channels are difficult to collect. This study utilizes a new dataset on distortions to agricultural markets

---

[29] In particular when the city-state of Singapore is omitted, the results hold. Singapore is always an outlier in the population data, and more so when using concentration in place of urban concentration. Using concentration, its score (100%) is roughly ten times the average—that is a distant outlier—while when using urban concentration its score (100%) is only three times the median, an outlier but less problematic one.

[30] One of the possible explanations for the decision to move the capital is entitled "isolating central administration from the larger population centre" (Myoe 2006). Other cases of nondemocratic regimes moving their capitals since 1960 include Lagos to Abuja (Nigeria) in 1991, Dar es Salaam to Dodoma (Tanzania) in 1986, Almaty to Astana (Kazakhstan) in 1999, and Karachi to Islamabad (Pakistan) in 1969.

[31] This is, of course, not always the case historically. For instance, the capital's move from the smaller St. Petersburg to the larger Moscow in the USSR occurs outside of the time range of the analysis. As documented in Wallace (2013), the results presented are robust to using capital cities instead of largest cities.

as a proxy for rural-urban redistributive policy.[32] The World Bank's Distortions to Agricultural Incentives project attempts to measure systematically the biases in governmental policy dealing with agricultural markets across a wide swath of countries. The measure used here, the *relative rate of assistance* (RRA), reflects the extent of government assistance to agriculture relative to other sectors of the economy.

The goal of the World Bank's Distortions to Agricultural Incentives project is to use the measures to suggest improved policies across a wide swath of countries.[33] As they say in their methodology report, a key purpose of the estimates is:

> To provide a long annual time series of indicators showing the extent to which price incentives faced by farmers and food consumers have been distorted directly and indirectly by own-government policies in all major developing, transition and high-income countries, and hence for the world as a whole (taking international prices as given).[34]

Estimates of these distortions are derived on a per-crop basis for each country-year and then aggregated up to national level estimates. The estimates include data based on border price differences, domestic market prices, exchange and inflation rates, price distortions for intermediate inputs (e.g., fertilizers), and international trading costs, among others.[35] The aggregate estimate for each country-year is the Nominal Rate of Assistance (NRA) to agriculture. As this represents a combined assessment of government policies in favor of agriculture, higher values represent more assistance and lower values represent less assistance. Lower values, then, represent policies that are more urban-biased.[36]

While NRA represents assistance to agriculture through policy, it is a measure of nominal assistance. Its utility as a measure of urban bias ignores the possibility that a regime might assist both agriculture and industry. The NRA methodology simply tallies many different aspects of assistance to agriculture but ignores

---

[32] Anderson and Valenzuela 2008.

[33] Anderson and Valenzuela 2012.

[34] Anderson et al. 2008, 5. The World Bank project is broader in scope than my own. In particular, it also addresses the rural-biased policies of the developed world and places these along with the urban-biased policies of the developing world on the same scale.

[35] Anderson et al. 2008, 5–19.

[36] The methodology of the construction of the NRA series consistently references agricultural producers themselves as the beneficiaries of positive NRA rather than the sector as a whole (i.e., urban consumers) giving one confidence that it is measuring urban-rural bias. However, the distribution of the assistance remains opaque and varying proportions of the assistance may go to urban/rural regions in different countries potentially reducing its utility of the measure of urban bias. As an example, the US farm subsidies often seem to be directed to agribusiness and land owners who may actually reside in urban areas.

industrial assistance. It is possible that a regime could receive a positive NRA but is actually helping its industrial sectors even more than the agricultural ones and thus is, to some extent, actually enacting policies biased against agriculture. Understanding this potential flaw in their variable's construction, the team created a second estimate that attempts to control for this possibility: the RRA.[37] Just as there was a construction of assistance to the agricultural sector in the creation of the NRA, a similar process assembles information on the assistance going to non-agricultural sectors. This "NRA to non-agriculture" is used to make a ratio of relative assistance to agriculture according to the following equation:

$$RRA = (1 + NRA_{ag})/(1 + NRA_{nonag}) - 1$$

This relative measure then shows not simply how much the policies of the state are assisting agriculture but also how much assistance is going to agriculture relative to other sectors of the economy. As it happens, in the universe of country-years under examination in this study, these measures are highly correlated $(r > 0.9)$.

RRA is the measure of urban bias in the analysis, which is an independent variable in table 3.4 explaining urban concentration and an independent variable accounting for regime survival in table 3.5; however, it measures support for agriculture. A shift in a negative direction in RRA is actually a shift toward further urban bias and vice versa. The measure used below, *urban bias*, transforms RRA such that increases in the assistance to agriculture are decreases in urban bias and reduced assistance to agriculture raises the level of urban bias.[38]

ON MIGRATION RESTRICTIONS

As noted above, the "migration restrictions" construct is a broad one, ranging from internal passport systems such as China's *hukou* to exclusionary policies that create slums to slum clearance policies. Cross-national data on migration restrictions are only available starting in 1981, and this limited time frame prevents their incorporation into the full statistical analyses below. The best available data come from the Cingranelli-Richards (CIRI) human rights data project, which codes US State Department Human Rights Reports across a number of policy dimensions.[39] Policies that limit "citizens'

[37] Ibid., 24. As the RRA measure requires additional information in order to be created, it is not surprising that it is available for a smaller set of the country-years under examination.

[38] In order to facilitate intuitive understanding of the analysis to come, I transform RRA by multiplying it by −100 so that an increase reflects higher levels of urban bias and its scale is proportional to the other variables.

[39] Cingranelli and Richards 2008, 2011. Another possible source of data comes from the UN, where its *Population Policies 2009* puts together answers for different countries on their self-reported population policies and the goals of such policies. I have serious questions about the quality of these

freedom to travel within their own country" are one such dimension, coded as follows:

> A score of 0 indicates that this freedom was severely restricted, a score of 1 indicates the freedom was somewhat restricted, and a score of 2 indicates unrestricted freedom of movement.[40]

I collapse this coding into a dichotomous variable noting the presence or absence of restrictions on the freedom of movement, as the coding rules state that internal passport schemes and work permits are consistent with a "somewhat restricted" score.[41] A possible concern is that curtailed freedom of movement within a country might not proxy for controls on the freedom to migrate to a country's largest, or primate, city. However, I find that lower levels of urban concentration are associated with these restrictions, suggesting that the CIRI data on restrictions on freedom of movement captures barriers to rural-to-city migration. Urban concentration exceeds the mean level in only 37 percent of regimes with migration restrictions, whereas over 60 percent of country-years without migration restrictions have concentration levels above the mean.[42]

I argue that China's migration restrictions have been part of the regime's economic development strategy. By discriminating against farmers, the regime was able to maintain social stability in cities that made investment there more attractive. Such discrimination against farmers continued in the private sector, where migrant laborers knew to temper their wage demands lest they be removed from the urban locale altogether. Migration restrictions might affect regime survival in multiple ways through different channels. First, migration restrictions may directly abet regime survival. For a given level of urban concentration and economic growth, regimes that restrict movement might endure. One could imagine that this factor would operate through mechanisms such as the maintenance of urban order through only winners being present in the prime cities. Second, migration restrictions might decrease urban concentration and

---

data. China is seen in 2009 as changing from limiting to encouraging the growth of urban agglomerations. It does not appear as if the UN data actually assesses policies independently or simply reports answers to the survey. As such, it is not used here.

[40] Cingranelli and Richards 2008.

[41] Ibid., 42. The results are robust to the inclusion of only severe or both severe and somewhat restricted categories as controls. See table A17 in the web appendix of Wallace (2013) for details.

[42] Of the 548 country-years without migration restrictions, 338 exhibit high levels of urban concentration. Of the 1,410 country-years with migration restrictions, only 533 have high levels of urban concentration (Pearson chi-square 91.1, $p < 0.001$). If one analyzes these four situations, three of them yield mean regime durations around five years. When migration restrictions are present and the urban concentration level is low, on the other hand, regimes endure for over 10 years on average. N.b. as noted in the text, the migration restriction data are only available from 1981 to 2004.

so increase regime duration. That is, such policies reduce the dangers of cities by limiting their expansion. Third, migration restrictions might increase economic growth, which also might be associated with improved chances of regime survival through a given period of years. Finally, migration restrictions might decrease the prominence or even existence of slums in ways that enhance regime survival probabilities.

The lack of long-running, neutral, and valid data on migration restrictions precludes the inclusion of this variable in the statistical analyses below. As the CIRI data series begins in 1981, it limits the number of regime-years in the analysis and censors long-lived regimes. Second, the source of the data may bias it to omit politically inconvenient references to restrictions in US allies in ways that could systematically distort the results. Finally, the "travel restrictions" data only cover part of the ways in which regimes attempt to slow urbanization and urban concentration. The discrimination against rural people in cities takes many forms, including the phenomena of slums and their removal.

ON SLUMS

The political danger of slums comes from the fact that they are areas of concentrated population and poverty. In addition, the symbolic power of a slum in a central city emerges from its status as a testament to the failures of the regime. Yet high-quality measures of the existence, location, and conditions of slums cross-nationally are elusive and so no measures are included in the statistical analysis to come.

UN Habitat data, for example, do not account for the spatial clustering or dispersion of these populations.[43] UN Habitat conducts surveys of individuals living in cities and includes questions about living conditions. The "slum" population in a city is based on the share of respondents answering that their living conditions are below some critical threshold. As such, what is actually captured is not an estimate of the slum population but instead an estimate of the number of impoverished individuals living in a given city.

As I have noted previously, in Chinese cities, the "slum" population does not reside in clusters, but rather is spread thinly throughout the urban environment. I believe that this dispersion reduces the ability of the urban impoverished to come together and act collectively, as each small community has individual concerns and hence less of a sense of a collective "slum-dweller" identity. Perhaps even more importantly, the lack of these easily identifiable clusters reduces their

---

[43] UN Habitat 2012.

political utility in intra-elite struggles as well as their ability to shape the narrative of a place's street politics.

It should be noted, however, that many consider China to have slums.[44] I would instead argue that China has exclusionary policies that discriminate against migrants in urban areas but that these policies create communities and migration patterns that differ from traditional slums that exist in the heart of major cities in most developing countries. To use the language of Wedeen, these areas in China are peripheral to the principal narrative of the city, whereas in other cities of the developing world, the slums are part of the core idea of the city's population and so are of substantial political importance.[45]

Consider the following counterfactual: if the hundreds of thousands of construction workers in Beijing clustered in one area of the city rather than dispersed in work sites, apartment basements, and other locales, then this inevitably slum-like community, teeming with those who have not benefited from the regime's policies, would be eyed warily, like a barrel of gunpowder. China's villages-in-cities (城中村, *chengzhongcun*) are slum-like but are not of the scale of what we generally think of as slums in the developing world's cities.[46] Even more importantly, they are not the result of land invasions where the state has failed to control territory while the slum dwellers rule. Instead, these are built-up areas where villagers rent out space to migrants. The conditions are shabby and point to the high level of inequality within the society. However, these villages-in-cities do not highlight state weakness as much as do slums whose origins lie in a regime's inability to control property rights over land. The visible presence of slums affects the political scene and adds tension even if the community itself were stable today.

ON PROTESTS

Systematic and accurate counts of collective action incidents in nondemocracies are difficult to obtain. The data that social scientists traditionally have used are media mentions of collective action incidents. In large part, this difficulty comes from regimes themselves suppressing protests and more significantly suppressing media reporting on protests that do in fact occur. Yet their public nature allows significant numbers of such incidents to be reported on and compiled.

---

[44] e.g., Feler and Henderson 2011; Miller 2012.

[45] Wedeen 2013.

[46] Miller 2012, 19. As Miller put it in an interview, China had slums but they were not like those in other countries, "The term slum has become associated with Bombay, Dakar, those kinds of [places]. We're talking very slummy slums." *Sinica Podcast*, 17 January 2013.

The collective action data come from two sources: first, the urban social disturbance dataset describes 3,375 events in African and Asian cities from 1960 to 2006 using Keesing's World Events and second, the Cross-National Time Series dataset, which compiles news reports of different kinds of contentious political actions.[47]

The number of cases where protests directly removed leaders is small.[48] But if one examines the histories of turnover where protests are not coded as the direct source of turnover, protests are often present. I analyze regime changes with all manner of irregular removals, including mass uprisings, coups, and democratic transitions. Urban concentration acts as a political stressor that makes a regime-ending collapse more likely even if protests are not coded as the proximate cause of the regime's death.[49] For example, in Peru's 1975 bloodless coup, General Morales replaced General Velasco as government chief. Although the transition is coded as a military coup not specifically involving collective action, tensions were building in the country and in the capital specifically, with violent riots, strikes, and student demonstrations taking place in Lima in the weeks and months leading up to the coup.[50] These pressures were part of the political calculus behind the military throwing its support to Morales over the ailing Velasco.

Methods and Data

The cross-national analysis provides an empirical examination of three different claims put forward by the argument. The first, the *danger of concentration hypothesis*, predicts that nondemocratic regime duration will decrease as urban concentration increases. The second, the *induced concentration hypothesis*, states that urban bias should be associated with increased levels of urban concentration. The third, the *Faustian bargain hypothesis*, expects urban bias to strengthen regimes in the short term but subvert them in the long term. Redistributive

---

[47] Urdal (2008) compiled the Keesings data; Banks (2011), the CNTS. The dependent variable data from the Banks portion of table 3.3 is produced by adding all of the totals of the collective action events from the Banks datafile, in particular: "Assassinations," "General Strikes," "Guerrilla Warfare," "Government Crises," "Purges," "Riots," "Revolutions," and "Anti-Government Demonstrations." The online appendix to Wallace (2013) also includes correlations with individual components of this joint collective action events data with urban concentration (see tables A16 and A17).

[48] Based on Archigos' codings, 3 cases where a "Leader lost power as a result of domestic popular protest with foreign support" and 26 cases where a "Leader lost power as a result of domestic popular protest without foreign support." Archigos 2.9 Codebook, 3.

[49] Urban concentration thus plays a role similar to that of decay in Kalyvas's (1999) treatment of the decay and breakdown of the European Communist regimes.

[50] Hofmann 1975.

policy favoring cities temporarily abets regimes but also induces urban concentration that undermines them.

As this study examines the causes and correlates of authoritarian regime failure, it uses survival analysis rather than other statistical methods.[51] The primary method of analysis is a Cox proportional hazard model, although the results are robust to other modeling choices, such as log-logistic or Weibull distributions.[52] In a Cox model, a positive coefficient for an independent variable indicates an increased instantaneous probability of failure, while a negative coefficient indicates a reduction in the hazard rate.

I analyze nondemocratic regimes from the post-World War II era, 1946-2004.[53] The regime data come from two primary sources: dichotomous regime type codings from Cheibub and Gandhi (2004), which update the Przeworski et al. (2000) project, and leader data from Archigos 2.9 by Goemans, Gleditsch, and Chiozza (2009), which collect information on leaders and their entries and exits.[54] Country-years are coded as nondemocratic if they fail any of the following four conditions:

1. The chief executive must be chosen by popular election or by a body that was itself popularly elected.
2. The legislature must be popularly elected.
3. There must be more than one party competing in the elections.
4. An alternation in power under electoral rules identical to the ones that brought the incumbent to office must have taken place.[55]

The universe of nondemocratic country-years is delineated by these coding rules following the Cheibub and Gandhi data.

---

[51] e.g., Bienen and van de Walle 1989; Geddes 1999a; Box-Steffensmeier and Jones 1997. Survival analysis helps this study as it allows for regimes that do not last an entire year to be examined, while other methods tend to restrict a country-year to a single observation. This is critical when considering country-years with multiple regimes and regimes surviving less than a full year.

[52] Results using other models as well as other robustness checks for the results presented in the tables of the paper are available in the web appendix. Cox proportional hazard models utilize a baseline hazard function that is shifted depending on the covariates for each case, making the calculation of explained variance, such as an R^2 value in OLS, essentially meaningless (Box-Steffensmeier and Jones 2004).

[53] The regimes data go back to 1946, but the city population data and hence the urban concentration measure, which relies on the city population data, start in 1950. Thirty-seven regimes are left-censored by at least one year, although only 25 of them have urban concentration data. All of these save Bhutan, Saudi Arabia, and Jordan failed by the end of the period under study. Dropping all left-censored regimes has no effect on the results (see table A16 in the web appendix of Wallace 2013).

[54] Przeworski et al. 2000; Cheibub and Gandhi 2004; Goemans, Gleditsch, and Chiozza 2009. The merging process is described in the web appendix of the paper (Wallace 2013).

[55] Cheibub, Gandhi, and Vreeland 2010, 69.

Legislatures, among other formal institutions normally seen in democracies, appear to enhance the durability of nondemocratic regimes.[56] Legislatures allow for safer negotiation between core members of the regime and outsiders, co-opting potential adversaries into the regime. When paired with elections, legislatures can also be a fruitful source of regime-enhancing information on both the preferences of the public and the quality of candidates.[57]

Level of economic development is generally seen as abetting autocratic regime survival, contra the classic works of modernization theory. Wealthier regimes have greater ability to act as rentier states and with lower stakes in their politics are less prone to revolution; both of these factors should aid a regime's chances of enduring.[58] Level of economic development data come from Gleditsch (2002), which fills in much of the missing data from the Penn World Tables and other datasets by inter- and extrapolation as well as examining electricity usage and other statistics.[59]

I also control for the presence of civil or inter-state conflict. Civil wars have tended to be fought in the periphery, although the dominance of rural insurgency-based civil wars is on the decline since the end of the Cold War.[60] Nonetheless, conflicts might hasten regime demise, whether they are intra- or inter-state in nature. *Conflict* is a dummy variable that takes the value of one in all cases where the UCDP dataset count of current conflicts is non-zero. There are 1,192 country-years where conflict takes a value of 1.

Analysis

Cities are dangerous as they grow in population and dominate the urban population of a country. Is urban concentration negatively associated with authoritarian regime longevity? For the 235 regimes with urban concentration levels above the mean level in the data, the mean duration is 8.6 years and the annual regime death rate is 9.1 percent. For the 198 regimes characterized by low levels of urban concentration, the incidence rate is only 5.7 percent and the mean duration is 12.2 years.[61] Regimes where the largest city dominates the urban landscape fail

---

[56] Gandhi 2008; Wright 2008.

[57] Blaydes 2010; Malesky and Schuler 2010.

[58] Lipset 1959; Ross 2012.

[59] The wider coverage of the Gleditsch data allows 800 additional observations into the analysis. The main results are unchanged if Penn World Tables GDP data is used (Wallace 2013, table A9).

[60] On insurgency as the dominant technology of civil war, see Fearon and Laitin 2003. Kalyvas and Balcells (2010) show that this dominance has eroded following the end of superpower support for regimes such as occurred during the Cold War. The survival analysis results presented in this chapter are not a Cold War artifact (Wallace 2013, table A10).

[61] Using medians rather than means yields almost exactly the same results.

nearly four years sooner and face 60 percent greater death rates. A similar pattern befalls regimes with large cities, regardless of the level of urban concentration. For countries with over 10 million in total population, 60 regimes face a largest city with over three million people, while 103 regimes do not have a city of that scale. The median case for regimes with such large cities is only a four-year dura- tion. On the other hand, without such a large city, the median regime survives for 10 years, more than twice as long. There is nothing particular about three million. A five million cutoff yields 37 regimes with a median duration of two years for regimes with large cities and 120 regimes with a median of nine years for regimes without them. This represents *prima facie* evidence in support of the danger of concentration hypothesis.

The inclusion of control variables does not affect these key results.[62] Table 3.1 shows a substantively and statistically significant positive coefficient for urban concentration across all specifications. The coefficient for 0.945 for the urban concentration variable from Model 3.1.1 translates into an increased risk of col- lapse of 43 percent when moving from one standard deviation below to one standard deviation above the mean level of urban concentration, controlling for autocratic regime type and other factors.

The control variables mostly have effects in the expected directions. When compared with the baseline of personalist and hybrid regimes, monarchies and party regimes are relatively resilient whereas military regimes are short-lived. Legislatures, similarly fitting with previous findings, are associated with dura- bility. On the other hand, wealth is not associated with an independent effect enhancing regime survival. This surprising non-finding comes from three sources. First, including monarchies as a separate category of regimes absorbs much of the explanatory power of wealth as monarchies tend to be both lasting and rich. Second, legislatures are more prevalent in richer regimes, as evidenced by the size of the coefficient for wealth increasing when legislatures are omit- ted from Model 3.1.3. Finally, the greater coverage of the Gleditsch GDP data includes many relatively poor but long-lasting regimes that are dropped when using the Penn World Tables data.[63]

I argue that large cities are dangerous. Table 3.1 shows that even once one controls for factors that other scholars have found to account for variance in regime survival, having higher levels of urban concentration decreases the expected length of regimes substantially. Table 3.2 shows that similar results are found when large cities are measured by their population rather than their share of the country's urban population (i.e., urban concentration) even after

Table 3.1 **Urban Concentration Harms Regime Survival**

Variables	Model 3.1.1	Model 3.1.2	Model 3.1.3	Model 3.1.4
Urban Concentration	0.945**	0.948**	0.846**	0.911**
	(0.388)	(0.387)	(0.383)	(0.385)
Military Regime	0.790***	0.797***	0.796***	0.864***
	(0.159)	(0.166)	(0.166)	(0.171)
Monarchic Regime	−1.026***	−1.009***	−0.896***	−0.974***
	(0.330)	(0.333)	(0.327)	(0.333)
Single-Party Regime	−0.916***	−0.911***	−0.905***	−0.818***
	(0.212)	(0.210)	(0.211)	(0.213)
Legislature	−0.338**	−0.336**		−0.425**
	(0.164)	(0.164)		(0.168)
Civil/International Conflict				0.267*
				(0.150)
GDP Growth				−2.539***
				(0.561)
Real GDP per capita (logged)		−0.019	−0.026	
		(0.073)	(0.074)	
Observations	3,694	3,694	3,694	3,597
Regimes	332	332	332	325
Failures	244	244	244	238
Log-Pseudolikelihood	−1155	−1155	−1157	−1101

Robust standard errors in parentheses. Cox Models.
***$p < 0.01$, **$p < 0.05$, *$p < 0.1$.

controlling for other causes of regime instability. The four models in table 3.2 are paired. The first two show that, after controlling for the size of the national population, larger cities also are associated with brief regime tenures. Moving from a city with a population one standard deviation below the mean to one with a population one standard deviation above it increases risk by 52 percent, using Model 3.2.1. Model 3.2.2 includes nondemocratic regime type controls as well as controls for legislature, conflict, and GDP growth.[64] The inclusion of these control variables causes some attenuation in the estimated coefficient for city population, implying that some of the estimated effect from Model 3.2.1 for city population's ability to decrease survival prospects for regimes is better

[64] Here using the Cheibub and Gandhi nondemocratic regime type codings.

Table 3.2 **Large Cities are Dangerous for Regimes**

Variables	Model 3.2.1	Model 3.2.2	Model 3.2.3 10 million +	Model 3.2.4 10 million +
City Population (logged)	0.209*** (0.069)	0.161** (0.082)	0.409*** (0.129)	0.408*** (0.154)
Total Population (logged)	−0.185*** (0.071)	−0.213*** (0.082)	−0.190 (0.147)	−0.193 (0.160)
Royal Dictatorship		−1.543*** (0.512)		−0.685 (0.736)
Military Dictatorship		0.179 (0.175)		−0.187 (0.277)
Legislature		−0.269* (0.147)		0.119 (0.237)
Civil/International Conflict		0.350** (0.139)		0.087 (0.216)
GDP Growth		−1.787*** (0.518)		−2.204*** (0.796)
Observations	4,306	4,155	1,929	1,863
Regimes	381	372	144	140
Failures	318	306	115	109
Log-Pseudolikelihood	−1601	−1497	−464.2	−428.2

Robust standard errors in parentheses. Cox Models.
***$p < 0.01$, **$p < 0.05$, *$p < 0.1$.

captured by other factors. Notably, positive GDP growth and status as a royal dictatorship aid regime survival.

The second pair of models drops all countries that have total populations under 10 million. Rather than dealing with nearly 400 regimes and over 300 regime collapses as in Models 3.2.1 and 3.2.2, the number of regimes in the final two models is only 144 with 115 failures.[65] Eliminating the small countries substantially strengthens the results either when including just the population variables (Model 3.2.3) or the full set of covariates (Model 3.2.4). The estimated decline in survival is now 49.3 percent for a one standard deviation move in population of the largest city. A final piece to note is that only GDP growth and city population

[65] 140 and 109 for Model 3.2.4.

appear to be linked to regime survival in Model 3.2.4; all of the other factors that the literature has found significant fail to approach non-zero estimated effects.

Support for the *danger of concentration hypothesis* is robust with the connection between urban concentration (table 3.1) and city size (table 3.2) and regime collapse. The type of survival model used or treatment of urban concentration as continuous or dichotomous does not affect the results. The findings are also unchanged by the addition of regional controls, dropping regimes with small or large populations, or using the Cheibub and Gandhi regime codings rather than those from Geddes and Wright.

Why are large cities dangerous? Cities make effective collective action easier and more dangerous and reduce the ability of the regime to observe its citizens. Realized collective action events are observable, even if isolating the specific trigger for a given instance of collective action is next to impossible.[66] High levels of urban concentration represent abundant kindling upon which a spark may engulf a territory. Urban concentration is tied to a greater chance of collective action, as seen in table 3.3.[67] All models report positive and statistically significant coefficients for urban concentration and city size on the number of collective action events. Increasing the size of the largest city by one unit (on its logged scale) translates into the expected difference in the logged number of events increasing by 0.50, while holding the other variables in the model constant. These results are not due to the particular data series being used; large cities are the modal location for significant incidents of collective action in other datasets as well.[68]

The Social Conflict in Africa Database (SCAD) of collective action is dominated by events in capital cities and other major urban areas. Using large city population instead of urban concentration in models akin to table 3.3 yields similar results. Although these databases may capture a greater percentage of collective action events that occur in capital cities than in peripheries,[69] those collective action events that are measured have a strong influence in terms of regime survival.[70] In this way, any potential bias in the reporting of events may reflect the real political importance of large cities. To wit, if a tree falls (or protest happens) and no one sees it, does it really matter?

Larger and more dominant cities are home to more collective action events. Do we find that such events are associated with regime collapses? Yes, but this result comes with many caveats. Namely, the event data in the Banks dataset are

---

[66] Kuran 1991; Lohmann 1994.

[67] The urban concentration and regime variables are detailed below in the data section and the web appendix.

[68] Salehyan and Hendrix 2011.

[69] Schedler 2012.

[70] Wallace 2013, tables A19 and A20.

Table 3.3 **Urban Concentration Linked to Collective Action**

Variables	Model 3.3.1 Banks	Model 3.3.2 Banks	Model 3.3.3 Prio	Model 3.3.4 Prio
Urban Concentration	2.59*** (0.44)		2.85*** (0.81)	
Real GDP per capita (logged)	−0.09 (0.08)	−0.10 (0.09)	−0.09 (0.12)	0.01 (0.11)
GDP Growth	−1.89*** (0.29)	−2.11*** (0.27)	−2.78*** (0.53)	−2.92*** (0.53)
City Population (logged)		0.22** (0.10)		0.50*** (0.20)
Constant	0.52 (0.67)	0.62 (0.96)	0.25 (0.99)	−1.98 (1.61)
Ln alpha	0.20*** (0.04)	0.24*** (0.04)	0.07 (0.08)	0.08 (0.07)
Observations	3,779	3,974	1,656	1,675
Year FE	YES	YES	YES	YES
Country FE	YES	YES	YES	YES

Robust standard errors in parentheses.
***$p < 0.01$, **$p < 0.05$, *$p < 0.1$.

aggregated up for the entire year, which means that running the analysis would allow for the possibility of anachronisms, such as incorrectly attributing certain events that happened after the regime turnover to having caused the change.

Yet even with collective action included in a survival analysis, urban concentration is associated with shorter regime durations. This suggests that while much of the explanatory power of dominant cities comes from protests, realized events do not account for the entire power of cities to undermine regimes. The argument here is that the political threat arising from the possibilities of riots can be felt in expectation and not only after they take place. Further, cities reduce the legibility of the regime's population and so this might undermine the regime's ability to detect and protect itself from a myriad of threats.[71]

One could ask, "How would one know that the threat of collective action did not operate in a given case (or in the entirety of the data)?" First, it is important to remember that collective action is but one of two channels by which cities

[71] Quantifying the legibility factor is beyond difficult. How does one measure the inability to measure or observe activity?

undermine the survival of authoritarian regimes. In the second channel, cities reduce the "legibility" of the population to the state, and so give potential opponents—be they from the elite or from the masses—more ability to organize effectively without state interruption. The task of governing a city increases in difficulty as its size increases. That being said, I do not claim nor intend for this to be a complete theory of authoritarian regime survival. In an individual case, regimes collapse for all manner of reasons. The modal regime failure is a military coup. Undoubtedly, there are cases where the leader of a successful coup never directly considers collective action or the threat of collective action or the size of the capital city as something that might undermine the stability of the *ancien régime*. However, a coup leader's cognizance of the political environment's structure—in this case, that larger cities are associated with shorter regimes and more collective action—is close to irrelevant to the determination of the importance of that structure. Further, it might be the case that plotting a coup without being discovered before the plan is fully hatched is easier in a larger city. Coups could also be more likely to succeed and be accepted in a country with large cities as the downsides of unclear leadership may be higher in complex, illegible environments. Leadership instability or fragmentation might seem particularly undesirable in an urban environment where order could collapse and large-scale violence erupt at a moment's notice, making a drawn-out leadership fight more dangerous than in a more stable urban context.

Even though cities and regime collapse are correlated, the relationship may not be directly causal. Urban concentration is a structural factor that has no agency to overthrow regimes itself. The mechanisms linking cities and urban concentration to regime collapse are collective action and legibility. But it is possible that structural factors themselves may play a role. For instance, weak regimes might be prone to both urban concentration and collapse simply through an inability to project power outside of the capital city. If weakness leads to urban concentration and subsequent collapse following the mechanisms outlined above, this is not problematic for the argument. More difficult to address is the chance that weak regimes have high levels of urban concentration but the concentration itself is not causing collapse. In this view, urban concentration might be a proxy for state strength and the patterns described in the tables reduced to the unsurprising finding that weak regimes fail to endure. However, the results point against this interpretation. First, urban concentration is uncorrelated with measures of state capacity.[72] Second, inclusion of GDP per capita in the analysis does little to change the estimated effect of urban concentration on collapse as shown in Model 3.1.3 of table 3.1. Third, using the largest city's population instead of

---

[72] The bivariate correlations of urban concentration with logged GDP per capita is −0.01 and with the imputed polity score is 0.05.

urban concentration to capture the danger of concentrated masses produces similar results. City size is less likely to be correlated with state weakness than urban concentration.

These results point to the dangers of large cities. The accumulation of risk inherent in an immense central city that towers over the political landscape represents a combustible situation but comes with a long fuse. Farmers moving to favored cities due to the discriminatory fiscal policies represent more kindling for potential urban explosions in the future.

The second hypothesis to be tested, the *induced concentration hypothesis*, argues that urban bias leads to urban concentration. The data on urban bias used here are only available for a subset of the country-years under examination in the prior tables limiting the scope of the analysis. As seen in table 3.4, using multiple regression rather than survival analysis techniques, the lagged value of urban

Table 3.4 **Urban Bias is Positively Correlated with Urban Concentration**

Variables	Model 3.4.1	Model 3.4.2	Model 3.4.3	Model 3.4.4
Urban Bias (Lagged 1 year)	0.023 (0.015)	0.026 (0.016)		
Military Regime (Lagged 1 year)		−0.005 (0.012)		
Single Party Regime (Lagged 1 year)		0.020 (0.012)		
Urban Bias (Lagged 10 years)			0.016** (0.006)	0.017** (0.006)
Military Regime (Lagged 10 years)				0.021*** (0.006)
Single Party Regime (Lagged 10 years)				0.019*** (0.003)
Constant	0.286*** (0.011)	0.276*** (0.018)	0.264*** (0.002)	0.250*** (0.004)
Observations	757	708	446	425
R-squared	0.223	0.210	0.033	0.073
Number of Countries	35	34	30	29
Year FE	YES	YES	NO	NO
Country FE	YES	YES	YES	YES

Robust standard errors in parentheses.
***$p < 0.01$, **$p < 0.05$, *$p < 0.1$.

Table 3.5 **Urban Bias and Concentration Have Opposite Effects on Hazard**

Variables	Model 3.5.1	Model 3.5.2	Model 3.5.3	Model 3.5.4
Urban Bias	−1.083***	−0.881***		−0.360
	(0.288)	(0.284)		(0.548)
Urban Concentration	2.515***		1.840**	2.375*
	(0.871)		(0.889)	(1.231)
Single-Party Regime				−0.980*
				(0.545)
Military Regime				1.214***
				(0.342)
Observations	836	836	836	761
Regimes	77	77	77	73
Failures	61	61	61	49
Log-Pseudolikelihood	−188.2	−190.8	−192.0	−136.4

Robust standard errors in parentheses. Cox Models.

***$p < 0.01$, **$p < 0.05$, *$p < 0.1$.

bias is positively associated with urban concentration, even in the presence of country and year fixed effects. Including controls for regime type strengthens this connection. This result shows support for the claim that urban bias induces urban concentration. The mechanism presumably linking these two is similar to the "blind flows" of rural-urban migration in China before the implementation of the *hukou* system: rural extraction inducing migration to favored cities.

The *Faustian bargain hypothesis* predicts that urban bias will aid regime endurance in the short run but also induce urban concentration, harming survival rates. The hypothesis is supported by the results shown in table 3.5. The method of analysis is again survival analysis and specifically the Cox proportional hazard model. When urban bias and urban concentration are placed together into a model, as seen in Model 3.5.1, the first and second-order effects of urban bias are pronounced. Urban bias is associated with endurance, and urban concentration is linked with collapse. When included separately, as seen in Models 3.5.2 and 3.5.3 for urban bias and urban concentration, respectively, these patterns still emerge. Despite the positive correlation between urban bias and urban concentration, the two variables show effects on survival rates in the expected opposite directions. When including control variables, however, the second-order effect of urban bias—induced concentration—dominates the countervailing direct effect of placating potential protestors, consistent with the Faustian bargain hypothesis. As seen in Model 3.5.4, when including nondemocratic regime types, the magnitude of the direct effect of urban bias on regime survival evaporates. The second-order effect of urban bias, that is, urban concentration, only suffers a 10 percent attenuation in explanatory power with these controls added. This difference is not due to the change in the number of observations between Models 3.5.1 and 3.5.4. Rather, the regime type variables, particularly that for military regimes, absorb much of the variation previously accounted for by the urban bias measure. In sum, after controlling for the type of nondemocratic regime, urban bias is detrimental to long-term survival, undermining authoritarian duration through urban concentration.

Conclusion

The survival of nondemocratic regimes varies dramatically across cases. While some of these differences are explained by the personal characteristics of elites and the institutionalization of regimes, mass politics also play a role. The results in this chapter demonstrate support for an old idea—large cities are critical for regimes—and point to the difficulties regimes face in appeasing urban grievances. Biasing policy in favor of the urban masses stabilizes cities in the short term. Over time, however, this bias reshapes the urban-rural dynamics of countries, increasing the level of urban concentration. Overly concentrated city systems—proxied here by the share of the urban population living in the largest city—are tied to brief regime tenures. As such, urban bias represents a Faustian bargain. Leaders facing immediate threats may implement such policies to maintain their grasp on power in the short term. By inducing mass migration to favored cities, however, the policy feedbacks undo these benefits as the level of urban concentration grows and with it the threat of urban protests.

These results point to the validity of the argument but leave open questions. First, the findings look at the downstream effects of redistributive policy across space, yet the argument advanced here has implications for the determinants of urban bias as well. Regimes facing different and shifting internal politics will differ in their redistributive policies including the level of urban bias. Nondemocratic regimes arise from different origins and have distinctive coalitions at their founding. Over time, changes in the makeup of a coalition likely will entail changes in the redistributive strategies of the regime. The makeup of these coalitions can shift as political demands, the whims of leaders, and international or domestic economic circumstances change over time. Some coalitions will be in favor of more extraction from the countryside and spending in cities than others. Given the short-term advantages and the long-term of costs of tilting policy toward cities, regimes facing crises may turn to urban bias in hopes of making it through the storm and risk the consequences afterwards. Regimes with longer time horizons or more resources, such as China in recent years, may reverse course and move away from urban bias to steer away from urban concentration and potential urban instability in the future. I return to examine this hypothesis in chapter 7 with cross-national data.

Second, rather than alter redistributive policy, regimes may enact policies that allow them to reap the advantages of urban bias without also harvesting the problems associated with over-crowded capital cities. Internal passport systems, such as China's *hukou* system, allow an authoritarian regime to pursue urban-biased policies while preventing a flood of farmers to favored cities.

The next three chapters dive into the case of the CCP-led regime in China to put additional meat on the bones of the argument. It describes how the CCP initiated its versions of "urban biased" policies, as well as what those policies looked like, evolved into, and resulted in over time. Of particular interest is China's migration restriction system, which attempted to preserve the political benefits of urban bias (stable cities) without yielding its political costs (unchecked inflows of urban migrants).

CHAPTER 4

China's Loophole to the Faustian Bargain of Urban Bias

> Right now it looks as if there are no problems in the cities, but it is hard to predict whether or not unexpected circumstances will develop. We must anticipate that it will become tighter (*jin*) in the cities, but if the cities are thrown into disorder, all sides will be influenced. If we do our work in the countryside well, serious problems can be entirely prevented, but the situation in the cities is still not clear now, so the problem is now that the cities and the countryside may not both be stable. But which side should be tighter? We have discussed this problem several times in the Central Committee and made reports to the Chairman, *we must tighten the countryside to protect the cities.* Would this be acceptable?. . . Could we dissolve the cities and all go back to the countryside, back to Yan'an? No, not a single person would approve this.
> —Premier Zhou Enlai, 1961, *on addressing the problems of the Great Leap Forward*[1]

> If no attempts had been made to affect rural-to-urban migration during the last three decades, China's urban population could be at least twice its current size. In particular, the urbanized populations of the primary cities would have mushroomed to several times their current number, producing the phenomenon of over-urbanization so common in developing countries today.
> —Judith Banister, *China's Changing Population*[2]

The CCP regime has ruled China for over 60 years and is one of the world's longest running authoritarian regimes. Numerous factors—institutional, structural, and contingent—help account for the regime's longevity. The regime's

---

[1] Wemheuer 2013, translating from Jin 1998, 4:1604–5; emphasis added.

[2] Banister 1987, 327. The use of "over-urbanization" here differs from my use of that term, as described in chapter 3. Over-urbanization is when a country has a larger share of its overall population living in cities than one would expect given its level of economic development, whereas Bannister's description that the largest cities "mushroomed" is an increase in urban concentration in my terminology.

party status, that it promised a return to greatness following China's near dismemberment by foreign empires, that it did so as a Communist regime, and that it rules over a huge and populous country all undoubtedly are partly responsible for its survival.[3] To say that a regime in a counterfactual reality without these characteristics would have collapsed with any certainty is a task closer to being impossible than merely difficult. Many have explored the ways in which these factors and others have shaped the regime, the lives of the people living under its rule, and the world at large.[4] The task of this book is to highlight the ways in which the Chinese regime has shaped urbanization, thereby aiding the regime's endurance.

The survival patterns of nondemocratic regimes since World War II show the dangers that large cities pose for regimes and that urban bias is a Faustian bargain, yet the politics of how these factors operate at fine-grained level remain to be explored. Motivated by fear of urban instability and desire for rapid development, the CCP-led regime biased policies in favor of cities to such an extent that farmers left the countryside and fled to cities to escape. To control these flows, the regime created its *hukou* system. The three puzzles of the book—the CCP's enduring rule, China's mass urbanization without the kind of slums seen in other developing countries, and the recent fiscal shift away from urban bias—are all intimately tied to the development, tightening, and loosening of the *hukou* system.[5]

The *hukou* system shapes China's political economy to this day in dramatic fashion.[6] Its modern origins come from the 1950s, when the CCP began following a Soviet-style development path that promoted industry, particularly heavy industry. The regime gave urban workers in that sector an "iron rice bowl" of lifetime employment, housing, and numerous other social services to which farmers in the countryside were not given access.[7] Streams of farmers desiring this better life as part of the urban proletariat flooded into cities, vastly outnumbering the jobs available and straining the infrastructure of cities. To prevent this wave from crashing and overwhelming the cities, the CCP created a *hukou* system that

---

[3] See chapter 3 for a discussion of the nature of party versus other types of nondemocratic regimes as well as how the CCP varied in its "partyness" over time. For China, in particular, regime legitimacy is seen to come from economic strength, national glory, claims to cosmic truth, and shared prosperity, among many others (Shue 2002; Perry 2008).

[4] See White (2009) for an excellent literature review of prominent arguments in the field.

[5] This is not to say that there are not individuals in Chinese cities living in conditions that are not slum like or even are slums themselves. The limited claim of the book is simply that Chinese cities are not overwhelmed by slums in a manner similar to most large cities in the developing world. This distinction is important because it fits the argument that the politics of Chinese cities are less dominated by the slums or the residents of would-be slums than in other places. For more discussion on the domination of the political narrative of a city, see chapter 2.

[6] In the conclusion, I describe some contemporary reforms to the *hukou* system. See also Miller 2012.

[7] Lin, Cai, and Li 1998; Fung 2001, 259.

quickly leapt from merely keeping track of individuals to limiting in-migration to cities.[8] In some periods, policies even expelled urbanites from their cities to go to the countryside. The CCP recognized that managing urbanization would require policies to deal with both the countryside and the cities. The *hukou* system is the main way in which the regime limited freedom of movement within the country and into large cities in particular.[9] Following Mao Zedong's death in 1976 and the initiation of economic reforms under Deng Xiaoping from 1978, millions of individuals were able to move away from the countryside as the restrictions on migration were relaxed. Yet migrants were treated as second-class citizens in cities and discriminated against by firms, the state, and city residents.[10]

The development of China's *hukou* system and its reform illustrate the central role that migration restrictions have played in preventing high levels of urban concentration in China and preserving stability in China's cities. First, without a *hukou* system, China would have substantially more people living in cities and especially in its largest cities, as Banister noted in the chapter's epigraph. Second, the origins and maintenance of the *hukou* system come from political concerns about stability associated with large urban populations. Third, migration restrictions served as a loophole to the Faustian bargain of urban bias. The CCP regime was able to treat its urban workers and residents with favored policies—housing, food, education, etc.—without inducing massive in-migration to cities because of the controls on population movement.

The CCP's management of urbanization also sheds light on the great tragedies of Mao era China—the Great Leap Forward and the Cultural Revolution. The famine of the Great Leap and the Cultural Revolution's waves of violence have strong geographic components. While urbanites survived, the extraordinary extraction from the countryside during the Great Leap left farmers with little to eat. The Cultural Revolution used urban collective action—particularly in Beijing, at the heart of the regime—as a source of leverage in an intra-elite power struggle. During the Cultural Revolution, Mao's mass following brought millions of students from around the country out onto the streets of Beijing and other cities to protest, as part of his effort to oust elite rivals. The political importance of urban protestors capturing symbolic spaces is also seen in Tiananmen Square Incident of 1989.

The regime's later reforms of the *hukou* system further demonstrate the continuing importance of geography in the regime's fears of population migration. Policies remain tilted to protect the living standards and status of those in China's largest cities and prevent them from being overwhelmed by migrants. Using

[8] Chan and Zhang 1999, 820.
[9] Cheng and Selden 1994, 644–45.
[10] Solinger 1999a.

local variation from an experimental *hukou* reform in the late 1990s, I show that local leaders restricted migration selectively: lowering barriers in peripheral cities while maintaining high walls around provincial capitals.

Origins of the *Hukou* System

China's *hukou* system is a thoroughly modern and dictatorial solution to problems inherent to industrialization. The system both limits the free migration of individuals around the country and discriminates against rural, agricultural migrants in cities. By restricting blind flows of peasants trying to escape rural drudgery and famine to enjoy a life of relative privilege as a member of the urban proletariat, the system has allowed the regime to maintain living standards in urban areas, avoiding slums and overrun major cities.

What is the *hukou* system? It is a system of registration that categorizes individuals in two dimensions, "one by socio-economic eligibility and one by residential location."[11] The first is the "type (类别) or nature (性质)," classifying individuals as agricultural or non-agricultural.[12] The second dimension is based on the locality of their *hukou* registration (户口所在地), which is referred to as the place of one's permanent or official residence.[13] Individuals actually residing in their location of official residence are referred to as having a local (*bendi*) *hukou* (本地户口), whereas those who reside elsewhere do not (and could be described as *wai di* (外地).[14] Chan and Buckingham provide a good illustration of these different categories with examples of four types of individuals living in Nanjing and its environs:

> To clarify this point, we use Nanjing (as one "local" place) to provide an illustrative example of these four types of people: first, those holding local (Nanjing) and non-agricultural *hukou* (including most Nanjing "urban residents," as they are commonly known); second, those holding local and agricultural *hukou* (most of whom live in Nanjing's outlying districts and counties); third, those holding non-local (non-Nanjing) and non-agricultural *hukou* (mostly migrants from other cities); and finally, those holding non-local and agricultural *hukou* (mostly migrants

---

[11] Chan and Buckingham 2008, 587. Article 10 of the landmark law of 1958 established the agricultural vs. non-agricultural distinction (and restrictions on movement between countryside and city) ("中華人民共和國戶口登記條例" 1958).

[12] Chan and Buckingham 2008, 587. These are 农业and 非农业 *hukou*.

[13] Ibid., 588.

[14] Ibid.

from the countryside outside Nanjing; a great majority of the *mingong* are in this category).[15]

Chinese governments have been moving populations for political purposes since before there was any notion of a unified China.[16] As Lee notes, "throughout Chinese history, the state repeatedly used migration as a major tool to further its policies of political and social integration, economic development, popular relief, and control of the rich and powerful."[17] The state often responded to floods and droughts by moving populations away from the affected territory. As leaders of Bronze Age dynasties conquered new territory, they encouraged colonies, often begun as military garrisons, to cement their rule.[18] Despite Confucian norms of filial piety and connection to home territories, individuals also moved on their own, not only at the behest of the state.[19]

The *hukou* system and its antecedents, most prominently the *baojia* system, represent one of China's oldest political institutions.[20] Registration predates the *baojia* system, and in fact was introduced as early as the Western Zhou period (1050–771 B.C.E.), predating the Qin dynasty from which the name China is derived.[21] The *baojia* system of registration and collective responsibility was put in place for the most basic functions of the state, taxation and stratification of the population.[22] This system allowed the state to extract resources and protect itself from the people by knowing who was where, improving the "legibility" of the population for the state.[23] Under the system as nationalized by the Qin in 221 B.C.E., "everyone was required to report residence, age, gender, and profession to the authorities," which the state verified three times per year. Under this system, official approval for relocations was also required.[24] Of course, it was impossible to register 100 percent of the population and many stateless areas persisted throughout many imperial dynasties.[25] The sophistication of the

[15] Ibid., 589.
[16] Lee (1978) is the main source for ancient Chinese population movements.
[17] Ibid., 21.
[18] Ibid., 21, 25.
[19] Ibid., 26.
[20] Wong 2009, 60; Wang 2005, 33; Dutton 1992. See Wang (2005, ch. 2) for more details on variation in the implementation of *hukou* and similar policies during the Imperial era.
[21] Wong 2009, 55.
[22] That is, if any member of a *bao* was found to have violated the law for illegally migrating, the entire *bao* (5-10 families (*jia*)) would be punished (Wang 2005, 42–43). See also Fei 1986a, 78–79. As opposed to the modern period, leaving the countryside was viewed as more problematic than settling in cities. That is, the emigration from the land, not the immigration to the cities, was the concern.
[23] For more discussion on legibility, see chapter 2 and Scott 1998.
[24] Wang 2005, 35.
[25] Lee 1978, 28. See also Scott 2010.

censuses, however, should not be doubted. Ming censuses even included esti-mates of under-registration.[26]

Yet while keeping track of the population was a clear motivation for the impe-rial registration system, limiting geographic movement was not. As Solinger put it,

> In sum, ambitious as the imperial-style projects of the dynastic rulers might have been, their objectives did not generally—and decreasingly so over time—encompass a strict regulation of the private movement of the subjects.... Except insofar as they could mobilize populations to assist in this cause [subduing and overcoming rivals], no leader before 1949 had the time or the power to direct the migratory behavior of the people.[27]

Similarly, Cheng and Selden put forward that no prior regime had controlled either intra-rural migration flows or rural-to-urban migration except in "con-tested zones in time of strife."[28]

By the Ming Dynasty, everyone in walled cities had to "hang plaques by their doors disclosing their *hukou* information, including native origin, number of household residents, and presence of any live-in guests," and visitors in a locality were forced to register.[29] The transparency of the plaques made their use by non-state actors simple. Strand notes how a sixteenth-century tax riot in Hangzhou turned the *baojia* system against its originators, the state:

> The control-oriented *baojia* system was turned in an instant by city dwellers (*shimin*) into the organizing principle of their rebellion. When rioters in 1582 seized control of the city, neighborhood by neighbor-hood, they counted and grouped households by tens as the government and tradition had taught them to do. The government's template of con-trol became the protesters' instrument of resistance.[30]

The system continued under various guises during the Ming and Qing Dynasties. During the Qianlong emperor's reign, "Chinese began to defy government

[26] Lee 1978, 28 n. 40, referencing Ming memorials from 1442.
[27] Solinger 1999a, 29–31.
[28] Cheng and Selden 1994, 646; Solinger 1999a, 28 n. 11; Wong 1997; Dutton 1992. These views contrast with Wang Fei-ling's emphasis on *hukou* as ancient and so accepted, although *Organizing through Division and Exclusion* focuses less on population movement and more on legibility (Wang 2005).
[29] Wang 2005, 41.
[30] Strand 1995, 400, referencing Fuma 1993.

prohibitions and move into southern Manchuria in large numbers, and also to populate the uplands of the Yangzi and Han River drainage areas."[31] These prohibitions, even if they were followed, were enacted for cultural and economic reasons (e.g., protecting the Manchu's dominance in Manchuria) rather than limiting the size of urban agglomerations.

Following the 1911 fall of the Qing, the final imperial dynasty to rule China, individual provinces became effectively sovereign but could do little to control movement of the populations under their nominal rule, either within their territories or between their own and neighboring units. Rather than be closed off, Chinese cities during the Republic/Warlord era were teeming with all manner of individuals, foreign and domestic. Chinese cities had foreign concessions where citizens of the foreign imperial powers resided and ruled.

The Nationalists (KMT) and CCP initially worked together to wrest territory from the warlords and reunify China, yet their political differences made them unable to maintain a united front. In April 1927, the KMT initiated the White Terror, aiming to destroy the CCP before it grew too powerful, leading to long-lasting changes in the party's ideology and Chinese history. The killing of thousands of Communist Party members and sympathizers in Shanghai and other cities led the CCP to withdraw to the countryside. First, the CCP retreated to the Jiangxi Soviet. The Nationalists, in their fifth encirclement campaign of that location, finally dislodged the CCP from Jiangxi and forced the Communists to flee in the fall of 1934. The Long March that followed pushed the CCP deep into the hinterlands of China.

The CCP's self-conception as a peasant party solidified in these violent episodes. The rural factions of the party survived while their urban counterparts perished, and party members changed their minds about the relative importance of the peasantry and urban proletariat.[32] By 1938, Mao had grasped control of the party, and he would not relinquish it until his death. The countryside had become the "center of gravity" for the party.[33]

During the Chinese experience of World War II with Japan and the civil war between the KMT and the CCP that both preceded and followed it, China was divided under three different regimes—the CCP, the KMT, and the Japanese occupation, all of which maintained different systems meant to identify and control the population. The Japanese created "a system of citizen's cards (*liangmin zheng*)" in occupied Shanghai.[34] In occupied Manchuria, Japanese alternated

[31] Spence 1999, 94.
[32] Lewis 1966, 900–903.
[33] On grasping control, see Hu 1980; Lewis 1966, 904. "Center of gravity" is from Mao.
[34] White 1978, 149. For more on Japan's use of identification cards limiting access and movement when it controlled Manchuria (Manchukuo), see Han 2004.

between limiting and encouraging in-migration as concerns shifted from stability to economic production and the need for labor.[35] The Japanese needed a way to know whom they ruled in order to police them and to fund war efforts on the backs of the conquered rather than the Japanese at home. Identification of the population was of political import for the Japanese as it aided in their ability to crush resistance and police territories that they controlled.

Following the Japanese defeat, KMT-ruled Shanghai had a system of identity cards (*shenfen zheng*) following the *baojia* framework.[36] These identity cards aimed to ensure that the KMT had the ability to police and protect the population of Shanghai as well as to improve its ability to arrest the possibility of Communist infiltration and anti-KMT violence.

At the same time, in Communist base areas, the principal focus was on controlling the border itself.[37] Concerns about infiltration of the territories by enemies were paramount. Despite vehement complaints about the use of such systems by the KMT, in areas under its control the CCP used policies of "connected assurance (*lianbao*)" where groups of five families were expected to protect against counter-revolutionary activities.[38] Despite the different names, the systems fielded by all three sets of combatants operated in similar ways toward similar ends.

The population migration patterns in China between the Japanese invasion and the victory of the CCP over the KMT in 1949 were principally driven by individuals attempting to escape from the violence that surrounded them. As Solinger puts it,

> Thus a great deal of the geographical movement that took place in these years was in the nature of a flight ordinary people made on their own from disaster of one sort or another. Both on the North China plain and in the region surrounding Shanghai, war and agrarian crisis in various guises propelled peasants off the land and into the big cities.[39]

China's cities swelled with millions of farmers who ran away from the conflicts taking place in the countryside.[40] What to do with this newly urbanized population was an important consideration for the CCP. The Central Committee released a new political line at a March 1949 meeting in Shijiazhuang: "The countryside must certainly not be cast aside and attention not merely paid to the cities. *But*

---

[35] Gottschang 1987, 464.
[36] Schurmann 1966, 370–71; White 1978, 149. These remained in force until the Shanghai government under the CCP issued residents' cards (*jumin zheng*).
[37] Wong 2009, ch. 4.
[38] White 1978; Wang 2005, 43.
[39] Solinger 1999a, 31.
[40] White 1978, 103; Cheng and Selden 1994, 647.

the center of gravity of Party work must be placed on the cities."[41] Before the "Chinese people stood up," millions of them had fled the countryside to the relative safety of China's cities. Addressing this urban threat and simultaneously leading China toward its industrial future challenged the regime from the moment of its triumph.

Mao's CCP in Power, 1949

The CCP desired economic development through industrialization. To fund the factories, the regime turned to extraction from the countryside. Chinese farmers attempted to join in the industrial future by moving to cities, but did so in numbers that the regime did not feel as though it could support. As a result, it instituted migration restrictions to allow its urban-biased policies without the attendant urban concentration. This narrative of China's management of urbanization builds substantially on the work of others who have chronicled the *hukou* system's development, but focusing on the urban-rural divide also provides a window into the full range of Chinese politics and political history during this epoch, in particular including the dual tragedies of the Great Leap Forward and the Cultural Revolution.[42]

China in 1949 was a poverty-stricken society with an overwhelmingly agrarian economy recovering from decades of conflict. Moreover, its cities teemed with jobless people. Upon taking power, the CCP treated the urban unemployed as a threat that the regime could not ignore. Yet keeping their bellies full is only one of two policies that the regime undertook to deal with the unemployment problem in China's cities. In a June 1950 speech to the CCP Central Committee, Mao called upon the Committee to "set aside two billion catties of grain to solve the problem of feeding the unemployed workers."[43]

The new regime addressed the problem of urban unemployment by de-urbanizing them, pushing the unemployed out of the cities. Many refugees fled rural conflict and remained in cities without jobs. The regime feared that the urban "dependent population" would revolt if their relative deprivation was not ameliorated. As Rao Shushi, a high-level CCP official, put it in 1950:

No more than three million of Shanghai's six million people actually take part, directly and indirectly, in productive work. . . . We should, first

[41] Steiner 1950; Lewis 1966; emphasis added.
[42] The narrative builds on the seminal works of Chan 1994; Solinger 1999a; Cheng and Selden 1994; and Wang 2005, among others.
[43] Cheng and Selden 1994, 646-47. This first policy of feeding the masses is old politics. Giving the plebeians bread and circuses, or at least just bread, to decrease the chances of riots harkens back to Juvenal (Juvenal 1999).

of all, mobilize a great number of refugees and unemployed masses to return to the countryside to areas flooded by the Yellow River in northern Anhui and salt-producing areas in northern Jiangsu.[44]

Much of the initial relocation was not coerced but voluntary.[45] Any success of the program was due to financial support and distribution of land to those willing to move to the countryside.[46]

Large numbers of unhappy urban dwellers represented an immediate threat to the regime, which responded with policies that kept the urban unemployed fed or ensured that they were no longer urban. The combination of relative deprivation and cities made for a potential source for instability that the regime feared. Reducing their poverty or their moving them out of the cities would reduce the threat.

Having established control of the territory and responded to the pressing threat of urban unemployment, the CCP began to move against the landlords in the countryside. It began by enacting a rural land reform law in June 1950 and implemented an even more radical version of the policy beginning in November-December 1950.[47] By improving the lot of farmers, the party fulfilled its promises and improved the economic situation of peasants, which kept them from heading to cities. Over 40 percent of China's arable land was seized from landlords and redistributed to the poor.[48] Even this figure understates the amount of transformation taking place in the south of the country since many northern areas had already undergone land reform prior to the establishment of the PRC. These seizures of land broke the power structure of the local elite across rural China, often through violence. Estimates place the number of people killed during land reform in the hundreds of thousands.[49] The small amount of land that was distributed to each family came with efficiency losses in farm

[44] 饒漱石 1950, pt. 2, p. 8. Part 2, p. 8. Quoted in and translated by Cheng and Selden 1994, 647. Rao Shushi is soon to be ousted in the Gao-Rao affair as the eponymous Rao.

[45] Chan 1994, 37: "To be exact, in the first two or three, still unstable, years of the People's Republic, while millions of previous urban employees and their families returned to cities after the war, there was a massive campaign to remove vagrants, prostitutes, the unemployed, ex-nationalist officials, and soldiers from major cities."

[46] Cheng and Selden 1994, 648-49. Of course, the fact that at the time there were no barriers to re-entering cities also makes the decision to leave the city seem less permanent than it turns out to be (Cheng and Selden 1994, 649).

[47] On the initial law, Tiewes 1997, 34. On the more radical revision, see Tiewes 1997, 35.

[48] The status of rich peasants and the classifications of individuals into different socioeconomic classes were critical to the politics of the land reform.

[49] Tiewes 1997, 36; Stavis 1978, 29. Stavis examines varying estimates and official/unofficial tallies, and ends up concluding that "it is possible that the rural revolution could have cost 200,000 to 800,000 lives."

production. Some of these inefficiencies were eliminated with the rise of mutual aid teams and later cooperatives.[50] As Unger put it, "in these, farmers received a portion of the harvest yields in exchange for having allowed their land and draft animals to be used by the cooperative and another harvest portion based on their contribution of labor."[51]

The CCP solidified its control over urban life as well. First, a more elite focused campaign during the spring of 1951—the Suppression of Counter-Revolutionaries—seized KMT assets and demolished various urban secret societies.[52] Then campaigns to drum up popular participation in the political activities during this time, including the Three-Anti and Five-Anti Campaigns during the winter of 1951-52, came to the fore. The campaigns targeted corruption in both the regime and state hierarchies as well as among capitalists.[53]

While the party's official line stated that the rights of the population to freely relocate would not be abrogated, other policies made it clear that the regime viewed the cities and the countryside as separate areas and that the people living in those areas would receive different treatment.[54] The people living in the cities of China would be looked after while rural people would fend for themselves. In fact, the registration system that would arise created a "bifurcated social order" where "urban areas are essentially owned and administered by the state, and their residents are the state's direct responsibility."[55] Urban governments supplied not only classic public goods such as policing and infrastructure for sewage and transportation but also jobs, housing, food, water, schools, and more for urbanites.[56] On the other hand, rural areas were left to their own devices with the state assuming no direct responsibility for their residents.

What are the origins of this different treatment? Some put forward an ideological perspective: "One reason for this hypersensitivity to urban problems is the fact that the new state accepted more or less axiomatically from the start (presumably derived from Soviet practice) a responsibility that no previous Chinese state had ever assumed: to provide jobs and subsidized food and housing for all

---

[50] These forms of agricultural cooperation between families were seen as voluntary, as opposed to collectives and communes institutions that would arise later in the 1950s.

[51] Unger 2002, 8.

[52] Lieberthal 2004, 91.

[53] Lieberthal 2004, 93. The Three-Antis (waste, corruption, and bureaucratism) targeted the state, while the Five-Antis (corruption, tax evasion, stealing state property, cheating on state contracts, and stealing state economic secrets) attacked capitalists.

[54] Cheng and Selden 1994, 645-46; Wang 2005, 88; Chan 1994, 52. In September 1949, a month before the takeover in October, the *de facto* constitution of the country as well as the first official constitution in 1954 puts forward that freedom of domicile and movement would not be infringed. No document after 1955 made this claim (Cheng and Selden 1994, 646).

[55] Banister 1987, 328.

[56] Ibid.

urban residents."[57] In addition to this ideological account, urban areas concerned the regime because that is where it believed possible threats would arise. The countryside was the base at the time of "liberation," so there was little reason to be concerned about a peasant uprising. On the other hand, cities were full of capitalists and had not been "penetrated" by the regime to nearly the same extent as the countryside; urban areas were full of landmines for the new government.[58] The regime assumed the responsibility to provide jobs, food, and housing in order to obtain the political support of urbanites. While Mao believed Marxism required localization to China's culture and economy, he believed that he had no choice but to build socialism in China from a Soviet model as there were no other models available.[59] In early 1953, Mao said, "We must earnestly study the advanced experience of the Soviet Union.... We must whip up a high tide of learning from the Soviet Union throughout the whole country [in order] to build our country."[60]

State provision of resources to the urban industrial sector and for urban dwellers induced millions of peasants to come to China's cities. All investment in the country was taking place in cities and industrial sites; in contrast, the agricultural sector was falling back on older, more labor-intensive practices.[61] Many fled this return to the past for an attempt to join the urban industrial future. The size of these migrant flows were, the regime feared, beyond the ability of the cities to cope with, either in terms of jobs, housing, and other goods and services. The 3 August 1952 State Council "Decision on Labor Employment Problems" describes the situation of this "blind" rural migration into cities:

> Urban and industrial developments and the progress of national construction will absorb the necessary labor from rural villages, but this must be done gradually, and cannot be accomplished all at once. It is therefore necessary to prevail upon the peasants and check their blind desire to flow into the cities.[62]

In 1951, concerns about the situation of cities and urban labor markets began to coalesce into a system of population control with "Regulations Governing the

---

[57] Cheng and Selden 1994, 650.

[58] Torpey thinks that "penetrated" is an overly masculine term and points to patriarchy, yet "embraced," Torpey's preferred term, fails to convey the party's hostility toward capitalists and cities (Torpey 1997).

[59] Lieberthal 2004, 61.

[60] Closing speech of the 4th session of the CPPCC, 7 February 1953 (Kau and Leung 1986, 1:318).

[61] Chan 1994, 62-67.

[62] Tien 1973, 352; Cheng and Selden 1994 offer the Chinese for the final line as *quanzu nongmin buyao mangmu jincheng*, not the more pejorative *mangliu* expression of 1954.

Urban Population," a proclamation from the Ministry of Public Security that was approved by the State Council.[63] The regulations created numerous categories attempting to place all individuals inside one bureaucratic box or another, to be urban or rural. The state forced individuals to tell the Ministry of Public Security when they transitioned from one box to another.[64] Knowing who was urban and unemployed was necessary to try to address their situation, either with food aid or with relocation to the countryside.

Despite policies that aided the common rural resident in the early 1950s such as land reform, and the pushing back of refugees and unemployed from cities to the countryside, the urban population increased.[65] In the first half of the 1950s, "pull" factors dominated because of "the attraction of urban employment that offered workers security, a range of benefits and prestige."[66] Of particular concern and matching the views in the Soviet Union about the population being divided into "productive" and "un-productive" groups, the State Council in 1956 noted that in large cities the "dependent population" had increased nearly three times as quickly as the labor force.[67] Migrants looking for work were bringing non-working family members along with them that added to the "un-productive" population of the cities.

In the mid-1950s, the regime grabbed control of the means of production and placed itself in the driver's seat of the nation's economy.[68] The state directly owned 95% of all urban land by 1956, and private housing markets were "transformed" so that the state controlled them beginning in 1956. They were eliminated completely by the mid-1960s.[69] At around the same time, the regime seized control of the market for food in urban areas. The unified purchase (*tonggou*) system was used for rural extraction, involving "compulsory sales to the state of specified amounts of grain at low state prices" to "assure ample low-priced food for urban residents and to channel the agricultural surplus from the countryside towards industry and the cities."[70] By 1956, the system had been effective enough at accomplishing these tasks that the policies were extended to nearly every significant agricultural product. At the same time, controls were placed on

[63] Cheng and Selden 1994, 649.
[64] Ibid.
[65] Chan 1994, 37-38.
[66] Cheng and Selden 1994, 653. Push factors, though, also played a role, including, "flight from poorer regions, discontent with co-operatives, and the loss of income-earning opportunities associated with the market as the state curtailed private commerce, set low purchasing prices for agricultural commodities, restricted and then largely eliminated opportunities for rural people to obtain seasonal or long-term work in the cities, and centralized agricultural processing in metropolitan areas" (ibid.).
[67] Koshizawa 1978, 10; Cheng and Selden 1994, 657.
[68] Naughton 2007.
[69] Zhang 1997, 437–39.
[70] Cheng and Selden 1994, 657. See also Chan (1994) for similar points.

the purchase of food and other goods in urban areas. Rationing was provisionally established in August 1955 for grain and then expanded to cover almost all food and basic goods.[71] Ration coupons were allocated by one's household registration.

STOPPING BLIND FLOWS INTO CITIES

With generous wages and provisions given to urbanites, farmers increasingly came to want to join the urban proletariat. Yet their numbers were too great for the cities to accommodate, so the regime implemented policies to stymie these "blind flows." The Chinese regime's leaders viewed urban laborers much like their compatriots in the Soviet Union: as the core of a future communist and socialist society. The favorable treatment of urban workers induced rural-to-urban migration through pressures both fiscal and ideological. Fiscally, the factories were paid for through rural extraction, using low state procurement prices as a means of taxing the agricultural sector. Ideologically, Mao during the 1950s still followed a notion of communist ideology that put the industrial workers first. Commenting on China's tiny industrial working-class share of the population, then only 12 million or 2 percent of the country's 600 million people, Mao said, "The whole society will be one of workers, and this is why only the worker has a future and all others are transitional classes."[72]

Aware of the incentives and opportunities in urban areas, peasants flooded into cities in 1953. The regime directed them to return to the countryside:

> On 17 April 1953, the State Council promulgated a "Directive on Dissuading Peasants from Blind Influx into Cities," referring above all to the largest cities. The directive, using persuasive language, urged the hundreds of thousands of peasants who had entered the cities in search of work to return to their villages.[73]

Yet efforts to convince peasants to go back to the countryside proved inadequate. By 1954, a more direct system of control replaced exhortation:

> On 12 March 1954, the Ministry of the Interior and Ministry of Labour promulgated a "Joint Directive to Control Blind Influx of Peasants into Cities."... The state proclaimed that all subsequent population and

[71] Cheng and Selden 1994, 657.
[72] Kau and Leung 1986, 455, cited by Cheng and Selden 1994, 652, with a different translation. This comes from the edited version of Mao's "On the Correct Handling of Contradictions among the People" speech from early 1957 but re-edited post-Hundred Flowers in June 1957. See Teiwes (1995) for more details.
[73] Cheng and Selden 1994, 653-54.

labour flows from the countryside to the cities would be determined by fiat.[74]

This 1954 Directive affected rural-to-urban migration by cutting employment ties between rural workers and urban work units (*danwei*). The severing of connections took place at all levels. Whereas previously local governments, firms themselves, and even individual workers could connect to individuals in their home villages to employment opportunities in cities, afterwards only local labor bureaus—not firms—had the right to contact rural people and villages to search for potential workers.[75] The directive also stigmatized the migrants by referring to them as blind migrants (*mangliu*), conjuring images of the term "hooligan" (*liumang*).[76]

The regime began formulating and implementing migration policies during the mid-1950s, but these restrictions had not solidified into the strict barriers that they would become. On 22 June 1955, the State Council passed the nationwide "Directive Concerning Establishment of a Permanent System of Household Registration," immediately prior to collectivization.[77] The directive codified specific procedures for changing residence; it "not only established formal administrative control over the rural influx to the cities, but monitored and regulated all intra-rural and intra-urban movement. Official permission was henceforth required *prior* to any change of residence, even within one's own township."[78]

Increasing the formal requirements to migrate decreased the rural-to-urban migration flows, from 6 million in-migrants in 1953 to 1.3 million in 1955.[79] In 1955, coercive repatriation occurred, sending "millions back to their villages," and marking the beginning of the labor-contract system.[80] Illegal migration could be punished as a crime but was usually dealt with by returning the violator to his home territory.[81] It is particularly important to note that only flows from low density to higher density localities were restricted. Records were kept of the movement of city residents to the countryside and those moving from a large

[74] Cheng and Selden 1994, 654.
[75] Tien 1973, 360–62; Solinger 1999a, 39.
[76] Cheng and Selden 1994, 654.
[77] Ibid., 655.
[78] Ibid., 656
[79] Tien 1973.
[80] Emerson 1982; Solinger 1999a. For the labor-contract system, see Perry and Li 1997, 100 (劳动合同制 a.k.a. Worker-Contract system). See also Han and Monshima 1992 and 中华人民共和国国务院 1983.
[81] Chan and Zhang 1999.

city to a smaller one, but limits were not imposed to constrain migration flows from larger to smaller communities.[82]

Even with these new strictures, rural-to-urban migration during this period was also influenced by the bounty of harvests and farmers' assessments of their ability to make ends meet with only farm-based income.[83] Movement was free enough for economic considerations to play a large role. For instance, a large move back to the countryside followed the 1955 bumper crop, while poor yields and agricultural incomes in 1956 and 1957 "led to an uncontrollable return to the city."[84]

As the plan enveloped the entirety of economic life, the food ration system hardened the wall around urban areas.[85] The state began to monopolize grain purchases in 1953, achieving control of all surplus grain in 1954.[86] In August 1955, the State Council put forth the "Temporary Methods for Supplying Grain Rations."[87] The system of rations was elaborate. Distinctions were made between

> residence, occupation and grade: city and town resident grain-supply card; industrial and commercial trade grain-supply card; city and town animal feed-supply card; city and town resident grain-transfer card; grain ticket for nation-wide use; local area grain card; and local area animal-feed card.[88]

Purchases of foodstuffs—via restaurants or grain stations—required food rations.[89] "Oil, cloth, fuel and many other products" were also rationed, and the "system severely restricted movement into the cities from the countryside and affected the ease of movement between urban areas."[90] Only the urban population had a state guaranteed food grain supply.[91] Urban rations were generous. For instance, they were greater than the amount that farmers were able to keep and not sell to the state.[92]

---

[82] Ibid.

[83] As the regime dominated all markets and prices, the incentives facing farmers were a function of policy choices not abstract market pressures.

[84] Howe 1971, 69.

[85] The connection between walls and cities in China is an intimate one, with the two sharing a Chinese character (*cheng* 城) (Chan 1994).

[86] Oi 1989, 17.

[87] Solinger 1999a, 43.

[88] Cheng and Selden 1994, 658.

[89] Davin 1999, 7. However, prior to 1960 restaurants tended to not enforce this requirement and until 1959 food markets still did exist (Cheng and Selden 1994, 658).

[90] Davin 1999, 7.

[91] Chan 2009, 212.

[92] Davin 1999, 8; Cheng and Selden 1994, 659. The state compelled farmers to sell to it all grain not for personal consumption. This personal use allowance was smaller than the urban rations.

The system of control was present everywhere. After 1960, purchase of inter-city public transport tickets required official approvals, and this was enforced "especially if the destination was Beijing and the time was politically sensitive."[93] Migrants found it "literally hard to survive in the urban areas"; even when visiting urban friends, the hosts would only have so many extra grain coupons to offer the visitor, making anything but short stays burdensome.[94]

The clear differences in rules between rural and urban individuals also necessitated clear demarcations between the city and the countryside, between who was rural and who was urban. As noted above, the *hukou* system has two layers of identification, the place of registration (*hukou suozaidi*) and the *hukou* status (*hukou leibie*), agricultural or non-agricultural.[95] While most people working in the countryside were given agricultural status, state employees were granted non-agricultural household status regardless of their urban or rural location and as such were allocated grain rations.[96] Strangers to urban communities were often reported to neighborhood committees and could be deported.[97]

The passage of the *hukou* law on 9 January 1958 formalized the system.[98] Under the *hukou* system, moving to a city from the countryside became exceedingly rare outside of state employees. "A formal, permanent change from rural to urban required the conversion of registration status from agricultural to non-agricultural (the so-called *nongzhuanfei*). Such a conversion was seldom granted."[99] The walls around China's cities and their urban denizens protected them from the worst ravages of disaster to come.

GREAT LEAP FORWARD

The dead in each province are the problem of that province, but deaths in
Beijing are a problem for the People's Republic of China.
—Peng Zhen, 1959[100]

The Great Leap Forward pushed farmers into vast communes, individuals into steel-making in backyard furnaces, and officials into inflating production numbers, resulting in one of history's worst calamities. Overwhelmingly, it was a rural tragedy. Thinking that China's development trajectory was too slow and

---

[93] Cheng and Selden 1994, 657 n. 40.
[94] Davin 1999, 7.
[95] Chan and Zhang 1999, 821–22.
[96] Cheng and Selden 1994, 658.
[97] Davin 1999, 7.
[98] Wang 2005, 45; "中華人民共和國戶口登記條例" 1958.
[99] Chan 1994, 76–77.
[100] Yang 2012, 340. For more in-depth analysis of the Great Leap, see Dikötter 2010; Yang 2012. Peng Zhen was a Politburo member and the Party Secretary of Beijing at the time.

a re-enactment of the Soviet experience, Mao initiated the campaign to take advantage of China's great strength: its population. Pressures to perform led to vast exaggeration of production levels, yet grain and taxes were extracted as if these lies were the truth, leaving nothing for the farmers themselves to eat. Ironically, Mao's desire to break with Soviet precedent led to a famine even more destructive than what the Soviet Union faced in the early 1930s.[101] The Great Leap Forward fits into the broader argument in three ways. It showed how rural extraction could cause massive migration to cities. It also highlighted the ability of the *hukou* system to control that migration. Finally, it demonstrated the party's inherent urban bias during the planned era.

From 1958 to 1960, China launched a disastrous economic policy, attempting to catch up to developed countries through intensive popular mobilization. The economic origins of the idea came from taking advantage of China's plentiful resource (labor) to substitute for its deficient one (capital) through sheer will, ignoring the necessary steps of capital and skill development.[102] Mao put forward the policies of the Great Leap in part to distance himself and the Chinese development path from that taken by the Soviet Union.[103] With a call to arms by asking "Why can't we innovate?" Mao pushed this disaster.[104]

Lies and subterfuge were also key features of Great Leap Forward policies that ultimately resulted in the worst man-made famine in history.[105] Just a few years earlier, the costs of criticizing the regime were made very public. In 1956, the comparatively open Hundred Flowers Campaign (百花运动)—where Mao called for "Letting a hundred flowers bloom and a hundred schools of thought contend (百花齐放，百家争鸣)"—lasted for just a few months. Those who had voiced new ideas were then attacked as Rightists during the subsequent anti-Rightist campaign. Political pressures on local leaders pushed them to vastly overestimate production; indeed, Li Choh-Ming's book *The Statistical System of Communist China* spends an entire chapter on the "Statistical Fiasco of 1958."[106] In 1959-60, leaders believed that harvests had produced double the amount of grain that was available. Only about 180 million metric tons were produced whereas production estimates and leader's statements put the figures at around 365 to 430 million metric tons.[107]

---

[101] On the Soviet or Ukrainian famine, see Conquest 1986; Davies 1980; Davies and Wheatcroft 2004; Fitzpatrick 1994; Fitzpatrick 1983. On comparing different famines and agricultural policies, see also Pryor 1992; Bernstein 1984.

[102] Bachman 1991. Often referred to as voluntarism, see Lieberthal 2004, ch. 3.

[103] Bernstein 1984, 341.

[104] Quoted by Bernstein 1984, 341 n. 11 from Mao 1968.

[105] Kung and Chen 2011.

[106] Bernstein 1984; Kung and Chen 2011. Also see Li 1962.

[107] Bernstein 1984; Li 1962.

The difference between Stalinist and Maoist policies during the Great Leap are present only at the level of intentions.[108] Under Stalin, there was a conscious effort to undertake deeply predatory behavior against the peasantry as a backward class. Under Mao during the Great Leap Forward, the real level of extraction from the countryside was similarly severe, but the center believed that extraction was occurring at normal rates. The "winds of exaggeration" had led to obscene over-taxation of the harvest.

Famines tend to be characterized by an odd syllogism: farmers grow food; people die of starvation in famines; most of the people who die in famines are farmers.[109] The death rates of urban areas during the years of the famine (1959-61) increased significantly—on the order of 20 percent; yet this increase is insignificant compared to what happened in the countryside where death rates skyrocketed to five times normal levels. Death rates in rural areas almost doubled from 1959 to 1960, reaching a peak of over 2.86 percent of the rural population dying in that year, as opposed to 1.27 percent on average for the previous three years.[110]

As starvation spread in the countryside, farmers attempted to flee to cities where food supplies were more available. Yet agents of the regime forcibly returned those who attempted to flee to cities back to their farms and communes. This behavior is most apparent in what Yang Jisheng refers to as the "epicenter of the disaster," Xinyang prefecture in Henan.[111] Officials were concerned about news spreading of what were thought of as local disasters to outside areas in addition to the possibility that cities might be overrun.

> To prevent starving people from fleeing and spreading news of the disaster, county party committees deployed armed guards to patrol borders and access roads. Sentry posts were set up on roadways, and checkpoints at every village. Bus stops were manned by police officers, and long-distance buses could be driven only by party members. Anyone discovered trying to leave had all his belongings confiscated and was beaten. Xinyang's rail depots were monitored by the railway public security bureau. The peasants could only stay home and await death.[112]

It was not only Xinyang that attempted to keep its rural dwellers in the countryside.

---

[108] Bernstein 1984.
[109] Lin and Yang 2000.
[110] Ibid., 145.
[111] Yang 2012, ch. 1.
[112] Ibid., 50.

The CCP Central Committee supported these suppressive tactics. In March 1959 the Central Committee and the State Council jointly issued an "urgent communique" designating those who fled the countryside as "vagrants" and ordering the detentions and repatriation of all rural dwellers who attempted to enter cities or industrial or mining regions. [113]

Farmers were part of communes and local officials closely observed their actions. They could not withdraw from the system.[114] For much of this period, food was served out of communal kitchens, making retreating from the commune impossible.[115]

The political significance of large cities and the regime's willingness to inflict suffering on the countryside led to differential starvation rates across the urban-rural divide. Politburo members argued that city dwellers and particularly those in Beijing counted more than did farmers; even Deng Xiaoping, who was born in rural Sichuan, claimed "a food shortage in Sichuan had less serious political ramifications than food shortages in the big cities."[116] Zhou Enlai's concern about urban stability during the Great Leap is obvious. "From June 1960 to September 1962, Zhou spoke of the food crisis 115 times, and 994 notations in his handwriting can be found in 32 statistical reports that have been preserved by the Food Ministry. His main concern was food supply to the cities."[117] Sichuan was particularly devastated due to policy decisions made by its leadership.[118] A provincial party secretary for agriculture from Sichuan later wrote in his memoirs:

> The central leadership explained that the political, economic, and other ramifications of the problems in Sichuan were less significant than those in Beijing, Tianjin, and Shanghai. This policy was subsequently known as "Better that people should starve to death in Sichuan than in Beijing, Tianjin, and Shanghai."[119]

[113] Ibid., 50.

[114] Scott 2010.

[115] Yang 2012, 159.

[116] Ibid., 340. English translation. The phrasing used is "When Deng Xiaoping went to Sichuan, his comments to Li Jingquan echoed Peng Zhen's" but then no quotation marks appear. The reference is to "conversation with veteran Xinhua Sichuan branch journalist Liu Zongtang in Chengdu on December 13, 2000." As noted above Peng Zhen at the time served as Party Secretary in Beijing. During the Great Leap, Deng was a Politburo Standing Committee member and head of the party's Secretariat.

[117] Yang 2012, 341. English translation.

[118] Ibid., ch. 6. See also Kung and Chen 2011.

[119] Yang 2012, 213.

By 1961, the regime faced the fact that it was not producing sufficient grain and imports spiked. "In order to import grain," Li Xiannian stated during a speech on 26 August 1961, "we must squeeze out each and every exportable item."[120] As summarized by Yang Jisheng in *Tombstone*, "export commodities such as pork, eggs, and oil had to be snatched from the peasants, but the imported grain that these exports purchased was supplied to the cities. Again the cities were preserved at the expense of the people in the countryside."[121]

In the end, estimates of the number of people killed due to the famine are astounding. Between 30 million to 45 million Chinese died from 1958 to 1962 in excess of prior demographic patterns.[122] The peasants who had backed the CCP's rise were decimated. In some counties and prefectures, more than 20 percent of the population perished.

The Great Leap Forward led to a twofold breakdown in the *hukou* system. First, prior to the height of the agricultural disaster, urban enterprises that were decentralized and commanded to grow flouted the rules and brought in needed workers.[123] Other projects, such as in irrigation, also pulled farmers away from their fields.[124] Second, later, starving masses of the countryside fled to cities looking for some way to survive. Despite millions of farmers being turned back by urban authorities, many escaped the desolate countryside. This breakdown was associated with a tremendous temporary urbanization. In just three years, the Chinese population in cities grew from 16.2 to 19.7 percent, a level of urbanization that China would not reach again until 1980.[125] Net inflow to cities was 15 million people in 1959 alone.[126] They were not to remain there long.

MAO STEPS BACK: THE LIU-DENG INTERREGNUM

The post-Leap recovery was characterized by substantial reverse migration to the countryside.[127] Following the calamity of the Great Leap Forward, Mao retreated from day-to-day administration to focus on his study of Chinese

[120] Ibid., 342. English translation.
[121] Ibid.
[122] Dikötter 2010; Lin and Yang 2000; Yang 2012.
[123] Cheng and Selden 1994, 665.
[124] Yang 2012.
[125] Chan 1994, 38. Cheng and Selden have an even more dramatic estimate: China's population living in cities shifted from 15 to 20 percent (1994, 665). Estimates are thus between 1.1 and 1.7 percent per year.
[126] Chan 1994, 38.
[127] Solinger 1999a.

culture, war, and history. Liu Shaoqi and Deng Xiaoping were the principal actors filling the Chairman's shoes. Economic activity and life returned to more normal circumstances following the famine in many dimensions, including population movements.

Most people who moved to cities during the Great Leap Forward, at least 20 million, were pushed out of cities following the end of that chaotic and calamitous period.[128] The ways that the regime pushed people out of cities in the post-Leap period was not through campaign tactics but rather through "more conventional methods" such as closing down small factories and encouraging the unemployed to leave cities in a "return to the village" (*huixiang*) campaign.[129] The regime also created a system of temporary peasant workers (*yinong yigong*) that aided urban factories searching for labor in a controlled manner.[130] Migrants under this designation did not have full urban rights as would local urban residents with proper *hukou*. However, their labor helped to build the cities and operate the factories that produced much of the interregnum period's economic growth. The tightening of the system of urban grain distributions also squeezed farmers who had fled to the cities during the famine. The policy pushed many out of cities and prevented others from relocating to cities.[131]

The ability of the system to limit urbanization was impressive. From 1964 to 1982 China's urban population essentially held steady, moving from 18.3 to 20.9 percent over the long 18-year period, an annual increase of only 0.14 percent.[132] As Solinger says,

> What had been constructed by the start of the sixties was largely locked into place for the two succeeding decades. This program of forcing farmers to remain in the fields, grow the foodstuffs to feed the workers and sustain the cities, had been achieved through a series of labor recruitment rulings, backed up by selective food allocation and a lack of residential space. It was not until the era of reform that the state offered the farmers a key to come in.[133]

Before reform took off with Deng's rise, however, lay the Cultural Revolution.

---

[128] Cheng and Selden 1994, 666; Selden 1993, 174.
[129] Schurmann 1966, 400. N.b. Schurmann uses the Wade-Giles *huihsiang*.
[130] Wang 2005, 47 n. 76.
[131] Chan 1994, 39.
[132] 2006 China Statistical Yearbook.
[133] Solinger 1999a, 44.

CULTURAL REVOLUTION

The Great Proletarian Cultural Revolution (1966-1976) was the second colossal human tragedy of the Mao era.[134] The focus here is on the ways that migration and urbanization played into the turmoil of the Cultural Revolution, specifically its early years (1966-69).[135] Mao launched the Cultural Revolution in 1966, calling on young people to revolt against the ossified leadership of the Communist Party who were taking the capitalist road. While the regime's management of urbanization reduced the likelihood of spontaneous urban collective action, Mao's deliberate desire was to have the people attack the political establishment on the streets.

During the early Cultural Revolution's chaos, old systems of control broke down, allowing massive flows of people to move into cities.[136] In the political chaos, some farmers moved to cities, and they were accompanied by students in support of Mao. Mao's Cultural Revolution used China's youth as the foot soldiers in attacking the political establishment, that is, the party apparatus—save, of course, Mao himself. These radicalized children, who came to call themselves Red Guards, viciously attacked their elders, teachers, and party members. They followed Mao's call to destroy the "Four Olds"—old thinking, old culture, old customs, and old habits—as part of bringing China into the modern world.[137] Children were given the ability to ride trains for free to attend rallies, the largest of which were held in Tiananmen Square in Beijing.[138]

Over time, rival factions of Red Guards came to fight in the streets of Beijing and other major cities over which groups were most in line with Mao and the radical ideologies of the moment.[139] These fights escalated into urban guerrilla warfare with different Red Guard groups having People's Liberation Army (PLA) soldiers and their weapons operating on their behalf. The fighting came to a halt when Zhou Enlai and Mao Zedong called for its cessation and for Red Guards to be dispersed into the countryside to be educated by the peasantry.

By December 1968, even Mao conceded that the urban bedlam caused by the Red Guard factionalism needed to be curtailed and agreed to encourage the policy of sending youths educated in cities "up to the mountains and down to

---

[134] Compared with the Great Leap, knowledge of the Cultural Revolution and its tragic elements are much more broadly known. Rae Yang's memoir, *Spider Eaters*, is one of dozens of amazing and widely read books about the period. Andrew Walder's research, including the 2009 volume *Fractured Rebellion*, is also of note (Yang 1998; Walder 2009). See also Thurston 1987; Liang and Shapiro 1983; Yüeh and Wakeman 1985.

[135] Wang 2005, 47.

[136] Chan 1994, 40. Many also fled the conflict in the cities that was to take place.

[137] Lieberthal 2004, 114; Spence 1999, 575.

[138] Jiang and Ashley 2000, 5; Thurston 1990, 160.

[139] Walder 2002, 2009.

the countryside" (*shangshan xiaxiang*).[140] While the policy predated the Cultural Revolution and even the Great Leap Forward, the numbers of youths rusticated by the program expanded dramatically in 1969 to over 2.67 million following Mao's decision the previous December.[141]

The initial purpose of the rustication policy was to decrease pressures on urban employment and coffers by sending people to the countryside. The policy responded to three specific problems, as Bernstein notes:

> The first is urban unemployment and growth. Second is the motivational difficulties of urban youths who have been educated in secondary schools but who can neither be accommodated in higher schools nor given white-collar jobs. The third problem area is that of rural development.[142]

The Cultural Revolution exacerbated these economic problems. Ideologically, Red Guards were unwilling to challenge the order to "be re-educated by the peasants" and so these radical students dispersed.[143]

Variation in the intensity of the program across different provinces and cities reflected concerns about the location of future urban growth. "Planners have sought to limit or even to reduce the size of the largest cities, while permitting some urban places of small or intermediate size to grow."[144] The policies mirror those the regime used upon taking power in 1949 to deal with cities filled with more people than jobs: de-urbanizing non-productive populations.

An enormous number of people were resettled to the countryside in the rustication campaigns. The programs for youth alone relocated 12 million individuals and some gross totals for emigration from cities run as high as 30 to 50 million.[145] The lower end of that spectrum, 12 million, represented 10 percent of China's urban population in 1970.[146]

---

[140] Bernstein 1977, 72; Chan 1994, 40.

[141] Pan 2002, 361. The policy began in 1953. During the Great Leap, some of the projects sending urban workers to irrigation projects fell under this umbrella (Peking Review 1976). The program is often referred to using Wade-Giles, "*shangshan hsia-hsiang.*" See also Chan 1994, 41.

[142] Bernstein 1977, 33.

[143] Chan 1994, 40. Chan cites Beijing Revolutionary Committee 1968 on the phrase "re-educated by the peasants."

[144] Bernstein 1977, 43.

[145] Ibid., 2; Chan 1994, 40–41, 78.

[146] Despite the rustication campaigns, official net urban population flow figures during the Cultural Revolution were positive. Why? The Third Front (Chan 1994, 41). From 1964 to 1975, the central leadership in Beijing believed that it was in a poor geostrategic position. Mao had split with the Soviets after Khrushchev's denouncement of Stalin and relations with the United States were still not on strong ground. As such, policies were undertaken to build an industrial base in the interior of the country—namely in Sichuan and Guizhou—that would be less vulnerable to bombing

Urbanites were given preferential treatment, even in policies such as the sending down of youths. Youths born in the countryside who moved to cities for schooling vastly overwhelmed the numbers of urban youth rusticated by the policy. In Fujian, of the nearly 1.25 million educated youths sent to the countryside, over 1 million of them were rural students who had gone to schools in towns and cities while less than a quarter of a million urban youths had to move.[147] Urban youths ended up in better villages than did the returned rural youths.[148]

Reforms

One of the principal changes of the Reform era was the relaxation of the effective migration restrictions that had prevailed for decades. Yet this increased freedom to move from countryside to city came with severe limits. Migrants were allowed to reside in or near cities but were not treated as full urban citizens. Further, the largest cities were the ones that did the least to remove their invisible walls. Preferential treatment of those born in urban areas remained in place. Consistent with the general argument, these reforms demonstrate that the socioeconomic and demographic makeup of the largest cities was prioritized by the regime for reasons of political stability.

Following Mao's death in September 1976 and the denunciation of the Gang of Four a month later, the CCP faced an elite competition for control between Hua Guofeng, whom Mao "helicoptered" up the hierarchy and designated his successor, and the long-time revolutionary Deng Xiaoping.[149] As Hua's legitimacy came solely from his connection to Mao, he put forward policies including the "Two Whatevers" and even copied Mao's image and haircut to project authority akin to that of the "Great Helmsman."[150]

In part to differentiate himself from Hua, Deng suggested that the party needed to reform the economic system of the country.[151] Upon Deng gaining the reins of the party in December 1978, these economic reforms began to take shape. The

(Naughton 2007, 73–77). The industrial heartland had been Manchuria in China's far northeast, which was seen as exposed to both US and USSR forces. Millions of farmers left the countryside to staff these new factories in the cities of the deep interior. The official statistics on migration during this time, however, are complicated by the fact that sent-down youth retained urban *hukou* and many rural migrants to cities kept their status as agricultural workers (Scharping and Chan 1987; Davin 1999).

[147] Bernstein 1977, 61.

[148] Ibid., 64–65.

[149] Lieberthal 2004, 149–50.

[150] On Hua's connection to Mao, see Lieberthal 2004, 127, 149–50. On Hua's haircut, see Hamrin 1984.

[151] Shambaugh 1993, 482–83.

chronological ordering of reforms underscores the regime's interest in preserving social stability, especially in cities. However, this concern did not mean that reforms were solely focused on the urban sector, in fact, quite the opposite.

Reforms began in the countryside to avoid disturbing the political economy and stability of China's cities, yet the rural reforms influenced China's cities by releasing a population no longer needed for agricultural work. The reforms were experimental and did reflect the notion of someone grasping for stones while crossing a river. Following the first sets of reforms, most decisions were made to put out fires that prior reforms had caused.

Initial reforms took place in the countryside, not in the cities, for a number of reasons. The Deng-led second generation of leaders believed that they understood how to improve the situation facing farmers, but they did not have as much confidence in their ability to reshape the urban industrial economy. This confidence came from theoretical beliefs, the relative simplicity of the agrarian economy, and the historical experience of the Interregnum period between the Great Leap and Cultural Revolution. Following the disastrous Great Leap Forward, Liu Shaoqi and Deng Xiaoping led a series of policies that saw the end of the famine and gave farmers more freedom in their operations.[152] There were fewer institutional adversaries in the agricultural sector that could oppose changes from the status quo. Agricultural producers benefited from lower levels of rural extraction, but the costs were diffused throughout the urban industrial economy. If the regime had reformed the industrial sector economy, then those producers losing prior privileges might have put up more resistance.[153]

Revising the status quo in the countryside was unlikely to yield explosions of effective mass opposition and so was safe ground politically. In moving away from the strict adherence to ideology, the regime faced serious political challenges. As farmers were often presented as at the heart of the CCP's political coalition—despite actual policies that extracted from agriculture and discriminated against them in cities—aiding farmers even through reforms resembling capitalism would be less jarring than other possible sites for reform. Farmers were a majority but faced discrimination; any movement to improve their situation could be portrayed as aiding "the people." Increasing state procurement prices for grains or offering freedom to make independent planting decisions was unlikely to cause protests that might have undermined the regime. The state bore the costs of these policies rather than transferring all of them on urban workers through higher food prices.[154]

---

[152] Putterman 1993, 12, 31–32; Shambaugh 1993, 482–83.

[153] Shirk 1993; Olson 1965. To the extent that some saw the agricultural reforms as bottom-up policies that the center accepted as a fait accompli. See, for instance, Shirk 1993, 41.

[154] Lin 1992, 36.

Land was de-collectivized—but not privatized—and agricultural production soared as a result of improved incentives and higher procurement prices.[155] The population density on Chinese farms was too high to use the available labor productively in the fields. The de-collectivization and the Household Responsibility System increased the efficiency of labor usage in the countryside, clarifying the reality of a massive labor surplus. The existence of "surplus labor" prior to the Household Responsibility System is debated, yet after the system went into effect, agricultural production increased while millions of rural dwellers also produced industrial goods.[156] The sources for this growth in agricultural production—improvements in technology, increased procurement prices, changed incentive structure, changed cultural norms surrounding accumulation—are known, even if their relative weights remain in dispute.[157]

De-collectivization also diminished the legibility of the population for the state, making it more difficult to ensure that rural farmers were not leaving en masse to cities.[158] Society under the planned economy was easy for the state and regime to observe and rule. The political and economic returns of growth outweighed the political costs of the comparative chaos and complexity of the reformed economy.

Surplus labor and a diminished capacity to monitor farmers led to a renewed fear of blind flows of migrants to cities. To soak up this labor force without having the population overrunning cities, the regime pushed rural industrialization. One telling expression, "leave the land but do not leave the village (*litu bulixiang*)" was "premised on the perception that it would be disastrous if all underemployed rural laborers moved to urban areas."[159] Many did stay in rural areas staffing small rural factories.

De-collectivization left local governments in the countryside without a source of revenue to fund their operations and led to Township and Village Enterprises taking off.[160] During the era of the planned economy, local governments were

---

[155] Oi 1989; Brandt et al. 2002. Ideological norms were also shifting. Deng offered that "it doesn't matter whether the cat is black or white, as long as it catches mice" and "some areas must get rich before others." It became politically acceptable for Chinese individuals to try to accumulate profit by working hard.

[156] Surplus labor is that which can be removed with zero loss in overall production following Lewis (Lewis 1954). On debates, see Xu 1999; Lin 1988.

[157] See Lin 1992, 43–45; Christiansen 2009, 566.

[158] Chan 1994, 113. Solinger 1999a, 45.

[159] Chan 1994, 110; Yang 2002, 25. As Yang describes, "The leading advocate of this policy (*litu bulixiang*) was the famous social scientist Fei Xiaotong. In recent years, scholars have proposed the oxymoronic phrase "rural urbanization" to describe the pattern of Chinese rural development," referencing Guldin 2001; Knight and Song 1999; Wang and Hu 1999; Yang 2002, 25 n. 31. See also Fei 1986a, b.

[160] Oi 1999; Huang 2008. It is only in the 1990s that private enterprises became dominant in terms of output, employment, and profits.

principally funded by the center, each according to its needs. This era of soft budget constraints came to an end with fiscal reforms in the 1980s.[161] Local governments were left to fend for themselves. Many rural counties seized the opportunity to produce consumer goods and other light manufactures which were undersupplied throughout the planned years, either by creating their own companies or supporting and taxing independent firms.[162] Initial reforms improved rural economic performance, thereby encouraging both rural stability and decreasing the incentives of farmers to migrate to cities.

In 1980, millions of sent-down youth returned to China's cities from their exile in the countryside. This influx of returnees expanded the problems of unemployment and unrest and pressured urban areas to continue reforms.[163] The state sector with its high capital-to-labor ratio could not employ the excess labor, requiring the expansion of the nonstate and more labor-intensive service sector that had been limited during the Mao era. Reforms allowing individual enterprises (*getihu*) to register with up to seven total workers began in 1981, and free markets in agricultural and other goods expanded from only a handful at the time of Mao's death in 1976 to around 3,000 by 1980.[164] These entrepreneurs became examples that rural migrants would follow in the years to come.[165]

In the early 1980s, China's reform and opening up led markets to emerge around the fringes of the planned economy, partially dismantling the invisible walls around cities.[166] For instance, one could buy food or other goods at a market without a locality-determined ration coupon. Despite the growth of Township and Village Enterprises employing a significant number of former farmers, the countryside still teemed with surplus labor. The reduced difficulty of migrating to cities created a dam near the breaking point. People were leaving the poor countryside to try to find higher paying jobs in urban areas. To manage these flows, by 1985, China had enacted a nationwide system of temporary residence permits for urban areas, following Wuhan's lead in 1983.[167]

The policy revisions allowed migrants freedom to move independently. The old system only allowed workers who had explicitly been recruited by an urban

---

[161] Oksenberg and Tong 1991; Oi 1999. Budget constraints are soft when breaking them is cushioned by funds coming from elsewhere to make up the gap and hard when no outside source of money exists.

[162] Oi 1999; Huang 2008.

[163] Chan 1994, 99–100.

[164] This limit is due to an obscure Marx quotation that anything under eight employees cannot be characterized as exploitation (Wu 1994, 189; Whiting 2000). Chan 1994, 100–101.

[165] Solinger 1999a, 47.

[166] Chan 1994; Solinger 1999a, 47.

[167] Solinger 1995, 122; Chan and Zhang 1999, 832.

firm through a rural commune to move to a city. Under the new system, on the other hand, individuals could choose to migrate "spontaneously" and remain in urban locales with the appropriate paperwork and associated fees.[168] The Ministry of Labor relaxed the recruiting system that had kept workers waiting for assignments, allowing individuals to strike out on their own.[169]

Migrants initially faced tough policies, but these hurdles were lowered over time. Yet a crucial piece remained: migrants did not receive urban *hukou*, and without it, they were not eligible for the full suite of urban benefits and rations.[170] While policies allowed migrants to move to market towns, relocation to larger cities, even county seats, remained frowned upon.[171] The abundant harvest of 1985 allowed goods that had been available only to local *hukou* holders in urban areas to be sold in a market setting without the need for ration coupons.[172] Migrants able to bring their own food with them could acquire a self-supplied grain *hukou* (*zili kouliang chengzhen hukou*).[173]

Larger cities were the desired destinations of many farmers, but entry into them remained more tightly controlled than small cities and towns.[174] This led to larger cities remaining the domain of urban incumbent *hukou* holders while smaller communities were relatively inundated by the flood of migration. As Davin describes,

> The differential effect of control is clear in evidence from the 1986 Survey of 74 Cities and Towns which showed the proportion of permanent in-migrant in the urban population was in inverse relation to the size of the settlement. Migrants were 7.3 per cent of the population of towns compared with 3.5 per cent in the medium cities and only 2.7 per cent in extra-large cities in the period 1985–6.[175]

While required, temporary residence permits were not always obtained by migrants who had little to lose. Many believed that given the low probability and costs of being discovered without a permit, they would not acquire one.[176]

---

[168] Chan and Zhang 1999, 832. Most common is the purchase of temporary resident permits, although some are purchasing urban "blue stamp" *hukou*.

[169] Solinger 1999a, 47.

[170] Solinger 1999a, 49.

[171] Solinger 1999a, 50.

[172] Solinger 1999a, 129, 158.

[173] Chan and Zhang 1999, 835–36; Mallee 1995, 14–15; Davin 1999, 41. Self-supplied grain *hukou* began as an experiment in 1984's No. 1 Document and disappeared by the early 1990s.

[174] Davin 1999, 36.

[175] Ibid.

[176] Solinger 1999a, 139.

"Floaters" shaped the calculus on all sides—cities and bosses discriminated against migrants so they did not put down roots.[177]

> Asked why they don't register, some say: "I didn't know about registration." Others say: "Registration requires paying money and it restrains you." The reporter then asks, "Aren't you afraid of violating the law acting this way?" An eighteen- or nineteen-year-old with a Henanese accent responds, unconcerned: "Afraid of what? Come to check on us, and we'll run away. Catch us, and we've no money."[178]

As Solinger notes, though, migrants were allowed to live in China's cities but were not treated as being of the city:

> A closer look reveals that these migrants remained confined within the rubric of the state's persisting imperative: to ally urban growth and productivity with cost-saving, and, as a "socialist" state, to provide for the city dweller while reserving the ruralite as docile, disposable trespasser, and drudge. Statism and urban bias, though more masked than before retained their wonted power to inform the relation between the Chinese migrant and the state.[179]

Migrants could move but were ill-treated.[180] They were disposable for urban states and could be "rounded up and returned to their villages when there was a downturn in economic activity" to ensure that they did not undermine social stability.[181] Yet despite this, people migrated anyway, on the order of 50 to 60 million by 1986.

Urban localities too were forced to find new sources of revenue. Governments in cities were able to take advantage of the desire by many farmers to move to cities by selling access to them. "Selling urban residency rights" to the newly rich became an important cash cow for these governments.[182] Full admission to the city proper via an urban *hukou* became a commodity to be sold as well.[183]

Costs varied for moving into different cities. Acquiring an urban *hukou* was expensive, and that expense strongly correlated with city size and status. *Hukou*

---

[177] Solinger 1999a, 140.
[178] Solinger 1999a, 141. Translated by Solinger from *Tianjin Ribao*, 4 December 1989.
[179] Solinger 1999a, 45.
[180] Solinger 1999a, 55.
[181] Davin 1999, 42.
[182] Chan 1994, 118–19.
[183] Solinger 1999a, 90. For more on prices and details, see Solinger 1999a, 90–91.

for large cities could come to as much as 40,000 yuan in 1994 but were less than 5,000 for cities and towns below the county level.[184]

Fundamentally, the regime relaxed migration restrictions, trading off social control for growth in the Reform era. The regime's management of this relaxation shows how attentive they remained to the political aspects of urbanization, both at the national and sub-national levels. Leaders remained skeptical of urbanization and especially urban concentration. In 1994, Zhu Rongji, then Vice Premier, noted:

> If we talk about the mass relocation of the rural population now, peasants will all wish to go to the big cities to make lots of money. How can this be tolerated? Nowadays about 20 million peasants are migrating to the cities each year. This cannot be tolerated.... Today, we still need to... make peasants stay in the rural areas.[185]

This statement was, of course, informed by the dramatic events of protest in Beijing and China's other major cities that occurred five years prior that nearly toppled the regime.

TIANANMEN

The social movement and protests that began in Tiananmen Square in April 1989 represented the gravest threat to the Chinese regime since the founding of the People's Republic in 1949. The vast literature describing and analyzing the Tiananmen protests cannot be summarized adequately here.[186] Yet these urban protests threatened the regime through mechanisms akin to those offered in chapter 2. Tens of thousands of protestors took control of the country's most symbolically significant space, while the regime's leaders—literally down the street—were unable to prevent it. That so many could descend on the square so quickly speaks to the power of proximity. The events called into question the competence of the regime—as a whole and its individual leaders—to audiences inside the walled leadership compound of Zhongnanhai and those outside.

Tiananmen, the Gate of Heavenly Peace and including the gigantic square that was built to its south, is the most important political space in the country. It served as the principal gate through which emperors would leave the Forbidden City and from which edicts would be pronounced.[187] The May 4th protests, "a

---

[184] Davin 1999, 45; Chan and Zhang 1999, 838.

[185] Rongji, via Solinger 1999a, 53. FBIS translation from Ching Pao, November 5 1994.

[186] Lubna Malik and Lynn White's "Contemporary China: A Book List" contains 56 "Tiananmen Books" along with over 100 books providing "additional background" as of 2008 (Malik and White 2008).

[187] Meyer 1991; Thornton 2010.

defining moment in the development of modern China," also took place on that ground in 1919.[188] Mao proclaimed the founding of the People's Republic from atop Tiananmen to throngs standing below him in 1949.[189] The space in front of the gate was expanded to hold one million people, modeled after Moscow's Red Square.[190] As Liu puts it, "As the national capital, Beijing had symbolic and strategic significance for the leaders. Moreover, symbolically what Beijing is to the nation, Tiananmen is to Beijing."[191] The political importance of Tiananmen and the square cannot be overstated: "In China, there is one universally recognized monument which overshadows all others in signifying both the hegemonic power of the state and the history of struggle against it, and that is Tiananmen or the Gate of Heavenly Peace."[192]

The loss of control of the square during the spring of 1989 severely damaged the perceived strength and political stability of the regime. Beijing's mayor during the incident, Chen Xitong, claimed that Liu Xiaobo and others said "as long as the flags on the square are still up, we can continue our fight and spread it to the whole country until the government collapses."[193] This claim rings true; as Hershkovitz put it, "Continued appropriation of the Square by the students presaged social chaos not only in Beijing but throughout the country; the reassertion of the state's domination over the disputed space was the prerequisite for a return to order."[194] With such massive populations of students, workers, and others disgruntled by the economic reforms and corruption in proximity to the Square, the protests could and did explode in size and spread across the country. If the regime's inability to command the territory at its doorstep were not enough, then the added scrutiny of the international media that came with Gorbachev's visit further inflamed the situation.[195] The proximity of the leaders' compound of Zhongnanhai to the square further escalated the tension.

The protests were violently put down on 4 June 1989. Maneuvering the tanks, military hardware, and personnel that effectively cleared the square to the center of Beijing was a difficult task. Debates rage over the nature of the

---

[188] Mitter 2004, 131; Thornton 2010, 303–5. Subsequent popular movements as well took place at the Square: a patriotic march on 18 March 1926; an anti-Japanese demonstration on 9 December 1935; an anti-KMT movement on 20 May 1947; among others (Hung 1991, 84; Hung 2005). Conquerors and military might was put on display over this space as well: the Allied Army's Victory March in 1900; General Zhang Xun's attempt to restore imperial order; the Japanese installment of its Chinese puppet regime; among others (Hung 1991, 84).

[189] Hung 1991, 88.

[190] Thornton 2010, 303–5.

[191] Liu 1992, 48.

[192] Hershkovitz 1993, 399.

[193] "Quarterly Chronicle and Documentation" 1989, 938.

[194] Hershkovitz 1993, 415.

[195] Ibid., 412.

violence—the competing estimates for the number of killed citizens ranges from a few hundred to multiple thousands—yet, in the end, the CCP regime endured.[196]

INCOMPLETE AND SEPARATED URBANIZATION

China's urbanization policy has been called "an 'incomplete urbanization' approach" in that it has pushed rural migrants to move temporarily to urban areas rather than permanently relocate to these cities.[197] These temporary workers, *mingong* or *nongmingong*, expanded from a population of 20 to 30 million in the early years of the reforms to over 150 million in recent years.[198] Precise estimates for the number of migrants are not available for the 1980s. The Chinese National Bureau of Statistics until 2000 used *hukou*-based lists for its surveys. As migrants often worked around the edges of the system and went undocumented, and hence uncounted, official estimates are generally taken to be lower than real values.

Migrants' continued connection to the land was in large part due to policies of the state, most especially their land allocation from the Household Responsibility System and the discrimination in cities that they faced due to the *hukou* system.[199] Farmers did not own the land that they farmed; rural agricultural land was retained by the collective. Migrants' inability to sell or sever the economic ties to their villages pushed them to view their migration as temporary. Solinger clarified the significance of migration seen as temporary as opposed to permanent:

> According to one migration specialist [Nelson, "Sojourners versus New Urbanites"], whether or not a sojourner eventually does stay on in town, his or her belief that he or she will return to the countryside has a major impact on all sorts of urban behavior, much of it relevant to his or her ultimate prospects for mobility. The person expecting to commit to the urban setting will try to form relevant skills and to build up a reputation, credentials, and contacts there. The reverse, of course, is the case for those who see themselves as only passing through. And in dozens of interviews with floaters I repeatedly encountered either a sense of total aimlessness about the future or else a plan to return home with a short, specified period of time, after accumulating enough cash

---

[196] Zhao 2001b; Wong 1996.
[197] Chan 2010b, 66.
[198] Ibid., 69.
[199] Solinger 1999b, 185.

to build a house or marry in the village. As one young shoe repairman from Zhejiang working in Tianjin told me flippantly when asked about his intentions, "Live a day, write off a day."[200]

The delay of economic reform in cities reflected a policy of maintaining urban-biased benefits for urban workers and showed that the potential for urban instability remained atop the hierarchy of the regime's worries. Urban state-owned enterprises (SOEs) were hemorrhaging funds, yet the government was unwilling to allow managers to fire workers and thereby improve efficiency.[201] The threat of urban instability should such reforms and layoffs occur loomed too large. The institutional power of the SOEs, likely an outgrowth of their significance in the regime's urban political economy, also delayed their reform.[202] The leadership wanted to postpone the concentrated large-scale layoffs that would follow SOE reform as long as possible.[203] In the mid-1990s, the regime finally let the small and medium SOEs go, while retaining its grasp on the large firms (*zhuada fangxiao*).[204]

Multiple tactics were undertaken to reduce the likelihood of resistance from laid-off workers, as well as the fallout from that resistance.[205] Restructuring or corporatization rather than privatization were the reforms of choice, in large part to prevent firms from laying off workers and unrest.[206] When layoffs did occur, the companies and government officials enacted policies fragmenting the workers to make collective action more difficult. Subsidies were given to some workers to reduce their incentive to agitate against the company or government. Layoffs were staggered across time for similar reasons.[207] The overall pattern of reforms— first in the rural agricultural sector and later in the urban SOE sector—is consistent with fears of urban instability taking precedence in the regime's calculus.

During the Reform era, China's urbanization has been rapid and, due to the size of China's population, massive in scale. The policy changes that took place to allow this urbanization to happen did not end the regime's discrimination against those born in the countryside. Migrants came to China's cities but did so as second-class citizens. Examination of the effects of these reforms across China's many cities can shed light on their political origins. These policies varied

---

[200] Solinger 1995, 122. 活一天，算一天.

[201] Naughton 1996.

[202] On the comparative institutional power of SOEs, see Shirk 1993.

[203] It is certainly possible that hypothetical large-scale layoffs in rural areas would be seen as dangerous and to be avoided as the urban layoffs were, yet as such factories and layoffs at a large scale by necessity imply urbanized locales, the counterfactual does not exist.

[204] Lee 1999; Oi 2005; Cai 2005.

[205] Cai 2002, 342–43.

[206] Oi 2005.

[207] Cai 2005.

over space. China's largest and most politically sensitive cities were consistently the most difficult for non-locals to access. Systematic analysis of variation at the sub-national level reveals that provincial leaders acted similarly to protect the stability of the most critical cities in their domains, even when putting forward reforms ostensibly to reduce migration restrictions.

HUKOU EXPERIMENTS

We will actively yet prudently promote urbanization.... We will relax eligibility for registering as urban households in small and medium-sized cities, guide the rational flow of the population, and enable more surplus rural workers to find nonagricultural employment in nearby towns and cities.
—Wen Jiabao, *"Government Work Report,"* 5 March 2012

China's *hukou* system is a national one, but, during the Reform era especially, its implementation has differed in different cities. In a few well-known examples, cities have adopted less restrictive *hukou* policies, notably Shijiazhuang and Zhengzhou.[208] At the time of their announcement, the party's propaganda apparatus trumpeted these reforms, but despite the ado, *hukou* restrictions for normal migrants and workers in Shijiazhuang ultimately were not relaxed in a serious manner.[209] The reform in Zhengzhou, on the other hand, led to a flood of migrants—the danger that so concerns *hukou* system adherents—and resulted in a quick policy reversal.[210]

In a major move, a 1997 State Council directive, *Guofa 20*, allowed provinces to choose a limited number of small cities and towns for experimental *hukou* reform to make transferring from agricultural to non-agricultural status easier.[211] Data on where these experiments took place and their effects on population change in these areas compared to their neighbors form the heart of this section of the chapter. Following the implementation of these experiments, national level policymakers expanded the reforms. In 2001, the State Council issued a second directive that in principle extended the possibility to enact similar reforms to all small and medium-sized cities across the land. Premier Wen Jiabao's 2012 Government Work Report described China's urbanization program as remaining focused on developing small and medium cities.[212]

[208] Wang 2005; Chan and Buckingham 2008. See also Miller 2012, 36–37.
[209] Chan and Buckingham 2008.
[210] Wang 2005.
[211] State Council 1997. The full name of the notification is: 国务院批转公安部小城镇户籍管理制度改革试点方案和关于完善农村户籍管理制度意见的通知.
[212] The conclusion discusses other reforms that have begun taking place by 2013, notably in Chengdu and Chongqing. I argue that these new reforms may presage another shift in Chinese urbanization policy.

Governing China's massive population has always been at the forefront of the party's political calculus, and the CCP's management of urbanization has continued through successive reforms. What effects should the liberalization of *hukou* policies have on population movement within China? I argue that political geography helps explain sub-provincial variation in the effects of *hukou* reform. The *hukou* system reflects political priorities in China at all levels: fostering growth while maintaining political stability. Yet these priorities vary over space. Political stability is more critical in core geographic units than in remote areas.

This desire for stability in the capital is reflected in the strictness with which migration is controlled in Beijing. As the head of the Judicial Affairs Office of Beijing Municipal People's Congress put it: "Economic development does not mean an uncontrolled population. As the capital, Beijing must control its population."[213]

At the sub-national level, local leaders face incentives that mirror those at the top in the regime's nested hierarchy. Just as cities exist above the countryside in the political hierarchy of the regime, similar distinctions exist between cities. In a given province, the provincial capital sits at the top of the pyramid as, by definition, the provincial party and state offices are located there. Instability in a capital reflects poorly on the province and its leadership. Provincial capitals are the dominant political unit under the purview of provincial leaders, and any unrest in them would negatively affect a leader's career prospects—more so than outlying population centers or minor cities under their jurisdiction.[214] The limited ability of the center to monitor local agents—especially in peripheral areas—crystallizes such distinctions.[215] As such, local leaders are more leery of allowing migrants to locate freely in provincial capitals than to cities in peripheral areas.

Why would migrants have negative associations for local leaders or be linked to the potential for instability in Chinese cities? Local governments are concerned with the burden of potential welfare costs that providing for migrants would entail. Similarly, blind flows of migrants are associated with crime and disruptions of public order.[216] As President Jiang Zemin put it in an August 1996 speech:

> At present, registered urban unemployment has already reached 5.2 million; 6.6 million workers have been laid off by enterprises that have either closed or reduced production; 22 million people are classified in the categories of either disguised unemployed or underemployed; and

---

[213] Xinjingbao 2010.
[214] Landry 2008; Smith 2009.
[215] Ong 2012.
[216] Wang 2006.

there are 130 million surplus farm laborers in need of nonagricultural work in cities. It can be said that one of the thorniest problems in deepening economic restructuring and changing the pattern of economic growth is finding jobs for everyone. At present, 60 million rural workers are engaged in migrant work, many of whom are working in large and medium-sized cities. This increases those cities' social supervision burden and aggravates the difficulties of social management. Law and order is currently not good, and crime is a serious problem in some localities. These problems have a direct relation to high underemployment rates and the blind movement of migrants.[217]

Indeed, one of the functions of the *hukou* system is to track criminals.[218] These political concerns—stability above all else—appear to have trumped calls for more relaxations of migration policy, since the system that assesses the performance of party and government officials focuses on measures of GDP growth and social stability along with family planning.[219] Stability is of paramount importance in the case of politically salient cities, namely provincial capitals.[220] As such, reforms have begun in small and medium cities, allowing the government to meet rising demands for urban residence permits without overwhelming the social and physical infrastructure and potentially jeopardizing "harmony" in the largest, most politically important cities. But even for small and medium cities, tension persists between the objectives of stability, on one hand, and economic growth and reduced inequality, on the other. As some areas—provincial capitals—are more critical for stability than others, it is to be expected that *hukou* policy operates more strictly under provincial capitals than in more distant locales.

My *political geography hypothesis* can be stated as follows: *hukou* reforms will systematically yield greater population gains in outlying regions than in core political areas. This contrasts with other expectations for the likely outcomes of *hukou* reform at the local level. One perspective believes that easing restrictions should produce an influx of migrants moving into that unit, as seen in Zhengzhou.[221] Yet others expect that *hukou* reform will have little to no effect on population movements due to limited employment, education, and housing opportunities.[222] Some variants of reform require the rural migrant to give

---

[217] Jiang 2010, 529.
[218] Wang 2005.
[219] Whiting 2000; Smith 2009.
[220] The only sub-provincial level city (a middle tier of city above standard prefectures but below provincial level municipalities) that is not a provincial capital in the data is Xiamen of Fujian province. No areas under Xiamen were on the Fujian provincial list of experimental zones.
[221] Wang 2005.
[222] Yang 2002.

up any claim to rural land of his or her home village, making a transition to the city a potentially costly one. Local level reforms in small cities will be less likely to trigger mass immigration. In this view, migrants are less attracted to the possibility of moving to a small city, so making such a move easier or more rewarding by making urban status in such cities easier for migrants to obtain will have little effect on migration decisions.[223] Unappealing destinations do not suddenly become magnets with a fresh coat of paint.

In contrast with either of these views where *hukou* reform strictly increases or has no expected effect on population movements, I argue that the effect on population growth will depend on the local context, with small cities growing and large, core cities maintaining effective limits that slow down population growth. Contrast this specific set of *hukou* reforms in the 1997 experiments with the general discussion of *hukou* liberalization above. On average, restrictions were lifted during the Reform era and individuals took advantage of economic opportunities to move to urban areas. However, an implication of my argument is that the implementation of these reforms should have differed, given the anticipated effects of urbanization on stability over space. I argue that local elites are likely to weigh economic and political factors in their implementation decisions. Urbanization may promote growth but also is viewed as linked with social instability. As such, provincial leaders are likely to encourage implementation that favors economic growth with political risks in outlying areas while preferring controlled growth and a more stable political situation in the political core of their territories.

The research design compares the population changes in areas that did and did not receive experimental *hukou* reforms in the late 1990s and early 2000s. The limits of the design should be clearly noted. This is a hard test of the importance of the *hukou* system. Failing to find an effect in population changes at the local level would not be strong evidence of the *hukou* system's insignificance on migration patterns in China in general. Rather, it would point to the limited impact of this "reform," either in the locations that were chosen to receive the reform or its implementation. Instead of a null effect, a non-finding could be due to (1) people already having made their migration decisions prior to the relaxation, (2) people being unaware of the policy reform and thus unable to make decisions based on it, (3) people anticipating that the partial relaxation presaged a broader relaxation to come.[224]

The data used to test the argument come from three sources: an original dataset of county level units that received the *hukou* reform "treatment," population data for county level units from the Barometer of China's Development

---

[223] Wang and Cai 2008, 184.

[224] The 2001 reform that allowed similar policies to be implemented in county level cities nationwide points out that (3) is in fact a correct belief.

(BOCD) dataset, and annual satellite imagery of nighttime lights in counties as an external measure of growth in those locales.[225]

The 1997 *Guofa 20* describes the experimental *hukou* reform to be undertaken at the local level.[226] The document makes explicit the limits of the policy. Reforms should take place at or below the county level. The policy explicitly bans increasing the size or scope of the experimentation, such as implementing the *hukou* reform in designated poverty counties. At the same time, the document makes clear that this reform does not end the *hukou* system. In fact, its preamble discusses the reform's purpose and significance, stating that strict control of the population of large central cities will continue, specifically naming "Beijing, Tianjin, and Shanghai, and other 'exceptionally large cities' (*teda chengshi*)" and stating that they will remain under strict population management.[227] The aims of the experimental reform are in keeping with the regime's narrative of developing of the countryside. Bringing rural surplus labor to nearby cities and developing the tertiary sector of the rural economy were the policy's dominant goals.

Provinces were assigned different numbers of experiments (*shidian*) based on their geographic region and socioeconomic characteristics. Western provinces were limited to 10 test locations, whereas central provinces were allowed 15 and eastern provinces 20. I searched news portals and law databases to find as many provincial lists of reform locations as possible, ultimately finding lists from 10 of China's 31 provinces.[228] These 10 provinces are Inner Mongolia, Fujian, Henan, Hunan, Guangxi, Guizhou, Shaanxi, Gansu, Ningxia, and Xinjiang. Figure 4.1 places them on a map to give a sense of their location. Each provincial document offered a preamble that in large part echoed the *Guofa 20* document, with different provinces referencing different guiding thoughts and principal targets of the reforms. These are categorized in table 4.1.

Most treated locations noted in the provincial documents are at the township level. The analysis examines patterns of population shifts at the county level rather than individual township level due to incomplete data for townships.[229] That is, each county that has at least one township listed on the province's *hukou* reform policy announcement is coded as receiving the policy reform treatment. I have found no evidence suggesting that the center was involved in selecting the reform locales; local officials—those from the provincial level and

---

[225] Image and Data for the nighttime lights processed by NOAA's National Geophysical Data Center. DMSP data collected by the US Air Force Weather Agency.

[226] State Council 1997.

[227] Ibid.

[228] China Academic Journals and Lawinfochina.com were used in addition to Internet searches using both Baidu and Google.

[229] Counties are one administrative level higher than townships. Implications of possible ecological inference problems are in noted the discussion section.

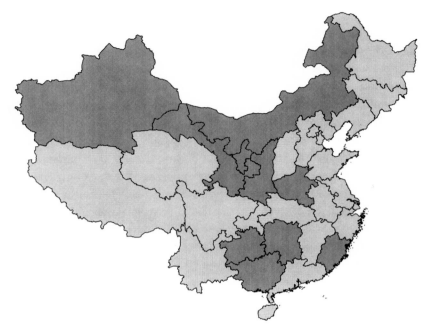

Figure 4.1 Map of Provinces with *Hukou* Reform Data. Note: Darkly shaded provinces are those with county level experimental hukou reform data analyzed in this section.

below—appear to have had full discretion in the choice.[230] A total of 119 counties are coded as receiving this treatment, slightly more than 12 percent of the total number of county level units extant in the provinces at the time of reform (989).[231] The *hukou* reform treatments began in 1997 and each province is coded based on the year the provincial list was released.

To distinguish core political areas versus outlying regions, I code counties by the status of the city above them. Counties administratively under provincial capitals are coded as core areas, and other counties are coded as being in peripheral areas. [232]

The population data come from the National County Population Statistics (*Quanguo fenxianshi renkou tongjiziliao*) compiled in the BOCD dataset project. The dependent variable is the total *hukou* population change in a county-year. It

[230] Chan and Zhang 1999, 840. This, like other negative claims, is very difficult to prove beyond the shadow of a doubt.

[231] There are a small number (9) of listed townships that cannot be placed into a given county due to matching names problems, that is, multiple townships having the same name across different counties in the same province.

[232] While at first theoretically appealing, a continuous analysis, using physical distance or travel time from the provincial capital, is at odds with the discrete metrics used in the evaluation of political leaders.

Table 4.1 **Provincial Objectives from Experiment List Preamble**

Objectives	Provinces	Province List
"Move excess rural labor towards towns"	7	Guizhou, Inner Mongolia, Ningxia, Gansu, Guangxi, Fujian, Hunan
"Social stability"	5	Inner Mongolia, Ningxia, Gansu, Guangxi, Hunan
"Promote development"	5	Inner Mongolia, Ningxia, Gansu, Guangxi, Fujian
"Develop socialist market economy"	4	Inner Mongolia, Guangxi, Xinjiang, Shaanxi
"Control population pressure in large or medium cities"	4	Guizhou, Inner Mongolia, Gansu, Guangxi
"Increase small town construction"	4	Inner Mongolia, Guangxi, Fujian, Hunan
"Accurate huji system"	2	Guizhou, Fujian

Note: Henan lists none of these objectives and instead references "rectifying negative effects of previous reform efforts."

should be noted that this test follows total population changes across counties, not directly assessing the numbers of individuals availing themselves of the new *hukou* permissions.[233]

To address the possibility that the local population data are problematic, I measure growth in these different regions by comparing changes in the amount of light that the territories emit at night. The US Defense Meteorological Satellite Program Operational Linescan System (DSMP-OLS) collects images of the nighttime sky globally. Cloudless nightly images are averaged over the course of the year with fires and gas flares removed and placed on a 30 arc second grid. Each pixel then receives a score from 0 to 63, with higher values reflecting more light emanating from that location. Using maps from the 2000 census, the grid is divided up into counties and with changes in the mean light level being the metric of choice below.

Many county level units change names and borders over time, complicating the analysis.[234] For example, many counties shift from counties to county level

---

[233] One estimate is that in experimental areas around 1.386 million individuals have begun to take advantage of the procedure (Tian 2005). More detailed sub-national data is not available.

[234] This is particularly the case for the nighttime lights data. Only county-years matching the GB code from 2000 are included those analyses.

cities to urban districts during the years of the analysis. In other cases, multiple counties are merged into a single county. A large number of counties appear and disappear due to these changes. For the purposes of this analysis, counties that receive the reform are compared with those that do not receive the reform, and the changes within those treated counties are tracked over time.[235]

ANALYSIS

At first glance, the experimental *hukou* reforms appear to have little effect. When analyzing county level effects of *hukou* reform for the pooled sample of counties, little effect can be discerned. Both treated and non-treated counties experience a slowdown of growth in the post-reform period due to a general decrease in China's national population growth rate during this time.[236] Treated counties tend to grow faster than do non-treated counties both before and after the time of treatment.[237] Both treated and non-treated areas see annual population growth decrease by little over 1,900 people on average as shown in table 4.2.

Yet separating counties by geographic status—outlying areas versus provincial capitals—tells a different story.[238] Nine of the 10 provinces in the data have designated at least one county under the provincial capital as an experimental *hukou* reform site.[239] The proportion of counties under provincial capitals that

Table 4.2 ***Hukou* Reform Comparison across All Areas**

	Pre-Reform Period	Post-Reform Period	Change
No Reform	4.86	2.95	−39%
	n = 7,787	n = 6,407	
Reform	5.88	3.91	−34%
	n = 845	n = 783	

Note: Values represent mean population changes for a given county-year for each category, measured in thousands.

[235] Due to renaming and border changing, the maximum number of counties that are coded as having received reform for a given year is 117 in 2000. The results below drop all cases where the absolute value of the change in population is coded as greater than 50,000 people in a given year as these are likely to be either coding errors or county mergers/border changes.

[236] Cai and Wang 2008.

[237] This difference in before treatment averages implies perhaps a selection bias toward attractive locales but, as discussed below, this potential does not undermine the political geography hypothesis.

[238] See table 4.1 for more themes from the preamble noted in the provincial lists.

[239] The exceptional case is Inner Mongolia.

receive the experiment is almost exactly the same as those in outlying areas (0.13 vs. 0.12). This equivalence shows no bias in the choice of experimental locales. Any difference across locations in the outcomes associated with *hukou* reform thus reflects *differences in effects* and not on *rates of experimentation* varying over space. The reform locations are not differentiated in the provincial lists in any way, yet the outcomes associated with the *hukou* reforms vary dramatically by their outlying versus center status.

The effects of *hukou* reform in provincial capitals and in outlying areas point in opposite directions. In outlying areas during both pre- and post-reform periods, treated counties grow faster than do counties without *hukou* reforms. By contrast, in provincial capitals, the same comparison yields the opposite result. Under the provincial capital, treated counties experience slower population growth when compared with the control group. This is a dramatic change from the pre-treatment period, as counties selected for treatment under provincial capitals grew faster prior to reform.

Table 4.3 summarizes these differences. The first column gives the mean values of total population change in counties before any of the provinces begin the experimental *hukou* reforms. In both outlying areas and provincial capitals, counties that would receive reform added more population than their counterparts. In outlying areas, this difference is around 1,000 people per year, and closer to 1,200 in provincial capitals. After the reforms, a difference across regions emerges. In outlying areas, both treated and control counties have reduced population growth in the post-reform period. The reformed counties experience less of a slowdown (−1,780) compared to their neighbors that did not receive the treatment (−2,220).

Yet under provincial capitals, the opposite occurs. Initial conditions in these core areas are the same, with areas receiving reform growing faster than the control group of counties. In precisely those counties where the experimental changes take place, however, a slowdown of growth occurs. This is counterintuitive. While unreformed counties under the provincial capital in the post-reform period remain very attractive to migrants and indeed increase their growth rates, those areas under provincial capitals receiving the experimental treatment experience slower growth. In fact, unreformed counties under provincial capitals are the only one of the four categories of counties to have faster growth in the post-reform period than prior to the reforms. The counties on the *hukou* reform list, on the other hand, lose 54 percent of their population growth on average. Whereas prior to the reforms the counties under the provincial capital that were to receive the experiment topped the population growth charts, after the reform experiments, they drop to just above the mean level of the bottom group, the outlying areas without reform.

China's population is growing, but experimental reforms tried to shape the contours of that growth and urbanization. Namely, reformed areas under provincial

Table 4.3 **Pre- and Post-Treatment Effects in Outlying Areas & Provincial Capitals**

		Pre-Reform Period	Post-Reform Period	Change (%)
Outlying Areas	No Reform	4.86 n = 7,293	2.64 n = 5,732	−46
	Reform	5.83 n = 719	4.05 n = 686	−31
Provincial Capitals	No Reform	4.92 n = 494	5.59 n = 675	+14
	Reform	6.18 n = 126	2.87 n = 97	−54

Notes: Values represent mean population changes for a given county-year for each category, measured in thousands.

Differences between the two pairs are always statistically significant, with the maximum p-value = 0.03.

capitals—rather than foster growth—have actually tried to slow population growth to those counties. While there was one national level policy directive that each of the provinces under question references in its policy, each province emphasizes different elements of the national level policy. Examination of the preambles summarized in table 4.1, however, does not lead to the conclusion that the content of the preamble connects to the outcomes in population terms of the policy. For example, provinces that explicitly mention "controlling population pressure in large or medium cities" exhibit patterns of population growth similar to those provinces that omit reference to this reform objective. Yet table 4.3 shows that the effects are consistent with reformed areas controlling pressure in politically important provincial capitals while allowing more unencumbered growth in outlying areas.

Regression analysis, as summarized in table 4.4, yields similar results. The general trend of population change in the counties in these 10 provinces has evolved over time. In table 4.4, all of the statistical models include year and province fixed effects, that is, they absorb year by year and cross-provincial variations in the data.[240] The coefficients that emerge reflect patterns of change controlling for the time effects within provinces. The dependent variable is the same as in tables 4.2 and 4.3, the total population change from one year to the next in a given county measured in thousands. With only a constant and the fixed effects

---

[240] County level fixed effects are not possible as location is fixed.

Table 4.4 **Differential Effects in Capitals and Outlying Areas**

DV: Total Population Change	Model 4.1	Model 4.2 Outlying Areas	Model 4.3 Provincial Capitals	Model 4.4
Hukou Reform	0.98	1.43**	−2.48	1.33**
	(0.56)	(0.52)	(1.61)	(0.53)
Provincial				1.81**
Capital				(0.56)
Hukou and Capital				−2.93**
Interaction				(1.17)
Constant	5.56***	5.42***	8.14***	5.46***
	(0.50)	(0.47)	(1.44)	(0.51)
Province FE	YES	YES	YES	YES
Year FE	YES	YES	YES	YES
Observations	15,822	14,430	1,392	15,822
Number of Counties	1,559	1,425	134	1,559
R-Squared	0.070	0.083	0.054	0.077

Robust standard errors in parentheses.

***$p < 0.01$, **$p < 0.05$, *$p < 0.1$.

as controls, in Model 4.1 *hukou* reform's estimated coefficient is positive but not statistically distinct from zero.

This model corroborates the mean comparison in table 4.2 showing no obvious effect in the pooled data. Yet this non-effect masks variation based on the location of the county as seen in Models 4.2 and 4.3, which separate the data and show that *hukou* reform points in opposite directions in these two different geographic contexts. For outlying areas, comparing the coefficient on *hukou* reform in Model 4.2 to its counterpart in Model 4.1 shows a near 50 percent increase in its magnitude. *Hukou* reform is associated with an average boost in population change of 1,430 residents when counties under the provincial capital are omitted. Rather than increasing the flow of people into a given county, *hukou* reform under provincial capitals is if anything associated with a negative effect.[241]

Model 4.4 again puts the two regions back together into a single analysis. Rather than separating the data, it separates the effect of *hukou* reform in

[241] Due to the large standard error on this estimate, confidence intervals usually used in political science for this coefficient would include zero; the *p*-value is approximately 0.15.

outlying areas and *hukou* reform in provincial capitals using an interaction term. The *hukou* reform coefficient and the constant estimate both track very closely those of Model 4.2. Counties under provincial capitals that have not received *hukou* reform are associated with the baseline constant level of growth plus an additional 1,810 individuals for a given year on average. The population change in reform areas under the provincial capital, on the other hand, was not much different than the baseline county in an outlying area that did not receive the *hukou* reform treatment. The sum of the coefficients for these three terms is 0.21, extremely close to the baseline. That is, although *hukou* reform and provincial capital status are individually associated with larger population gains, when both are present, population growth drops to barely above the baseline. These findings point quite strongly in support of the argument that the *hukou* system, even in the presence of reform, will be applied more strictly in areas of political import than in other places.

These results are confirmed using analysis of the nighttime lights data as shown in table 4.5. The change in the brightness of territories follows the exact same patterns as when using the population change data as the dependent variable. The satellite data begins in 1997 and so only has adequate data for post-treatment years. In these years, just as in the population change data, outlying areas that are reformed exhibit faster growth than their neighbors who were not on the reform lists, while that pattern is flipped under provincial capitals. The statistical differences between the two pairs are always significant, with the maximum *p*-value 0.03.

Table 4.5 **Nighttime Lights in Outlying and Central Areas**

		Post-Reform Period	Difference
Outlying Areas	No Reform	0.142 n = 3,294	0.07 $p < 0.04$
	Reform	0.212 n = 482	
Provincial Capitals	No Reform	0.593 n = 348	0.372 $p < 0.02$
	Reform	0.221 n = 70	

Note: Values represent mean changes for a given county-year for each category in the nighttime lights measure. 1 sided t-tests.

DISCUSSION

The analysis of experimental reforms in 119 counties across 10 of the PRC's 31 provinces enhances our understanding of *hukou* reform's effects in population terms and suggests the continued role of political and geographic factors in shaping urbanization at the sub-national level. Yet how narrow or broad is that understanding? What lessons can be gleaned from it? Four topics—potential selection effects, potential ecological inference problems, the lack of control variables, and the quality of Chinese population data—need to be addressed.

The study does not directly address the problem of selection effects. That is, it does not problematize why these localities in particular were chosen to receive the *hukou* reform treatment. Two potential lines of concern are the following: first, instead of the *hukou* reform treatment having any causal effects on the areas in question, the selected areas might have characteristics likely to produce similar outcomes absent the reform; second, being selected could induce changes in measurement that appear to be changes in outcomes. There are three responses to these potential concerns.

First, the principal result is the change in treated counties before and after treatment in different locales, not in comparisons between control and treatment groups. Within the set of treated counties, patterns of population change before and after treatment based on their status as core or peripheral areas. A naïve analysis sees a decline in the population change in these counties connected to treatment. Core areas with *hukou* reform experience a drop in population growth of 54 percent, while the decline is relatively modest in outlying areas (31 percent). Comparing the treated counties to the control counties in the respective jurisdictions allows one to gauge the baseline pattern of population change in these provinces. Thus, rather than concluding that *hukou* reform slows down population growth generally but especially in core areas, one can conclude that controlling for province and time, *hukou* reform boosts growth in outlying areas and reduces it in the center (table 4.4). Selection effects do not undermine this case.

Second, the possibility of *hukou* reform changing measured rather than real outcomes does not fit with the finding that the treatment effect differs in outlying and core areas. Such measurement effects would only change the magnitude of the story, not the direction. Imagine that *hukou* reform increases the share of migrants who register and are enumerated in a county. That is, rather than inducing more people to migrate to a county, reform simply improves the counting of those already there. If one could isolate and estimate this potential effect on measurement, then perhaps the estimated boost in growth associated with *hukou* reform in outlying areas might no longer remain statistically different from zero. However, in the end, as long as the measurement effect is unidirectional across space, this concern does not undermine the differential effect between core and outlying areas at the heart of the analysis; any effect would be to alter the baseline.[242]

Third, if the selection mechanism differed across space in ways that align with the argument, then the results could be weakened. Rather than *hukou* reform causing changes in population growth, the areas selected for treatment might differ across regions (i.e., faster growing outlying regions and slower growing capital cities might have been disproportionately chosen to receive treatment). However, table 4.3 attests to the similarities (not differences) in the kinds of areas selected for *hukou* reform. Both in outlying areas and under provincial capitals, *hukou* experiments were undertaken in areas growing faster than the mean during the pre-treatment period, with counties under capital cities growing faster than outlying counties. This suggests that reforms were adopted in counties that were already attractive to migrants (rather than slapping a fresh coat of paint on an unattractive locality) in both regions—outlying areas and under the capital. This argues against differential selection effects. However, even if experiments targeted counties with slowing growth rates under provincial capitals and counties with rising growth rates in outlying regions, this would support the *political geography hypothesis*—that the regime and local leaders are concerned about population growth in core areas more than outlying regions. At the same time, since the effect is different despite the similarity in observed treatment across jurisdictions, it is clear that there are other factors at work. Further investigation of these unobserved mechanisms and factors is called for. The significant but inconsistent effects of the *hukou* reforms align with the importance of political geography for local leaders.

A second cause for concern is the potential for ecological inference problems. The possibility exists that attributing population changes at the county level to the *hukou* reform experiments, which occur mostly at the township level, could be flawed. If the argument claimed that *hukou* reform made little difference, the possibility of ecological inference problems might be a real concern. That is, variation in the other townships in a county might swamp any systematic change in the reformed townships pointing to a null effect. Yet what the results show is an effect at a higher level of analysis than the treatment. As such the claim seems strengthened rather than weakened. Township level experimental areas affect county level population change; counties with townships receiving reform behave in different ways under provincial capitals and outlying regions, even though "counties receiving treatment" sometimes only receive treatment on a portion of their territory. That said, the data used to assess the claim are not

---

[242] This would be the case unless the reform encouraged only local officials in outlying counties to improve their counting of migrants or to do so more than in core areas, yet no rationale or logic along those lines appears plausible.

at the level of the treatment. Whether individuals moving into the experimental *hukou* townships drive the county level results remains unclear; some other cause—as unlikely as that may be—could be at work. A scenario along these lines is presented below.

Inside a county, townships and township level officials compete along numerous dimensions. One township is granted *hukou* reform status. Other townships do not have the official imprimatur to initiate *hukou* reforms but as the stringency of migration restrictions is often a function of implementation rather than law, the other townships become substantially more attractive to migrants. These changes by other township level units that were responses to the experimental *hukou* reform, and not the *hukou* reform itself, could be associated with the population growth accompanying *hukou* reform at the county level in outlying areas.

Even if this scenario were true, it does not explain the differential effect across outlying and capital city counties. In the outlying areas townships compete in ways that bring in more individuals, while in core areas they compete to slow down growth. As above, the broad claim of the section that the system manages urbanization in ways that control large cities more than periphery areas is supported at the expense of the more concrete claim related to the *hukou* reform treatment itself.

A third concern is that the study does not include control variables other than the year or province in the analysis. As other factors undoubtedly account for some of the variation in population change, the separate causal effect of the *hukou* reform remains potentially clouded. First, to be sure, other factors such as economic growth, attractiveness of climate, investment levels, availability of high paying jobs, and the like, affect migration decisions and ideally would be included in an analysis of the impact of *hukou* reform. Yet these variables interact with each other and with *hukou* reform in complex and indeterminate ways making any analysis a causal thicket difficult to disentangle. Questions such as the following would need to be asked and answered in a convincing manner: Did *hukou* reform cause the economic growth that led to the population growth? Or did *hukou* reform lead to population growth which in turn induced investment producing economic growth yielding further population growth? The political geography argument of the analysis rests on population-based evidence and, to be sure, would be strengthened if the described impact of *hukou* reform withstood the inclusion of control variables into a multivariable regression. As a baseline, this study shows that local variation in population policy produces differential effects on population growth across space. Further study to understand the micro-dynamics involved in the differential effects across space at work at the township and county levels is warranted.

A final concern is the study's use of official population figures, which are notoriously divorced from reality in the Reform era. First, the nighttime lights corroboration of the results from the official population data should address this concern. Second, while it is well documented that population data at the sub-national level in China during the Reform era are problematic, these problems mostly accrue because of difficulty in tracking and accurately locating migrant populations.[243] That said, these data are the best available, as census records only reveal snapshots of the population distribution that do not allow analysis of annual changes. Third, if the *hukou* reform should lead to any changes in the measurement of populations, the expected effect would be an increase in reporting rather than differential effects across regions. As such, this effect is similar to that seen above, where errors associated with measurement may affect the absolute magnitude of the estimated impact of the *hukou* reform but the differential across the regions should persist without distortion.

With these concerns addressed, the patterns in the data support the *political geography hypothesis*. Areas under core cities that receive the *hukou* reform treatment grow at slower rates while those in outlying areas increase their growth rates. Interpretation of why this is the case is less directly observable. I argue that local officials implement the policies leading these outcomes because of background concerns about social stability. Five of the provinces do explicitly mention social stability as part of their objectives in implementing the experimental reforms.

A slightly alternative view is that leaders fear overly massive cities for reasons other than social stability. The decision-making process interior to the leaders' minds remains a black box. As noted above, no patterns could be discerned based on the stated objectives placed in the various preambles to the experimental lists shown in table 4.1. One could imagine situations in which leaders of core cities—frustrated by traffic, pollution, and other congestion costs, as well as the inability to monitor activity—do all that they can to hamper the growth of these cities while promoting other locales. Instead of political pressures inducing behavior and replicating central political dictates at local levels, then, the patterns could be seen as the result of petty preferences of the leaders as individuals rather than political actors. Yet even here the problems leaders are seeking to avoid are the problems of large cities. Even if not directly operating through the social stability channel, the leaders are implementing the policies in ways to urbanize without increasing levels of urban concentration.

---

[243] Chan 1994. These measurement problems have led to severe misestimates not only in the population of different areas (despite having a registered population of less than 2 million, Shenzhen is usually home to more than four times that many people) but also in numerous socioeconomic indicators which use population as a denominator in some "per capita" metric. For instance, GDP per capita is grossly overestimated in cases that ignore large migrant populations (such as Shenzhen).

Conclusion

The Chinese regime's *hukou* system short-circuited the Faustian bargain of urban bias. By tilting toward cities but constraining farmers in the countryside, the regime reaped stability by placating urbanites without leading to cities overwhelmed with migrants desperate for opportunities and willing to live in slums to earn them. China's *hukou* system institutionally separated rural, agricultural populations from the urban, non-agricultural society. Its reforms arose out of economic necessity. The regime allowed for people to transition out of agriculture and move to urban factories, trading improved economic performance for decreased control of society. Even with economic reforms and partial relaxation of the *hukou* system, farmers moved to cities only as temporary migrants and second-class citizens.

Reform era China has seen a relaxation of the *hukou* system, at the national and sub-national level. Yet China's loophole to the Faustian bargain of urban bias remains a critical fact affecting the political economy of the regime. Just as national leaders have demonstrated concerns about the makeup of the county's largest cities because of their significance, local leaders have attempted to manage urbanization in their own areas of administration to balance growth and stability. As the regime has chipped away at the *hukou* system's restrictions on migration, there has been increasing pressure and eventually movement to reduce the level of urban bias in the country. The next chapter explores the fiscal shift that China has undertaken since the late 1990s toward rural and interior areas that I argue in part serves as a substitute to the *hukou* system.

CHAPTER 5

The Fiscal Shift

MIGRATION, INSTABILITY, AND REDISTRIBUTION

This year, we will completely rescind the agricultural tax throughout the country, a tax that China has been collecting for 2,600 years. This is a change of epoch-making significance.
—Premier Wen Jiabao, *March 5, 2006*

As the Chinese regime moved away from strict limits on population movement and allowed the migration barriers to wither, it also began to redirect fiscal resources to the neglected interior and countryside. After consolidating its fiscal powers, the regime began emphasizing the development of lagging areas and moving away from urban bias to reduce pressure on coastal cities, which the regime feared would be inundated with migrants. By 2006, the fiscal extraction from Chinese agriculture had been simplified, cut, and replaced with subsidies with "industry feeding agriculture in turn," changes described by Premier Wen Jiabao as of "epoch-making significance."[1]

This chapter details the fiscal shift toward the countryside and points to the ability of China's move away from urban bias to reinforce the *hukou* system's management of urbanization. Migration restrictions gave the regime the opportunity to lavish cities with resources for decades from the 1950s to 1970s while those in the periphery languished without the ability to escape their plight. As that system began to be disassembled, the underlying political problem that it addressed—potential instability arising from too many people in too few cities—remained. Abolishing agricultural taxes, increasingly subsidizing poor and rural areas, and promoting development in the rest of the country—and not just

---

[1] Xinhua 2006b. Oi refers to the idea that rural industry helped fund agriculture in the early Reform era in similar terms: "using industry to subsidize agriculture (*yigong bunong*) policy" (Oi 1999, 21).

the coastal enclaves—became part of the policy solution to this dilemma. By improving economic opportunities in the interior, the Chinese regime encouraged a more diffuse pattern of urban development rather than concentrating its industry and population growth dangerously in a few megacities.

The Chinese regime tacked away from its previous urban bias only after its political and economy stability blossomed in the mid-1990s. Economically, the central regime grasped control of government revenues from localities with a recentralizing fiscal reform in 1994. Politically, the regime had passed through the post-Tiananmen doldrums and quashed dissent. With its short-term future secured, the regime eased the fiscal burdens of farmers. The timing of the fiscal shift is in line with the general argument that urban bias is a deal with the devil that is most attractive when alternatives are lacking. When the regime could avoid the long-term negative consequences of urban bias, it chose to do so.[2]

China's fiscal shift aiding the countryside was not uniform across the country as localities near unstable cities received more assistance than other areas. To be sure, the national change away from urban bias was in part a response to the rise of rural unrest associated with the fiscal burdens that peasants carried. Yet increased transfers to the countryside did not only reflect the concern over instability in the countryside. On the contrary, sub-national variation in transfers suggests that increased monies sent to the countryside also reflected concerns that additional migrants might inflame urban instability. Sub-national officials targeted money to counties near unstable cities, aiming to expand economic opportunities in these rural areas to decrease marginal migrants from relocating to these unstable cities. While central state agency in these patterns remains unclear, the size and direction of transfers follow the logic of the argument. In the end, even the shape of the fiscal shift to the countryside also appears to reflect concerns over urban instability.

China's Fiscal Shift

Chinese governments have relied on agricultural taxes to fund their operations for millennia. The agricultural tax has a documented history of over 2,600 years.[3] These taxes built China's historical cities and paid for the luxurious palaces and

[2] As described in chapter 3, most developed countries exhibit pro-rural bias in fiscal policy. China's moves away from urban bias come earlier, at much lower levels of economic development than seen elsewhere.

[3] The Zhou Dynasty era Lu state put forward a system of agricultural taxation in 594 B.C.E. (Loewe and Shaughnessy 1999, 577). For a more limited 2,200-year history, that is, since the Han Dynasty, see Zhao 1986, 103. Often the taxes were paid in kind creating the phrase "imperial grain (皇粮)."

playgrounds of the emperors. Urban bias was also present in the anti-disaster efforts of regimes. Strand notes that "an urban bias became detectable in some elite-led relief programs," particularly referring to Zhejiang province's Shaoxing in the late Qing, where relief for rice shortages was "concentrated in urban areas."[4]

Despite Mao's rhetorical affinity for the farmer, the CCP followed the example of these previous Chinese regimes, extracting from agriculture to fund its urban operations. Breaking from this precedent, Deng's reforms began agricultural de-collectivization and higher prices for farmers' grain. These yielded quick boosts in rural incomes and reduced urban-rural inequality. Incomes rapidly increased in the countryside from 1979 to 1984.[5] Yet in 1985, after giving farmers a chance to "catch their breath," redistributive policy turned once again away from rural interests.[6]

In response to growing regional and urban-rural inequality, the regime in the late 1990s moved aggressively to turn the dial in the direction of those in the countryside and interior. To be clear, China's economic policy remains urban biased but has been decreasingly so since the fiscal shift began. The regime's efforts to tilt back to the countryside have served in part as a substitute for an increasingly lax *hukou*-based migration restriction regime. However, before the central government could initiate these changes in its urban-rural redistributive policy, it would need to deal with budget problems stemming from the marketization of the economy. An important precursor for the regime's fiscal shift was the recentralization of funds in the central state whose coffers had emptied due to the reforms.

1994 FISCAL REFORM

China's fiscal system went from the plan in the 1970s to ad hoc contracts in 1988 to a reformulated centralization in 1994. While the economic reforms initiated by Deng in the late 1970s generated tremendous growth, they also undermined the economic institutions of the PRC, which had been designed for a planned economy. Under a planned economy, the center was able to manipulate prices to ensure that excess profits would be concentrated in a few firms, from which revenues would then be extracted. Yet with marketization came the destruction of the regime's ability to collect revenue in this fashion as firms would sell goods

[4] Strand 1995, 402. On Shaoxing, see Cole 1986, 55.
[5] Lü 1997, 117.
[6] Zweig 1986; Bergsten et al. 2009, 138. See also Park 2008, 52–53. The countryside continues to take off in the latter half of the 1980s, only with Tiananmen does urban bias increase (Oi 1999; Huang 2008).

at market prices outside of the plan rather than accept the substantially lower plan prices for their goods.[7]

The 1994 fiscal reform strengthened the center. The center took over a substantially larger share of government revenues from the provinces that had controlled them prior to 1994. Beijing argued that the dramatic transformation of the regime's economy and revenues in the wake of the economic reforms since the late 1970s necessitated this centralization of revenues. To recentralize the fiscal system in 1994 past opposition from relatively developed coastal provinces, the center temporarily bought off these richer provinces with side payments. These deals came at the expense of the country's poorer areas, resulting in the fiscal system's regressive skew in the late 1990s. By the early 2000s, the regime took advantage of its excess revenues to shift transfers in a pro-poor, progressive direction. Both the centralization itself and the subsequent move away from this regressive policy were critical to "hold China together."[8] The former changed the fiscal system so that the center could afford to fund the shift that took place with the latter.[9]

As reforms took hold in the economic sphere, the revenue structure that had been put in place during the planned economy ceased to function appropriately. In 1988, the government created ad hoc fiscal contracts with firms and provincial level units to try to replace revenue lost due to marketization.[10] Yet this fiscal contracting system failed to reverse the central government's eroding fiscal position.[11]

The center's fiscal decline continued to such an extent that observers of Chinese politics increasingly saw parallels to a splintered Yugoslavia when contemplating the middle kingdom's future. The CCP was an underfunded regime with centrifugal forces from different regions pulling it apart to such an extent that disintegration seemed like a possibility.[12] Local governments shifted their revenue streams from shared taxes to off-budget fees that they were not required to share with the center. Christine Wong provides an example:

> Under the planned economy Shanghai remitted more than 80 percent
> of its revenues to the central government. This high "tax" on Shanghai

---

[7] Naughton 1992a, b.

[8] This is the title of a 2004 Naughton and Yang volume.

[9] Chen argues that the effect of the first reform actually makes the second more necessary by, unintentionally, increasing peasant burdens (Chen 2008).

[10] Wong 2005.

[11] Wong 1991; Wong, Heady, and Woo 1995; Naughton 1995; Wong 2005, 5.

[12] Naughton and Yang (2004, ch. 1) refer to this literature as "disintegrationist." *China Deconstructs* is a prominent volume; see also Goldstone's "Coming Collapse of China," as well as Gordon Chang's book (Goodman and Segal 1995; Goldstone 1995; Chang 2001).

revenues created incentives for collusion between the municipal government and its subordinate enterprises and the potential for informally sharing the "saved revenues" within Shanghai.[13]

The economic power of localities was beginning to undermine the central regime's political power.[14]

The notion that the local governments in the provinces could constrain the center from poaching their local revenues was also popularized, leading to the image of CCP-run China as a fiscal federalist state.[15] The 1994 fiscal reform, which grabbed control of the fiscal system's reigns from localities, reversed the central state's weakening position.

The 1994 reform modernized the administration of taxes, but its most important component was the creation of the Tax Sharing System (TSS).[16] As Wong puts it, the TSS "fundamentally changed the way revenues are shared between the central and provincial governments, by shifting from a negotiated system of general revenue sharing to a mix of tax assignments and tax sharing."[17] Most critically for the central government, the Value Added Tax (VAT), which accounted for almost half of all government tax revenue, went from being a purely local tax to 75 percent central and 25 percent local.[18] The TSS was a dramatic change that flipped the script; whereas prior to this reform local governments sent transfers to fund the central government, afterwards, local governments depended on transfers from the center to pay for their operations. The central government's share of revenues, as depicted in figure 5.1, shows the immediate effect of the TSS. The central government would have resources to dole out to address threats and by grabbing funds from localities directly countered the emerging threat of localism.

While the central coffers were quickly filled by revenue from the newly shared taxes, the reform actually exacerbated regional inequality in the years immediately following its implementation.[19] Urbanized and coastal provinces, whose political strength was undermined by the reform, demanded and received a commitment from the center for tax rebates. The tax rebates operated essentially as transfers to provinces based on a share of the growth of VAT and excise taxes. These tax rebates dominated the center-to-province fiscal transfers in the

---

[13] Wong 2005, 4. See also Oksenberg and Tong 1991; Wong 1991.
[14] See the disintegrationist literature, e.g., *China Deconstructs*, in n. 12 above.
[15] Shirk 1993; Weingast, Qian, and Montinola 1995.
[16] *fenshuizhi*, 分税制.
[17] Wong 2005, 6.
[18] Ibid.
[19] Ibid.

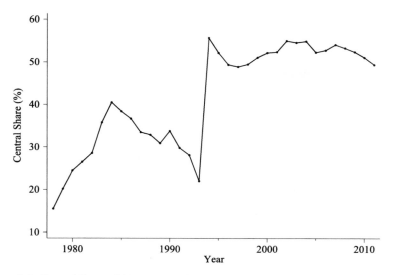

Figure 5.1   Central Share of Government Revenue. Source: Data from the National Bureau of Statistics, China Statistical Yearbook, various years (http://www.stats.gov.cn/tjsj/ndsj/2012/html/H0802e.htm).

mid-1990s, at around 75 percent of them, whereas transfers to equalize the fiscal position of the provinces "were only 1-2%."[20] Such inequalities in local revenue are reflected in local government expenditures as well, leading to reduced levels of public goods and services in poor regions.[21] Whereas in 1990 the five poorest provinces represented 14 percent of government expenditures, by 1998, that figure was down to only 8.6 percent.[22]

Having consolidated its budgetary position, the regime could embark on projects to reduce these disparities. By 2004, taxes and intergovernmental transfers moved toward rural areas with the Develop the West campaign, the tax-for-fee (*feigaishui*) reform in the late 1990s, the abolition of agricultural taxes, and the shift at the provincial level away from their prior urban, regressive character. These moves reduced the level of urban bias by shifting resources to provinces that were more rural as well as cutting the fiscal burden placed on the rural population.

---

[20] Wong 2005, 9 n. 11; 2002, 19. World Bank (2002) specifically refers to "Transition Transfers"; other transfers from the center are of tax rebates, quota subsidies, specific purpose grants, and final account subsidies. As the growth rates differed by province, the flat rebate rate was effectively regressive with more rapidly growth provinces receiving larger rebates on their tax revenue growth.

[21] Park et al. 1996, 771–75.

[22] Wong 2002, table 2.6. Also Wong 2005, table 3 "Fiscal Development Paradigms."

THE DEVELOP THE WEST CAMPAIGN

The growing disparity in economic development among regions has already been widely noted both at home and abroad. We must realize that the widening gap between rich and poor is not just an economic problem, but also a political one. The experience of some other developing countries demonstrates that when income disparities between members of society and between regions become too great, clashes break out between ethnic groups, between regions, between classes and between central and local authorities. This can lead to a country on the brink of chaos.
—President Jiang Zemin, *6 August 1996*[23]

The areas along China's coast grew substantially more quickly than did the more rural interior provinces in the first decades of the Reform era. With the 1994 fiscal reform locking in regressive tax policies through tax rebates, the Western provinces fell even further behind.[24] Richer provinces continued to pull ahead in GDP terms, but the differentiation in government revenues and expenditures was even starker. Despite their association with China's most glittering metropolis, Jiang Zemin and Zhu Rongji and their Shanghai clique began to move away from the urban bias of the previous decade. The Develop the West Campaign, the first major component of the fiscal shift, was announced in Xi'an in June 1999 by Jiang.[25]

Policies to develop the economies of the interior and western provinces had already begun to take form prior to this official announcement. As the quote from Jiang Zemin demonstrates, Beijing had realized the difficulties inherent in allowing these disparities to grow. As Goodman noted about the Develop the West Campaign, "the new emphasis on the interior is intended more as an addendum to the current regional development strategy than its replacement."[26] The coastal provinces had received preferential policies that aided their growth during the 1980s.[27] A division between coast and interior while China pursued export-led development was inevitable. The GDP-per-capita rankings of the provinces in China's west, particularly the northwest, dropped precipitously during this period.[28] Even while regional inequality metrics declined through the 1980s, the perception of coastal areas taking off and leaving the rest of the country behind threatened the regime.[29] The political salience of China's regional divergence

---

[23] Jiang 2010, 530.

[24] Wong 2002, table 2.6. Also Wong 2005, table 3 "Fiscal Development Paradigms."

[25] Later slogans include "industry aiding agriculture in turn" and "city helping the countryside." The Develop the West Campaign is referred to by different names (e.g., Open the West and Western Development Program. 西部大开发).

[26] Goodman 2004, 319.

[27] Naughton 2004, 255.

[28] Ibid.

[29] Ibid., 258.

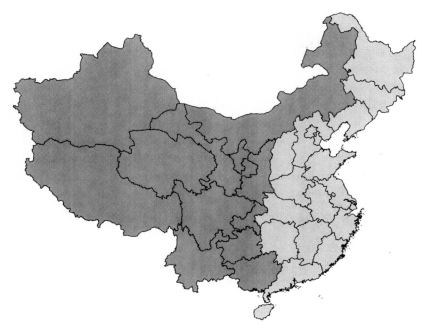

Figure 5.2 Provinces of the Develop the West Campaign

came in part from the ability to draw the economic divisions on a map. The CCP faced two Chinas—a rich, coastal one and a backward, interior one.[30]

The 12 provinces included as part of the West for the purposes of the campaign are shown in figure 5.2.[31] Guangxi and Inner Mongolia, two minority autonomous regions, were added to the traditional western provinces as areas targeted by the campaign.

The size of the program was substantial and included 20 large-scale investment projects in 2000-2001, valued at 400 billion yuan, or around 5 percent of national GDP at that time. Measuring such projects as "part" of the Develop the West campaign is controversial as many of them were begun before the start of the campaign and were relabeled to be part of it post-hoc. Yet, it remains the case that the state was investing significant resources in its western provinces and that these investments were politically significant in part because they were branded as part of the Develop the West campaign.

Much of the program's effort has been spent developing regional infrastructure. The Develop the West program consisted of tens of thousands of kilometers of new roads and four thousand kilometers of new railways, with estimated

---

[30] Of course, the regime faced numerous divisions, not just the coastal-interior one. The urban–rural divide remained important, as did the northeastern "rustbelt" region of the country.

[31] 中国西部开发网 2013. Darkly shaded provinces are the recipients of the Develop the West campaign.

costs running into the hundreds of billions of dollars.[32] A 2008 Xinhua news item put the total investment at 1.3 trillion yuan by the end of 2007.[33] Another component was a natural gas pipeline connecting Xinjiang's resources to eastern parts of the country with the demand.[34] Other energy projects also were part of the campaign, such as the West-to-East electricity transfer project, which was a "major feature" of the campaign in Guizhou.[35]

In the end, the purpose of the Develop the West campaign was not, for example, to turn Gansu into the equal of Shanghai but to demonstrate national level concern about all of the regions of the country and arguably to lay a foundation for the future economic growth of the interior. As Barry Naughton put it in his chapter in *Holding China Together: Diversity and National Integration in the post-Deng Era*:

> The WDP [Western Development Program, a.k.a. Develop the West campaign] is a public demonstration of the government's concern with national unity, inequality, and poverty; one strand of an energy policy; an environmental program; and a catalyst for further measures of economic liberalization.[36]

Centrifugal forces threatened China. By attempting to develop the west, the regime responded, both in real and symbolic ways, keeping the chasm separating the west and east from expanding further. The regime spread the spoils of its development to backward, interior areas of the country to integrate these two Chinas.

THE TAX-FOR-FEE REFORM

While China's regional divide could be seen on a map, harder to depict—but even starker in practice—was the rural–urban divide. Peasants increasingly suffered under a heavy fiscal burden imposed on them by local governments starved for revenue. Two reforms—tax-for-fee (*feigaishui*) and the abolition of agricultural taxes—reduced, simplified, and ultimately eliminated these burdens and represent a shift from taxing to subsidizing agriculture and farmers.

---

[32] Roberts 2000; Holbig 2004; Herd 2010.
[33] http://www.chinadaily.com.cn/bizchina/2008-06/22/content_6784587.htm ("China to Launch 10 Key Projects in Western Regions" 2008).
[34] Naughton 2004, 270.
[35] Oakes 2004. For more details, the Develop the West program is associated with the NRDC (http://xbkfs.ndrc.gov.cn/ and http://www.chinawest.gov.cn/web/index.asp).
[36] Naughton 2004, 255.

The post-1994 recentralization of revenues left poor provinces and the lower level governments underneath them in a difficult place in terms of collecting funds to use to provide public goods and services. To a large extent, local governments attempted to raise revenues through fees as such funds were wholly owned by the locality. In addition to mandatory labor, fees were collected for highway maintenance, to control soil erosion, handling traffic accidents, registering a birth, and even for children parking a bicycle at school.[37] Taxes, on the other hand, were shared with the central government. These fees took a heavy toll on the agricultural producers of China, who following the brief flourishing during reform's early days, remained poor and continued to fall further behind their urban and industrial countrymen. In 2000, Li Changping, a scholar of the Chinese countryside, wrote an open letter to Zhu Rongji lamenting the state of the countryside and coined the term the "three agricultures" (*san nong*), which he uses to describe the situation in rural areas: "peasants' lives are truly bitter, villages are truly poor, and agriculture is truly in danger."[38]

The taxes and fees piled on China's farmers came to be labeled peasant burdens. Bernstein and Lü give five structural sources of the peasant burdens: "the vertical and horizontal de-concentration of power; performance pressures on local cadres and officials; state sprawl—the costly expansion of the bureaucracies down to the townships; muddled finances at the township level; and deeply embedded opportunities to engage in corruption."[39] Chen goes as far as to argue that the centralizing nature of the 1994 fiscal reform shaped rural fiscal structure and essentially forced subsequent reforms because of the extent to which it removed revenue from townships.[40]

The fiscal burdens of peasants were heavy, regressive, and arbitrary.[41] As a share of peasants' income, fees took up to 20 percent or more in documented cases.[42] These farmers remained desperately poor.[43] The number of fees could be more than the "hairs on an ox."[44] For farmers, irregular fees and charges seemed endless and had "no boundary."[45] The fees were used for purposes outside of what farmers thought

[37] Bernstein and Lü 2002, 52–57. Fines for not registering a birth were also common.

[38] "农民真苦, 农村真穷, 农业真危险" (Li 2002). The common formulation became the "three rural problems (*sannong wenti* (三农问题))" (Li 2002).

[39] Bernstein and Lü 2002, 84.

[40] Chen 2008.

[41] Lü 1997.

[42] Ibid., 118–21.

[43] While no longer starving as they did during the Great Famine, tens of millions of Chinese farmers remained poor by any measure. China's official rural poverty line, 300 yuan per person per year (Ravallion and Chen 2007, 5), despite being much lower than the international poverty lines of $1 or $2 a day, still classified 5.12 percent of rural Chinese as not meeting this threshold. In the cities, the number was .20 percent, although this estimate does not include rural migrants (Ravallion and Chen 2007, 4).

[44] Bernstein and Lü 2000, 745.

[45] Lü 1997, 118.

acceptable, such as the feasting of officials when local teachers went unpaid, and even sparked unrest and riots in some locales.[46]

The central government, realizing that these fees had begun to spiral out of control, initiated in the early 1990s the literally titled "tax-for-fee (*feigaishui*)" reform, also known as rural fee reform (RFR).[47] The reform transformed the fiscal burden placed on farmers away from arbitrary fees to a standardized system of a single agricultural tax paired with one surcharge on that tax. Like many national policies, tax-for-fee reform had first been a local experimental policy, though its precise origins are disputed.[48]

The tax-for-fee reforms clearly reduced the farmers' fiscal burdens.[49] On the other hand, the reforms also deprived poor localities of funds. Areas without industrial bases to tax were left without much recourse to extract from the agricultural sector. After all, the fees arose to fund rural governments facing hard budget constraints that were unable to otherwise pay for government services and salaries.[50]

The primary purpose of the reforms was to reduce the level of peasant burdens.[51] As Premier Zhu Rongji explained in 2000:

> "Promoting the RFR is the fundamental strategy for protecting the legal rights of farmers and reducing their burdens. The basic approach in the RFR is to raise—by an appropriate amount—the existing rates of the agricultural tax and the agricultural special products tax, while abolishing all administrative fees that are levied on farmers."[52]

Agreeing with this as the first of two "twin objectives," Fock and Wong argue that in addition to lightening the fiscal load on farmers, the reforms attempted to "impose a more structured framework for financing government at the

[46] Lü 1997, among many others.

[47] In Chinese, 费改税 or 税费改革. As seen in n. 48 below, the chronologies differ as to the precise origins and timing of the reform.

[48] Zhu, Liu and Ou, Yep, and Bernstein and Lü present different chronologies, with some referring to an early experiment begun in 1990 in Inner Mongolia, followed by similar experiments in Anhui (1994) and Hebei (1996). However, Liu and Ou differentiate these from the Wugang experiment by noting that only Wugang actually eliminated extralegal fees altogether; the others reduced peasant burden by limiting fees and having them collected simultaneously with tax (朱守银 1998; 刘建民 and 欧阳煌 2000; Yep 2004; Bernstein and Lü 2002).

[49] Yep 2004, 50–54. To be sure, a decrease in service quality of local governments also followed from the RFR as discussed below.

[50] Chen 2008.

[51] Yep 2004, 43.

[52] Speech at the CCP Economic Work Conference, 28 November 2000 (Guowuyuan nongcun shuifeigaige gongzuo xiaozu 2001, via Fock and Wong 2008).

grassroots levels by bringing previously extra-budgetary revenues and expenditures on budget."[53] By removing off-the-books fees and creating a tax-based rural fiscal system, the central government hoped to curb the abuses of illegible fees by local dictators.

In addition to rationalizing the funding of the status quo, the reforms pressured local governments to cut positions and salaries, which dominated budgetary expenditure. The center's aim here was to reduce the size of the bureaucracy at the township level.[54] In particular, it followed on prior efforts to increase the efficiency of the state bureaucracy and represented a continuation of "soft centralization," which replaced local influence over state bureaucracies with administrative control from their functional superiors.[55]

The tax-for-fee reform completely remade township finances. The reforms abolished the five township levies (*wutong*) that "were fees collected on a per-capita basis for financing expenditure on (1) local education, (2) militia training, (3) road construction and maintenance, (4) welfare for veterans and households with special hardships, and (5) birth control."[56] The reforms prevented townships from creating similar fees with different names to pay for education or public works.[57] A modified agricultural tax replaced the revenue from these closed off streams. The agricultural tax would be set at 7 percent of estimated land productivity based on a survey of production over the past five years. This reflected a decrease in the rate, which was previously set at 15 percent. However, in some circumstances, the new estimates of land productivity were so much greater than the old ones that farmers had to pay more after the reforms.[58]

Village level taxes and fees were also jettisoned. The three village levies (*santi*), which funded local collective investment, welfare, and cadre compensation, were also abolished.[59] Villages replaced the funds from the eliminated *santi* with an agricultural tax surcharge of 20 percent of the amount paid for the agricultural tax.[60] The reforms also lifted the burden of forced labor by farmers. Yep notes that in Anhui, which initiated one of the most important experiments

[53] Fock and Wong 2008, 45.

[54] The tax-for-fee reform took the tactic of explicitly eliminating the possibility of ad hoc fees with the hopes that placing limits on local government revenue sources could help reduce the size of bloated bureaucracies at the lower levels. Wen Jiabao speech on 4 November 2000 (Guowuyuan nongcun shuifeigaige gongzuo xiaozu 2001, via Fock and Wong 2008, 48).

[55] Yang 2004b; Kennedy 2007; Mertha 2005.

[56] Yep 2004, 48–49. For more details on these township fees (*tongchou*), see Oi 1999, 45.

[57] Yep 2004, 49; 刘建民 and 欧阳煌 2000, 35; Fock and Wong 2008, 44–49.

[58] Li 2000; Yep 2004, 49–50.

[59] Yep 2004, 49; Jianmin et al. 2000, 35. The village retained funds (*tiliu*) were theoretically limited to 5 percent of a peasant's household income but often exceeded that limit by 2–3 times (Oi 1999, p. 21).

[60] Yep 2004, 49; Fock and Wong 2008, 44–49.

of the *feigaishui*, rural workers were previously required to donate 10-20 days of labor (or its equivalent in yuan).[61]

There is no question that the reforms lowered the rates of extraction from farmers. As Oi and Zhao describe,

> In the eighteen townships in our sample that had implemented the policy, peasant payments to township and village authorities had been substantially reduced. In one village peasant burdens had been cut by 38 percent over the previous year. In another village the new policy resulted in a 40 percent drop compared to the previous year. Our findings are in line with a 2002 State Administration for Taxation report that indicates an average 31 percent reduction in the per capita tax burden in Anhui, 30 percent in Jiangsu, and over 25 percent in the other pilot areas.[62]

Bernstein and Lü agree, "In 2000, the average burden in Anhui province decreased by 25.6% from the 1997 level."[63]

The revenue losses for local governments coming from reductions in peasant burdens were not replaced by funds from higher levels. The decline in revenues coming in to townships decimated their budgets. As Bernstein and Lü point out, "the Anhui [*feigaishui*] experiments had an enormous downside: Township and village finances, already in trouble, were plunged into an even more difficult situation. According to a ten-village study, the new system resulted in an average 62% decrease in village public revenue."[64] Kennedy describes substantial cuts in social services in Shaanxi that took place due to the reform from 2001 to 2003; some localities, for example, ended living subsidies for teachers and reduced funds for school repairs.[65] The cut in funding for township level government also spurred the merging of different towns and township governments.[66]

The central government at this time was able to replace some of the revenues that local governments lost access to due to the reforms.[67] But the center was not going to sign checks to replace all of the fee revenue that local governments had been collecting.[68] Central transfers to aid in the fiscal gap left by the reforms

---

[61] Yep 2004, 49.

[62] Xiao 2002; Oi and Zhao 2007, 82.

[63] Bernstein and Lü 2003, 202.

[64] Ibid.

[65] Kennedy 2007.

[66] Ibid., 57; Fock and Wong 2008, 25.

[67] Fock and Wong 2008, 46.

[68] Wen Jiabao speech on 4 November 2000 (*Guowuyuan nongcun shuifeigaige gongzuo xiaozu* 2001), via Fock and Wong 2008, 48.

varied by region. Agricultural Western provinces received all of the revenues they lost due to the tax-for-fee reform in transfers, while coastal non-agricultural provinces received no replacement transfers.[69]

The tax-for-fee reform clearly reduced peasant burdens but simultaneously undermined the provision of public goods and services that the burdens funded. However, in terms of "urban bias," it is clear that the *feigaishui* reforms represent a move in favor of rural areas as rural tax levels are reduced with at least some of the old revenues replaced by central transfers from non-agricultural funding sources. It is difficult to detect the net effect on farmers, their incomes, and their migration decisions because upon the reform's completion, the regime took the even more sweeping step of completely abolishing the newly reformulated agricultural taxes.

ABOLITION OF AGRICULTURAL TAXES

In the annual Government Work Report before the 2004 National People's Congress, Premier Wen Jiabao laid out a radical agenda of completely eliminating the agricultural tax within five years.[70] By 2006, agricultural taxation was rescinded throughout the country.[71]

The initial announcement posited a plan to reduce the newly reformulated agricultural tax until it was eliminated within five years. The reductions would phase in by 1-2 percent per year until the 7 percent agricultural tax and the additional associated surcharge dropped to 0 percent. The revenue losses represented around 1.7 percent of total government revenue at the time of the announcement.[72] In an increasingly industrial and service-oriented China and following the 1994 Fiscal Reforms, the central government could afford such losses. The regime pursued the abolition not simply because it could afford to do so but as "a response to the growing complaints that the agricultural taxes were unfair."[73] The inequity between urban and rural individuals was clear. While the first 9,600 RMB in income of urbanites was exempt from taxation, all farmers paid the reformulated agricultural tax and surcharge regardless of their level of poverty.[74]

As in the tax-for-fee reform, the agricultural tax abolition had consequences besides simply the reduction in peasant burdens. It undermined the second

[69] The four levels of replacement were "(i) central and western provinces that are grain "exporters," 100 percent; (ii) central and western provinces that are not grain "exporters," 80 percent; (iii) coastal provinces that are grain "exporters," 50 percent; and (iv) coastal, non-grain-exporting provinces, 0 percent" (Fock and Wong 2008, 46 n. 45).

[70] Wen 2004.
[71] Wen 2006.
[72] Lu and Weimer 2005, 321.
[73] Fock and Wong 2008, 49.
[74] Ibid., 50.

order objectives of the previous rural tax reform such as reducing the size of local bureaucracy. By eliminating the newly restructured sources of local government revenue, it allowed townships to escape the potential hard budget constraints based on those newly redesigned revenues.[75] Local governments unable to fund their own operations and pay their salaries pleaded and often received support from higher levels. One county official in Heilongjiang told me in a 2007 interview that he expected that the national level would give more money in fiscal transfers to make up for the gap from reducing local revenue sources.[76]

Following the rural fee reform and the subsequent abolition of these reduced and simplified agricultural taxes, farmers were without any fiscal burdens. Neither local governments nor the central government expected or demanded any taxes or fees from the farmers.[77] In fact, the farmers were now subsidized. A prior policy established by Zhu Rongji in the 1990s supported farmers by in effect guaranteeing a price floor for their rice production.[78] If the market price fell below this floor, then the central government would make up the balance to farmers. Yet in 2004, the market price greatly exceeded this floor, leaving the funds free for other uses and "a subsidy was paid directly to grain farmers in the 13 major grain producing provinces."[79]

Two additional reforms to aid rural government finances were also taking place in the wake of the abolition of taxes and fees in the countryside. First, in December 2002, local governments were notified that the same system of tax sharing that the 1994 fiscal reform implemented at the provincial level would be "completed" at the sub-provincial level.[80] The sub-provincial tax sharing of the mid-2000s was considerably more sensitive to issues of inequality across prefectures and counties than was the 1994 provincial level implementation.[81] The second related reform is referred to as the "3 Rewards and 1 Subsidy (三奖一补)." This policy rewards those poor counties and townships that are able to increase the size of their local tax base as well as provinces for aiding these counties, local governments for "streamlining" their workforces, and agricultural counties for increasing their grain production. It also subsidizes those local governments that

---

[75] Ibid., 50–51. As an unsurprising consequence, it is unclear what, if any, personnel reductions have occurred at the township level despite the fact that the abolition of agricultural taxes removed their primary funding vehicle.

[76] Heilongjiang Interview 2007071501.

[77] The exception is tobacco (Lu and Weimer 2005, 326).

[78] OECD 1999, 36 and 66.

[79] Lu and Weimer 2005, 326.

[80] Fock and Wong 2008, 55–56.

[81] Ibid., 56–57.

have already succeeded in overcoming such difficulties (to "avoid whipping the fast ox (避免鞭打快牛))."[82]

The combination of abolishing fees and taxes and subsidizing rural localities with replacement funds from non-agricultural tax sources had a strong effect on the economic attractiveness of the countryside. The abolition of agricultural taxes boosted the incentives to farm and is linked to higher rural incomes.[83] As Fock and Wong put it, the "government efforts to channel resources toward pro-poor, pro-rural programs continue to gather momentum."[84]

FISCAL TRANSFERS

One can see the fiscal shift most dramatically by examining the pattern of fiscal transfers. Intergovernmental fiscal transfers represent a critical piece of China's post-1994 fiscal system. With central coffers full and expenditures located at the local level, transfers from higher to lower levels of the state hierarchy permeate the system. The changing nature of these transfers demonstrates that the Chinese fiscal system has shifted.

Two features in figure 5.3 illustrate the shift. First, there is a clear move from an urban-biased pattern of transfers to a non-tilted level, that is, more urban areas received larger transfers in 1999 than in 2004. This shift can be seen in the change in the slope of the regression line from strongly positive in 1999 to essentially horizontal in 2004. In 1999, the largest per capita transfers were directed to two poor Western provinces, Qinghai and Ningxia, and to China's two most important municipalities, Beijing and Shanghai. The general pattern is regressive. As percent urban correlates highly with level of economic development as measured by GDP per capita, this can also be seen as a move away from regressive transfers tilted toward the rich. It is a progressive shift, albeit one that ends well short of transfers that are actually progressive. The correlation between transfers per capita and percent urbanized is 0.45 in 1999 but only 0.03 by 2004. Second, the scale of transfers per capita increases dramatically. The largest transfer was only 511 yuan per person in 1999, but by 2004 eight provinces received transfers that large, with the largest per capita transfer, Qinghai's 1,187 yuan per person, more than doubling the previous high.

These changes have been implemented on the ground. In each of the dozen counties that I visited during my fieldwork from 2005 to 2007, agricultural taxes were in the process of being (or had already been) eliminated, replaced with

---

[82] Ministry of Finance 2005. The intent here is to reward all localities that have accomplished these goals, not only those doing so after the enactment of the policies.

[83] Lu and Weimer 2005, 321–22.

[84] Fock and Wong 2008, 57.

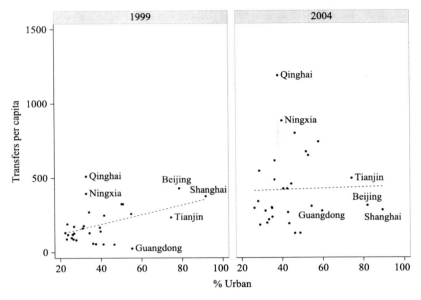

Figure 5.3 Illustrating the Fiscal Shift: Transfers per Capita (in yuan) in 1999 and 2004 by % Urban. Source: Transfers data is from the Government Finance Yearbook (Caizheng Nianjian) and Local Government Fiscal Statistics (Difang Caizheng Tongji Ziliao), various years. Calculated as (transfers from center less system remittances)/population. It also should be noted that Tibet is excluded from this data; Tibet is an extreme outlier in terms of transfers per capita due to its small population, minority status, and unique political position.

subsidies for seeds, fertilizers, and agricultural machinery. Individuals that used to pay hundreds of yuan in taxes and fees every year are now receiving subsidies, sometimes on the order of hundreds of yuan.[85] Given that rural income per capita is usually estimated at less than RMB 3,000, this shift represents a dramatic change in the economic calculus of potential migrants.

Even those not predisposed positively were forthcoming about the reduction in their fiscal burdens. During a complaint about local teachers being chosen for political rather than merit-based reasons, a Heilongjiang villager traveling between counties did allow that he no longer had to pay any fees to the local government. For some workers near the bottom of the economic totem pole in Beijing, government policy changes, as well as increased policing of the city, led them to consider moving back home. Pirated DVD sellers outside of shopping centers in Beijing related to me that their business was less and less profitable

[85] Heilongjiang interview, May 2007.

and that they might return to their homes in the countryside where city admin-istrative officials (*chengguan*) would not hassle them.[86]

The central government spending on agriculture, rural areas, and farmers was reported as 297.5 billion yuan in 2005, a 30 percent real increase from 2003.[87] The abolition of agricultural taxes and fees is estimated as a total reduction of the peasant burden of 125 billion yuan a year.[88] Budgeted spending from central cof-fers on rural compulsory education from 2006 to 2010 was 125 billion yuan.[89] At the same time, the New Cooperative Medical System (NCMS) expanded medical coverage in the countryside. Begun in 2003, by 2006 it covered 40 per-cent of China's counties.[90] With the fiscal shift, China has increasingly focused village level investments in public goods projects in poor and minority areas.[91]

These "populist social policies" have clearly been sold by the state as efforts to combat inequality.[92] The government trumpeted the abolition of agricultural taxes, the revenues of which, from 1991 to 2001, exceeded 374 billion yuan.[93] These policies and the changes in the nature of the fiscal transfers make clear that the regime has shifted its fiscal system away from urban bias. Again, by the mid-2000s China remained urban-biased, but much less so after enacting these reforms.

Improving the progressiveness of government policy toward farmers serves multiple purposes. Aiding the poor in the countryside is symbolically impor-tant for a Communist Party that still produces propaganda about how it values socialism and aiding all Chinese. Even in 2013, expanding the urban social safety net to all comers is a long-term aspiration rather than a concrete task close to being accomplished.

What accounts for the fiscal shift? I argue that marketization reforms under-mined the regime's fiscal system, which in turn forced the centralization of the 1994 fiscal reforms. The centralizing reforms of 1994 succeeded but also exacer-bated inequities across regions and across the urban-rural divide. The Develop the West Campaign, the tax-for-fee reform, and the abolition of agricultural taxes were simultaneously real and symbolic acts that responded to the growing

---

[86] Beijing Interview, April 2007.

[87] CPI data from the China Statistical Yearbook, 2005. The 2005 data is Xinhua 2006a.

[88] Xinhua 2006c.

[89] Xinhua 2006d.

[90] Yan et al. 2006. Also see Xinhua 2005.

[91] Zhang et al. 2006.

[92] Yang 2006.

[93] 2002 China Government Finance Yearbook, 353. Included are the agriculture tax, special prod-ucts tax, arable land use tax, forest products and contract taxes (*nongye geshui baokuo nongye shui, gengdi zhanyong shui, nongye techan shui, he qi shui*). The figure is in real 2001 yuan, CPI data from 2005 China Statistical Yearbook. It should be noted that agriculture is shrinking as a share of GDP

inequality. The timing of the fiscal shift toward the countryside and away from urban bias is not aligned with the arrival of Hu-Wen at the top of the CCP hierarchy.[94] The Shanghai clique of Jiang Zemin and his compatriots began many of the measures that shifted the Chinese fiscal system away from purely extracting from the farmers. Instead, the fiscal shift's timing coincides with the regime's centralization of resources following the 1994 fiscal reform and its renewed emphasis on political stability in the wake of the 1989 Tiananmen protests.

At the same time, while inequality and rural poverty were significant factors that led to a shift in focus toward the countryside, the story is more complex. Eliminating peasant burdens did some of the work of reducing rural grievances, as did replacing locally generated revenue with transfers from non-agricultural regions. But while the regime did loosen control of migration during the Reform era as detailed in the previous chapter, it did not eliminate the *hukou* system and its distinctions between people of rural and urban origin. Indeed, the regime managed urbanization with money but also with repression, particularly of migrants living in cities.

REPRESSION AND DISCRIMINATION

While the principal claim of the chapter is that the Chinese regime has moved away from the planned era's purely force-based migration restrictions to a more porous, incentive-based system as reforms have progressed since the late 1970s, repression and discrimination of migrants in cities remain central. The system continues to treat migrants as second-class citizens. Examples of this kind of behavior are the detention and repatriation of migrants, demolitions of migrant housing, and the forced closure of migrant schools.

The death of Hubei native and graduate of Wuhan Technical Institute, Sun Zhigang, in March 2003 in Guangzhou's "Custody and Repatriation" center showed the level of abuse that migrants received in cities and became a *cause célèbre* that led to some reforms.[95] Sun had not been able to obtain a temporary residence permit nor was he carrying his identification card and was taken into police custody for suspicion of being an illegal migrant. He was sent from a police

in China, and as such tax revenue from agriculture was also diminishing as the share of all revenue before the abolition of these taxes (World Bank WDI 2012).

[94] Naughton 2004, 255.

[95] Hand 2006. Sun Zhigang (孙志刚). Custody and Repatriation (收容遣送). The brief narrative here is principally derived from Hand's, as well as the original reporting from *Nanfang Dushibao* (南方都市报) and the SCMP. ("被收容者孙志刚之死_深度_南都网" 2003; "Seeking Answers to a Death in Detention | South China Morning Post" 2013; "Probe into Death in Custody Leaves Many Stones Unturned | South China Morning Post" 2013). Also Human Rights in China 1999; Zeldin 2003.

substation to the Guangzhou Custody & Repatriation center after an overnight stay.[96] On 18 March, he was sent from the Custody & Repatriation center to a medical facility, where he died two days later. Unconvinced by the official reports, his friends and family took his story to *Nanfang Dushibao* (Southern Metropolis Daily), where an investigative report exploded into the public consciousness.[97] While the initial official medical reports pointed to complications from heart disease, later revelations showed that he was healthy when arrested and died of injuries related to blunt force trauma in custody.[98] The furor roused by the case pushed the regime into action.[99] The State Council moved to end the Custody and Repatriation system in June 2003.[100] In an interview with a migrant assistance nongovernmental organization in Beijing in 2007, the abolition of this system was listed as the policy change that most directly affected workers' calculations as it "lowered the cost of coming to the city."[101]

Discrimination against migrants can continue past their deaths. Chongqing was the scene of a traffic accident in December 2005 that took the lives of three girls. This tragedy illuminates not in its occurrence but in its consequences. As is often the case in instances of wrongful deaths, financial considerations were offered to the families as compensation for their loss. While two families were given RMB 200,000 (US$25,000) in compensation, the third was only offered RMB 58,000 (US$7,000).[102] The discrepancy was due to the third family's *hukou* status. Despite having lived in the city for over 10 years, the members of the third family officially remained rural residents; as compensation in such cases is determined by average income in one's official residence, the rewards differed dramatically.[103]

Migrant housing has also been demolished and migrant communities often raided. In 1995, authorities demolished Zhejiangcun, a large settlement of

[96] The law behind repatriation (1982) predates national adoption of temporary residence permits (1985) (Hand 2006). See chapter 4 for more details (Guo 2006).

[97] A recent Lexis-Nexis search found 232 mentions of his name in Major World Publications.

[98] "被收容者孙志刚之死_深度_南都网" 2003; "Seeking Answers to a Death in Detention | South China Morning Post" 2013; "Probe into Death in Custody Leaves Many Stones Unturned | South China Morning Post" 2013.

[99] See Hand 2006, among others.

[100] Zeldin 2003.

[101] Beijing Interview 20070709.

[102] US$ estimates using a conversion rate at the time of near 8 yuan or RMB (renminbi) to the US dollar.

[103] Compensation is based on "average disposable income" in urban areas and "average net income" in rural areas. The facts of the story are from (Z. Wang and Zhou 2006). As noted above, the discrimination is not inherent to the *hukou* system, that is, various other government departments give differential benefits and services based on one's *hukou* status. For simplicity, the text uses the phrase "*hukou*-based discrimination" to describe this phenomenon.

migrants from Zhejiang living in Beijing.[104] Such sporadic raids were disruptive to the economic activity of migrants and forced them into difficult business arrangements with local Beijingers.[105] Uyghurs living in Beijing's Xinjiang villages were repeatedly pushed out when their homes were demolished by city authorities in the late 1990s.[106] Similar villages full of migrants from other regions and in other cities have also been affected.[107] Despite demolitions and discrimination, the resiliency of the communities is strong.[108] Prior to the Beijing Olympics, Zhejiangcun, perhaps the most famous of these migrant villages, was again destroyed.[109]

The education of migrants and migrant children is another area of clear discrimination against migrants. While progressive policies have pushed for free compulsory education in the countryside for rural *hukou* holders, children of migrants in cities do not have access to the superior urban school systems. In fact, many cities have gone so far as to close down or destroy migrant schools in their districts. One prominent and illustrative story is the destruction of 24 migrant schools in Beijing during August 2011.[110] The government's order of closure came in between June and mid-August, affecting the lives of up to 14,000 children. Officially, the schools did not meet safety and hygiene standards.[111] Yet these complaints on the part of the city officials often fell on deaf ears given the dilapidated condition of facilities in the countryside. As a Sichuanese woman put it when her child's school was closed in Beijing's Fengtai District in 2001 as the school year began: "Now that all of our family work in Beijing, if the child was sent back to our ancestral village, who would look after her? She's not well suited for that place. Also, the conditions in the schools of our home village are far worse than those at the migrant school."[112] Some of the schools were simply torn down over the summer—parents who arrived to register their children for the new school year found only piles of rubble where the buildings once stood.[113] As with the sporadic raids on migrant villages, a school closure is not necessarily a permanent condition because schools can re-open. The saga of the Tong Xin school in Beijing's Chaoyang district is illustrative. The founder believed that permission from local authorities had been secured

---

[104] Liu and Liang 1997, 96; Beja and Bonnin 1995.

[105] He 2003.

[106] Baranovitch 2003, 731.

[107] Xu 2008.

[108] Solinger 1999b, 238.

[109] Xu 2008, 648. See also Miller 2012, 25–27.

[110] Miller 2012, 28–30.

[111] Mao and Duncan 2011.

[112] 赵 2001, author's translation. Original: 现在全家都在北京打工，送回老家孩子谁照顾？孩子也不适应那儿了。而且老家的学校条件比这里的打工子弟小学也差远了。

[113] Jiang 2011.

when the school opened in 2005 but received a closure notice from the township in July 2012. Despite pushback from the school and aided by celebrities who lent their voices to keep it open, the township cut the school's water supply in August. Yet with parents' going so far as to lay down in front of bulldozers, the school was not demolished. Subsequently, it opened.[114]

To give a sense of the scale and breadth of the practice of migrant school closures, I collected dozens of stories about these events. These stories were then compiled into box 5.1, which represents news reports on over 850 school closures from 2001 to 2012.[115]

The system of migration restrictions has been supplemented and in part supplanted by incentive-based measures related to the fiscal shift, yet repression and discrimination against migrants continue. Consistent with the emphasis on the political stability of dominant cities, Beijing dominates the list of school closures, with the large-scale closing of all migrant schools in Shanghai joining it in significance.

The regime paired this repression and discrimination with the fiscal shift to continue to manage its urbanization. By reducing the difference in economic opportunities between urban and rural life, the regime accomplished the task of reducing the attractiveness of migration and migrant work. This decreased the threat of uncontrolled urbanization during this era of economic transformation. More broadly, the fiscal shift may have aided rural dwellers in their rural homes, while simultaneously being motivated by concerns over urban instability.

Sub-National Analysis

China's redistributive policy during the Reform era moved away from urban bias as the regime's economic and political houses were put in order. Going beyond the national level can illuminate internal variation in manners consistent with the general argument. In particular, some locations may receive additional funds because ensuring their stability and reducing emigration from those locales may be especially important. Sub-national analysis of Chinese fiscal transfers demonstrates that funds are allocated over space in ways consistent with the aim of improving the economic situation nearby and reducing the number of marginal migrants to specific locales. Rather than purely reflecting concerns over size, however, extra funds are transferred to areas near unstable cities.

---

[114] For instance, see Cheung 2013; "崔永元等致信教育部长 呼吁保留农民工子弟校-搜狐教育" 2013.

[115] Links to news reports of school closures available from the author.

Box 5.1 **Migrant School Closures**

City	Province	Year	Schools Affected
Beijing	Beijing	2001–12	253
Shanghai	Shanghai	2007–10	242
Taiyuan	Shanxi	2011–12	201
Urumuqi	Xinjiang	2011	81
Sunan	Jiangsu	2001	41
Xingyi	Guizhou	2010	39
Haikou	Hainan	2001–12	38
Chengdu	Sichuan	2005	28
Guangzhou	Guangdong	2005–9	16
Lanzhou	Gansu	2011	10
Taizhou	Zhejiang	2011	7
Fuzhou	Fujian	2006–11	6
Nanjing	Jiangsu	1999–2012	5
Hangzhou	Zhejiang	2006–10	4
Zhenjiawu	Zhejiang	2012	3
Foshan	Guangdong	2012	1
Ningbo	Zhejiang	2004	1
Yongkang	Zhejiang	2010	1

Note: Tianjin in 2004 is noted as having "many" schools closed without a specific number offered. Similarly, news outlets reported that Zhengzhou in Henan closed "a lot" of schools in 2008 without more specificity.

The core analysis combines county and prefecture level data showing that counties that are near unstable cities, *ceteris paribus*, tend to receive larger fiscal transfers from higher levels of government. That is, the conditions of cities outside of the counties themselves correlate with the funds directed to the counties. The correlation follows the pattern seen in the broader argument, that there is an attempt to direct resources to areas where out-migration to nearby cities is occurring and might be curtailed if local conditions can be improved. Numerous factors affect a given county's intake of fiscal transfers from higher levels of government, and many have been documented in the literature.[116] This analysis documents the sending of money to counties nearby unstable cities in part to help alleviate pressure on the city itself.

My fieldwork in two pairs of counties in Heilongjiang Province in China's far northeast clarifies how counties acquire transfers and how they are affected by these transfers.[117] The selection of pairs of counties followed a "most-similar" technique.[118] I chose by matching on basic socioeconomic and demographic characteristics but different levels of transfers to best isolate the effects of different levels of transfers in otherwise similar environs. The main data source is interviews with different county level officials. The focus here is on the fact that counties lobby higher level governments for funds, relaxation of regulations, and to host experimental policies.

As noted in the previous chapter, the state hierarchy of the PRC, a large nation-state with the world's largest population, can be overwhelming in its terminology. China is divided into 34 provincial level units with 31 operating under normal central control from Beijing—31 plus Hong Kong and Macao Special Administrative Regions (SARs) and Taiwan. The awkward "provincial/prefecture/county level unit" language is necessary as in addition to the normal type of units at each level (provinces, prefectures, and counties), there are numerous other types. Provincial level units include 22 provinces, 4 municipalities, and 5 autonomous regions. I refer to these as China's provinces. These 31 provinces are then broken down into 333 prefecture level units as of the end of 2006. Prefecture level units are designated prefectures and cities, the latter of which is now the dominant designation regardless of the character of the areas themselves (i.e., rural areas can still be designated as "cities"). I refer to these as prefectures to avoid confusion about the urban-ness of an area. Counties lie under these 300+ prefectures. As of the 2000 census, there were 2,870 populated county level units in the country, leaving the average population of county level units slightly over 425,000. County level units include counties, county level cities, urban districts, and variously designated minority regions (e.g., banners in Inner Mongolia).[119]

[116] e.g., Shih and Qi 2007.

[117] The counties are unnamed at the request of the government officials whom I interviewed. The selection of Heilongjiang as a research site was done for reasons of access to local officials.

[118] Lily Tsai's book deftly uses both most similar and most different case selection methods (Tsai 2007.

[119] Underneath counties are townships, which are the last unit of the state. Villages, which exist beneath townships, are technically levels of administration rather than of government.

HEILONGJIANG: AN INVESTIGATION

This analysis tests whether the Chinese central government uses redistributive policies to shape the process of urbanization through the distribution of resources to rural areas. First, as a baseline, it is necessary to show that resources directed toward counties do have an effect of reducing outward migration. The presumed mechanism is reducing the opportunity costs of remaining in the county as opposed to leaving to work in another city.[120] Migrants in China tend to be drawn out of their villages by friends and networks and often to nearby cities rather than coastal destinations.[121] Once this is established, then I show the pattern of transfers is consistent with a government strategically directing resources to counties based on factors including those outside of the counties themselves, namely the stability situation of nearby cities, the likely destination of migrants. The passive construction here is intentional. I cannot establish that this pattern is a central directive. Its source may well lie in the aggregation of political calculations of local and central officials, each agent pursuing some combination of self-interest and dutiful representation of the desires of the regime.

In four counties, I conducted two matched-pair analyses of counties within Heilongjiang province to see the extent to which the transfer of resources to counties and individuals within those counties affected migration patterns.[122] The county pairs had similar official statistics on a number of socioeconomic factors, including GDP per capita and industrial-agricultural mix of economic structure, and were under the same prefectural government. However, one of each pair received substantially larger fiscal transfers from higher levels.

After selecting these counties, I traveled to them in the spring of 2007 and interviewed numerous county level government officials and individuals within the county. The counties that I visited were relatively land-rich compared with other regions with one county reporting 6.7 *mu* as the average acreage per person.[123] The officials reported that the abolition of agricultural taxes in these counties did push them to reduce staff as the replacement funds from higher levels were inadequate.[124] However, it should be noted that this contrasted with

[120] Obviously, many forces lead individuals to seek to leave the countryside and try their luck in factories or cities away from where they were born. These factors can increase or decrease independently of these policy choices. The goal here is to see if there is a marginal effect that increased funds to counties make out-migration less likely and less attractive.

[121] Solinger 1999a, 176.

[122] Heilongjiang was chosen for reasons related to access but the choice of counties within the province was unrelated to factors other than those described in the above text.

[123] Heilongjiang Interview, 2007051601. A *mu* is a Chinese measure of land area equal to 1/6 of an acre or 1/15 of a hectare.

[124] Ibid.

the view of a local soybean farmer who was frustrated that "the salary of the government officials is so high and has risen so fast."[125]

Annual economic and migration data needed to provide a statistical test were not forthcoming from the authorities.[126] However, government officials did provide anecdotal evidence of the economic successes, including some of the headaches associated with reverse migration from individuals returning to the countryside after some time away.[127] It was clear that the officials believed that policy decisions about resources, taxes, and subsidies affect individuals' decisions about farming and county government's ability to attempt projects or to develop industries in the expected direction. That is, more resources are welcomed by county residents and their governments and make the county more attractive as an economic entity.

The process by which officials are successful in their efforts to acquire funds from higher levels is critical to understanding the politics of the situation. County officials "work out" with higher level officials whether they will receive a project or not.[128] Essentially, lower levels lobby for funds from higher levels. This lobbying often includes written reports with arguments about why the situation in one's county is especially suited to this project or in need of funds; connections and other methods are also used at this stage.[129] The meaning of "other methods" was left vague in the interviews but the impression was conveyed that the policy process at this stage involved provincial officials taking advantage of their influence in decision-making. Counties would compete with arguments but also bribes or favors to these higher level officials in order to secure success to these transfers and policies. One county that I visited improved its chances of winning these competitions by underestimating its income to maintain poverty county status, which they used to win transfers and projects from higher levels.[130]

Every anecdote from villagers to county officials in Heilongjiang or other areas of China accords with the idea that as a county government receives more resources and uses those resources for developing industry and subsidizing farmers, residents are more likely to stay in that county or return to it, all else equal. The phrase, "all else equal," of course, masks huge variation at the local level. Corruption, the competence of local officials in making efficient use of resources, and the strategic gambles that localities make all affect the economic

[125] Heilongjiang Interview, 2007051402.

[126] Similarly, because of complex endogeneity between growth, transfers, and migration and lack of overlapping data, I do not use migration data in the statistical analysis of this chapter.

[127] Heilongjiang Interview, 2007051401.

[128] Heilongjiang Interview, 2007051802.

[129] Heilongjiang Interviews, 2007051701 and 2007051802.

[130] Heilongjiang Interviews, 2007051701. Although the interviewee mentioned that the charade was coming to an end because of the agricultural census.

vibrancy of a territory. Such vibrancy is also a function of private firms, deciding whether to locate a factory in a county or its neighbor next door. In the analysis below, I do not claim to control for these factors.[131] Funding spent on transportation linkages and also education has been found in other developing countries as well as China to have mixed effects on migration.[132] Building a road connecting a heretofore isolated mountain, forest, or desert village to cities decreases the barriers for those in such a village who desire to exit and as such should be expected to increase emigration rates. Similarly, education opens up new possibilities for higher paying positions in urban areas that might not exist in rural ones. In the counties that I visited, however, basic transportation connections have been present for generations and while there are academic elites who leave communities to pursue post-secondary education, much of the bulk of the migrant labor force that officials discussed were low-skill workers in the private policing sector (*bao an*) as well as the classic *mingong* work of construction and factory jobs.

The interviews that I conducted in rural Chinese counties with government officials, especially in Heilongjiang, provide information on how the mechanics of preferential policies and funds are doled out. The importance of economic and political self-interest cannot be oversold in the telling of this narrative.

County officials fixate on economic opportunities that their counties can take advantage of. The same could be said of township and village level officials. This is unsurprising and a large literature has described the entrepreneurial drive of local government officials.[133] Opportunities include investing in factories of all kinds and creating business parks for plant locations.[134] The officials compete for promotions, with the principal measuring stick being economic growth statistics.

One of the aspects of the political economy of rural China that officials illuminated in interviews is the process of selection of pilot projects. In some cases as soon as higher levels announce their intention to participate in a new program that county officials believe will be beneficial, to themselves and/or the county, they make clear to the higher level the county's interest in being the site for such experimentation. It is at this stage in the selection of pilot projects that the pilot project's value to the locality can accrue to higher level decision-makers. More clearly, as being selected for a new transfer or subsidy is valuable to county level officials, they have an incentive to utilize informal networks to influence decision-makers to choose their locality for the new policy. Influence can be anything from payoffs to argumentation.

---

[131] What I do, however, is to assume that these omitted variables are not correlated with the level of unemployment in the nearby city, the independent variable of consequence for the argument.

[132] e.g., Brandt et al. 2002.

[133] e.g., Oi 1999.

[134] The counties where I conducted these interviews were relatively distant from cities of note, so activities related to land sales for urbanization were not on the table in these remote outposts.

Underlying all of this detailed focus on outperforming other counties for economic growth numbers is a baseline concern about stability. Higher level officials will not promote officials that have a poor track record of ensuring stability
in territories under their jurisdiction. One of the principal methods that the
government itself uses in assessing officials and the levels of stability of the jurisdictions under their watch appears to be statistics related to Letters and Visits
(*xinfang*) offices. The officials in charge of the Letters and Visits offices were constantly bombarded with indignant villagers complaining about the misconduct
of officials and the injustices borne by the common people (the Chinese *laobaix-
ing*, or old hundred names).[135] However, these officials also are assailed by their
fellow officials who often dispute a complaint's registration status in an effort to
keep their records relatively free from blemishes.[136]

Connecting the importance of lobbying higher levels and officials' dual focus
on growth and stability leads one to understand how provincial and city governments are persuaded to send resources to rural areas near unstable cities.[137]
Cities with high levels of unemployment are happy to see resources flowing to
areas that are the source of potential migrants. The reasoning is that these areas
have a relatively high likelihood of becoming problematic for higher level officials. The problems come from potential protests, a declining economic situation for residents, or frustration with local government officials that could erupt
from any number of causes. High unemployment in a city encourages officials to
direct resources to the city itself but also to the surrounding countryside. These
arguments hold currency for officials making transfer allocations because of
political self-interest.

RESEARCH DESIGN AND NEARBY INSTABILITY
HYPOTHESIS

As described in a large literature, the Chinese government's fiscal system is complicated and multi-tiered.[138] Resources are collected in localities and different
taxes are transferred to higher levels at different rates. Some portion of those

---

[135] Heilongjiang Interview 2007051503. The leader of the *xinfangban* of the county, while a relatively low-ranking position, is actually relatively politically powerful as the reported levels of complaints can affect everyone's chances of promotions. The interviewee spoke of being buttonholed to
not count various petitions as official because of technicalities often in direct conflict with the rules.

[136] For a view of the Xinfang Bureau at its weakest, see Smith 2009.

[137] Actual instances of incidents or protests would blemish a local official's assessment and hurt
career prospects, so manufacturing protests to increase transfers would be a losing political strategy
in China as opposed to Treisman's account of post-Soviet Russia (Treisman 1999). Suggesting that a
locality needs funds to avoid potential instability, on the other hand, is pervasive in China.

[138] e.g., Oksenberg and Tong 1991; Wang 2004; Wong 2005.

taxes, theoretically determined by rule, is returned to local governments. As described above at the province level, in addition to the tax side of the budget ledger, local governments receive various transfers from higher level governments. The analysis presented below examines these transfers controlling for county level factors and sees if factors outside the county have some impact on the funds that the county receives. Transfers are in part rules-based and in part ad hoc. It is with the ad hoc transfers where negotiations and lobbying play a major role.[139]

The principal claim, the *nearby instability hypothesis*, is that counties that are nearby unstable cities receive larger transfers than similar counties that are near cities that are relatively stable to decrease incentives of marginal migrants to these locales, *ceteris paribus*.

> Nearby instability hypothesis: Counties that are near unstable cities receive larger transfers than counties not near an unstable city.

Here, I analyze the unemployment statistics—as an indicator of instability— for the prefecture above the county. Each county under a given prefecture then receives the same official unemployment "treatment" for a given year. The hypothesis simply states that controlling for other factors, counties under prefectures with higher levels of unemployment will receive larger fiscal transfers.

If evidence in support of this hypothesis is found, then it is clear that factors outside of the county are responsible, at least in part, for differing levels of transfers to counties. This test is not the ideal test of the theory for a number of different reasons. First, it is possible, and follows the cross-national analysis, that politically salient cities, namely capitals, are the most important to keep stable for an autocrat. In the Chinese case, this would imply that resources should be flowing to areas nearby Beijing or Shanghai, as those are the most politically salient cities in the nation. Second, proximity alone is not an ideal measure of the likelihood that migrants from a given county are likely to end up in a given city. Migration patterns are complex and well-studied phenomena, both generally as well as in the case of China and suffer from substantial non-linearities. However, for the time period under study two-thirds of migrants remained within their home provinces according to the 2005 *Quanguo 1% Renkou Chouyang Diaocha Ziliao* (1% Population Random Sample Survey).[140]

In addition to the nearby instability hypothesis, a number of control variables at the county level are expected to affect the county's level of transfers. First,

---

[139] Heilongjiang Interview, 2007051802.

[140] http://www.stats.gov.cn/tjsj/ndsj/renkou/2005/html/1206.htm. The 2000 Census shows three-fourths of rural migrant laborers stayed in their home provinces.

larger counties will receive larger transfers, all else equal. Second, counties with more fiscal dependents will receive larger transfers, all else equal. Third, richer counties will receive smaller transfers, all else equal, as the transfers are supposed to be progressive in nature. In the next section, I describe the methods by which I define these various terms and the sources of the data that allow me to make the determinations.

DESCRIPTION OF DATA SOURCES AND DEFINITIONS

A happy legacy of the Chinese imperial system for contemporary students of China is the emphasis on record keeping that must in part account for the incredible output of information released by government ministries and localities on an annual basis.[141] The county level analysis combines the Barometer of Chinese Development (BOCD) datafile with city level statistics from China's National Bureau of Statistics compiled by the University of Michigan's China Data Online service.[142] In addition, latitude and longitude data are used to calculate the distance between counties and their relevant prefectural unit as well as the national capital.[143]

Instability is a concept that requires a definition for this analysis. The measure used here is the total number of urban registered unemployed workers. Shanghai has the highest total number of officially registered unemployed persons while Shenyang and other cities of the Northeast join it on the top of the rankings in terms of the unemployment to population ratio. While there is a large literature which argues that the official registered unemployment rate in urban areas represents an undercount of the actual numbers of unemployed individuals, it does provide some information relevant for perceptions of instability.[144] While

[141] Previous versions of this section have described the developed and verbose statistical system as the "happiest" legacy of the Chinese imperial era; however, upon reflection, in this author's opinion that slot is taken by things culinary.

[142] This is the same county level data used in the sub-national analysis in chapter 4.

[143] Thanks to Pierre Landry for sharing the location data. Given the difficulties of compiling complete county level data in China, I had previously conducted an analysis similar to the one here on a sample of 80 county level units (Wallace 2009). The BOCD data can confirm that the patterns observed in the sample hold for the population.

[144] e.g., Solinger 2001; Giles, Park, and Zhang 2005. One could argue that higher levels of official unemployment actually come from cities that are doing relatively well, as it is only in stable areas where there are the resources to give to the unemployed who register that makes registration worthwhile for someone without employment. For example, in this line of thinking, for a poor city without resources, the official registered unemployment rate will more dramatically undercount its unemployed than in a rich city that does have money to give to the unemployed. However, even following this line of argument, it seems difficult to have this negative correlation work with changes in the unemployment rate. Whereas it might have once been the case that the unemployed only bothered

an undercount, this analysis takes the unemployment data as correlated with reality, with levels and changes representing higher levels of official unemployment are regarded as being associated with actual levels and changes of unemployment increasing, and thus represent a more unstable area. Jiang Zemin, as quoted above in chapter 4, is just one official who believes the official unemployment figure as worthy of reference and, indeed, concern.[145]

In the discussion section below, I take up how one should interpret the impact of this variable on the level of transfers. Higher levels are operating in a relatively low information environment when assessing the economic situation and political stability of their subordinate territories. Local leaders have incentives to manipulate the impressions that superordinates have for reasons dealing with assessment. As described in the previous chapter, local officials are judged by their performance along a number of dimensions but the ability of higher-ups to glean accurate assessments of the situation on the ground is limited at best. The official unemployment rate, then, is a quantifiable figure that purports to contain information about a locality's employment situation. It might be used as such by those officials who collect and report it.

Finally, I define the dependent variable of net transfers in the following manner. There are three principal sources of on-budget local government revenue: self-raised funds, returned taxes, and transfers.[146] The second and third categories are sent down to counties from higher levels and thus can be considered transfers. While the returned taxes category should be governed by rule, the actual budget data show wide divergence between the amounts of revenue that counties receive and other measures, which points to this "rule-based" source of funds also being subject to discretion and hence adjustment based on the political situation.[147] As noted above, the third category there has seen a proliferation in the number of different types of transfers. To ensure meaningful year-by-year comparisons, I combine various transfers and returned taxes together into "non-normal revenue" streams. While there are many restrictions on the use of funds, the county level government officials interviewed made clear that local budgets possess a high degree of fungibility. I then subtract out transfers to higher levels from the non-normal revenue estimate to create the

to register in rich cities, the fact that more registered in year 2 than in year 1 is hard to square with anything other than a negative turn for the city in question.

[145] "Law and order is currently not good, and crime is a serious problem in some localities. These problems have a direct relation to high underemployment rates and the blind movement of migrant" (Jiang 2010, 529).

[146] Extrabudgetary items, which for various periods of the 1980s and 1990s were an extremely large and growing portion of local government revenues, have been reduced in their importance by reform measures by the central government (Oi 1999; Wong 2005).

[147] Wong 2005.

"net non-normal revenue" metric that is used below.[148] For simplicity, I refer to this total as the county's net transfers for a given year. A second metric is also used, ad hoc transfers. The difference between these is that ad hoc transfers ignore returned taxes. Yet in the analysis here, their correlation is 0.96 and over 0.98 when examined in per capita terms. The results are robust to the use of either measure.

The net transfers make up large percentages of a county's total budget, on average, totaling around half of a county's total revenue in 2005. Net transfers increase over time as central coffers are filled with industrial taxes and returned to lower level governments. The mean net transfer more than triples from 1999 to 2005 and increases dramatically every year.[149]

Rather than attempt to control for a multitude of county level factors, most of the analyses utilize county level fixed effects. This absorbs factors that are invariant across time but that are likely to affect a county's level of transfers. Most notably, a minority county status has been shown elsewhere to be associated with substantially greater transfers than a county that is similar in other dimensions but is not designated minority.[150] An alternative specification, using provincial level fixed effects, allows for county level invariant factors to be included such as distance to the prefectural capital or to Beijing.[151]

Time-varying factors at the county level also might affect the size of transfers. The control variables included in the analysis are a number of county level economic variables.[152] The size of the county is another control variable. The expectation is that larger counties would receive larger transfers, all else equal. A county's size is gauged by two separate measures, its population and its level of wealth by gross county product in per capita terms.[153] As there is time dependency in the data, fixed effects for years are included to absorb the change over

[148] For complete transparency, the net non-normal revenue figure is created as follows. First, the local revenue (本年收入) is subtracted from the total revenue (收入合计) for a given county-year from the *Quanguo Dishixian Caizheng Tongji Ziliao*. This is then the amount of non-normal revenue in a county. From this figure four upward transfers are removed (原体制上解, 专项上解, 出口退税专项上解, and 单列市上解省), producing the net non-normal revenue figure. Ad hoc transfers take this net non-normal revenue figure and subtract returned taxes (收入税收返还收入).

[149] 1999 to 2005 represents the full range of the data here. City level unemployment records in the China Data Online archive have high levels of coverage only beginning in 1999, restricting the utility of prior fiscal transfer data in this analysis.

[150] e.g., Shih and Qi 2007.

[151] Remote counties might be expected to not receive large transfers as they are off the beaten path. On the other hand, improving the economic opportunities in remote areas was seen as a winning strategy in the previous chapter and might be associated with greater transfers here under a similar logic.

[152] Data on official registered unemployment at the county level is unavailable.

[153] As these data are right-skewed, logged values are preferred.

time in the average level of transfers. As noted above, the overall size of transfers increases dramatically during this time period. This systemic change is controlled for by the year fixed effects which turn the analysis to focusing on the factors that change over time and the distribution of transfers over space.

ANALYSIS

An implication of the argument is that counties near unstable cities, all else equal, will receive larger fiscal transfers in part to improve the economic conditions of rural areas near cities that already have unemployment problems. To clarify, take the following example. Huinan county in Jilin province and Lingchuan in Guangxi are two counties in different parts of the country that are similar along a number of dimensions but are, obviously, nearby different cities. Their populations and GDP are comparable, 350,000 and 353,000 and 2.80 billion and 3.02 billion yuan, respectively. Yet the net transfers per capita going to these counties are dramatically different. While Lingchuan receives 445.2 yuan per capita, Huinan receives more than one-third more, over 600 yuan per capita.[154]

I argue that some of this difference can be accounted for by contrasting the economic and political situation in the cities nearby these counties. Guilin is a successful economic center in Guangxi, whereas Changchun has serious issues with unemployment. Changchun has three times the number of officially registered unemployed and twice the unemployment to population ratio of Guilin. The larger transfers that Huinan receives, thus, are in part to reduce the pressure on Changchun from its surrounding rural areas.

Supporting the nearby instability hypothesis, the level of unemployment in nearby cities is associated positively with the level of transfers that counties receive. I describe the models below. The statistical results are summarized in table 5.1. The total number of unemployed residents in the nearby city, the proxy for instability in that city, has positive and statistically significant effects on the levels of transfers received in counties. These effects hold under numerous alternative measures of the dependent and independent variables, fixed or random-effects models, and the removal of outliers.[155] An increase of a single standard deviation of the nearby city's unemployed population—from 30,000 to 69,000 people—would translate into a 0.4 yuan increase in net transfers per

---

[154] All figures are for 2004.

[155] An appendix is available showing similar results for analyses using other transfers per capita, total ad hoc transfers, and spending per capita as positively related to unemployment levels in the nearby city, either contemporaneously or using lagged values and controlling for numerous other factors along with year and county fixed effects. Both of the tables in the chapter and in the appendix omit Shanghai Pudong Xin Qu due to its status as an extreme outlier in net non-normal transfer

Table 5.1 **Higher Nearby City Unemployment Yields Larger Transfers**

DV: Net-Non-Normal Transfers PC	Model 5.1	Model 5.2	Model 5.3	Model 5.4	Model 5.5
Urban Unemployment, (in 1,000s)		0.01*** (0.00)	0.01*** (0.00)	0.01*** (0.00)	0.01*** (0.00)
County GDP Per Capita (logged)			−0.41*** (0.16)	−0.47*** (0.16)	−0.47*** (0.16)
Fiscal Dependents (per 1,000 population)				0.06*** (0.02)	0.06*** (0.02)
City Population (in millions)					−0.12* (0.07)
Constant	1.29*** (0.05)	−0.40 (0.49)	2.99** (1.39)	1.95 (1.37)	2.58* (1.44)
Observations	21,226	14,944	14,590	14,590	14,590
R-squared	0.38	0.33	0.39	0.39	0.39
Number of Counties	2,982	2,430	2,405	2,405	2,405
Year FE	YES	YES	YES	YES	YES
County FE	YES	YES	YES	YES	YES

Robust standard errors in parentheses.
***$p < 0.01$, **$p < 0.05$, *$p < 0.1$.

capita. Multiplied by the median population of a county, around 363,000, yields a not insubstantial 145,000 RMB to the county budget.

Transfers to counties vary. They do for as many reasons as there are counties in China. Controlling for fixed features of counties as well as for the year of transfers, the level of unemployment in the prefectural city is consistently associated with increased transfers to counties under that city. Interestingly, there is not a systematic pattern of counties nearby larger cities receiving greater transfers—city population is if anything negatively correlated with transfers per capita in the regression analyses—but the number of unemployed individuals in the city does seem to matter. While this might bring pause given the argument of the book, it is critical to note that areas around two of the most important cities—Beijing and Shanghai—did receive above expected levels of transfers.

The unemployment rate, similarly, is less correlated with higher transfers than is the total number of officially registered unemployed persons. Cities with large masses of unemployed people are perhaps viewed by local officials allocating transfers as more threatening than a large share of unemployed in a relatively small city.

An alternative account may see large transfers to counties surrounding cities with high unemployment as natural counter-cyclical economic activity, yet this is not the case in the data. This pattern of transfers only emerged in 2002. While the results from table 5.1 show that the pattern exists in analysis looking at the full dataset, table 5.2 shows that transfers since 2001 drive this pattern in the overall data. Unemployment in the nearby city is only associated with greater transfers in the second half of the data, that is, when the transfers increase in size with the advent of the fiscal shift.[156] The coefficient estimates for the first half of the data are exactly at zero, implying that the unemployment levels of nearby cities did not affect transfer levels during that period. It is only in the post-2000 period that the positive relationship supporting the nearby instability hypothesis is in evidence.

As Chinese central government revenues increased and the economy grew during these years, a shift toward policies increasingly focused on the medium to long term came to be implemented. If urban bias is a Faustian bargain, then in times of plenty, regimes are likely to move away from such deals with the devil. In the Chinese case, this desire is heightened by the relaxation of the migration restricting *hukou* system, which had operated as a loophole in the Faustian bargain during the prior four decades. The shift of resources to the countryside coincides with the strategic realization that the regime possessed the resources to consider problems and challenges that they would face in the future rather than only having the ability to muddle through the problems of the present. Concerns about rural-urban instability linkages are easily dismissed in moments of crisis or deprivation but take on significance when one has the wherewithal to look ahead of one's own two feet.

Conclusion

The CCP-led government of the PRC shifted its fiscal policy to reduce the level of urban bias in the country. I argue, however, that this increased attention and level of resources directed to the countryside are in part a function of long-term

---

terms. Including Pudong strengthens the results here substantially, so if anything its omission understates rather than overstates the relationship.

[156] N.b. on these results, only when using the lagged value of the unemployment level do we find the results. The general regressions work with the lagged value as well as the contemporaneous value. There might be reasons to believe that either one fits the data more reliably depending on the private budget and transfers policies in question. If transfers are decided at the beginning of the year, then the lagged value should take precedence as it is the most recent information available. If, however, one believes instead that the local levels are reassessing throughout a given year and sending additional transfers to areas in need, then the contemporaneous data may be used in that process.

Table 5.2 **Nearby Instability Hypothesis Support Only Comes with the Fiscal Shift**

DV:	Model 5.2.1	Model 5.2.2	Model 5.2.3	Model 5.2.4	Model 5.2.5	Model 5.2.6
Ad Hoc Transfers per capita	1999–2001	2002–2005	1999–2001	2002–2005	1999–2001	2002–2005
Lagged DV			0.31*** (0.07)	0.68*** (0.07)	0.31*** (0.07)	0.61*** (0.04)
Unemployment (Lagged, in 000s)	0.00 (0.00)	0.01** (0.00)	-0.00 (0.00)	0.01** (0.00)	-0.00 (0.00)	0.01** (0.00)
GDP PC (lagged, logged)					-0.11** (0.05)	-0.14 (0.09)
Fiscal Dependents (lagged, per 1,000)					0.00 (0.01)	-0.01 (0.02)
City Population (in millions, lagged)					0.05* (0.03)	-0.17 (0.13)
Constant	0.49** (0.20)	2.37*** (0.10)	0.24 (0.27)	1.28*** (0.13)	0.79 (0.60)	3.63*** (1.18)
Observations	4,016	8,773	3,792	8,667	3,689	8,467
R-squared	0.23	0.25	0.27	0.42	0.28	0.50
Number of Counties	2,137	2,328	1,974	2,299	1,940	2,272
Year FE	YES	YES	YES	YES	YES	YES
County FE	YES	YES	YES	YES	YES	YES

Robust standard errors in parentheses.

*** $p < 0.01$, ** $p < 0.05$, * $p < 0.1$.

concerns about the instability of urban areas. That is, these funds going to farmers are meant to stabilize not only the countryside today but also cities in the future through the mechanism of affecting migration decisions. That a durable regime has enacted such a long-term policy is understandable. Counties near unstable cities receive extra transfers compared with similar counties surrounding cities that are doing better economically. The center's macro policy of decreasing the burdens on peasants as a way to manage urbanization is accompanied by local level decisions attempting to discourage further migration to cities that are already plagued by unemployment.

Another critical piece of China's continued management of urbanization, which will be discussed in the next chapter, is the inability of rural residents to sell their land. Rural land remains collectively owned and until an individual transfers their rural *hukou* for an urban one, then they retain a connection to the agricultural economy. Land allocated by the household responsibility is described by some as a social safety net of last resort.[157] During the Great Recession, tens of millions of migrants who thought that they had left rural China and agriculture behind found themselves in the midst of an economic collapse. In droves they returned to the countryside from which they had come.

---

[157] e.g., Riskin 1994; Gilboy and Heginbotham 2004; Deininger and Jin 2005.

CHAPTER 6

Return to Sender

HUKOU, STIMULUS, AND THE GREAT RECESSION

Should Chinese-style growth prove unsustainable—thus exacerbating
already volatile social conflict—the party's mandate of heaven could be
torn asunder even as the nation is plunged into chaos.
—Willy Lam, *Chinese Politics in the Hu Jintao Era*[1]

The first decade of the 2000s ended with a great global economic crash. The crisis originated largely in the developed world, yet China too was hit.[2] Europe and
the United States faced economic collapse on a global scale unknown since the
Great Depression three generations prior and drastically cut purchases of goods
made in China. In the first five months of 2008, nearly half of the shoe exporters in Guangdong province shut down operations.[3] Tens of millions of Chinese
workers lost their jobs in 2008.[4] Such a dramatic economic decline also could
have threatened to undermine the regime politically.

However, despite large decreases in external demand for products made in
China and a brief dip below the symbolically important 8 percent growth mark,
the Chinese economy and the CCP weathered the storm.[5] Many accounts of China

---

[1] Lam 2006, 248.

[2] Global imbalances—excess savings in China and excess consumption in the West—contribute
to the crisis.

[3] "前5月珠三角近一半出口鞋企因汇率变化退出市场_产经动态_新浪财经_新浪网"
2008, as cited by Naughton 2008. Over 2,300 factories of the 4,750 that had been in operation at the
end of 2008 had ceased operations. Smaller operations were particularly hit hard as seen by the share
of factories closing their doors greatly exceeding the decline in exports, which decreased 15.5 percent
through May 2008 compared with the same period of time in 2007.

[4] e.g., Huang et al. 2010.

[5] Both 2008 quarter 4 and 2009 quarter 1 saw Chinese GDP growth below 8 percent (Chinese
National Bureau of Statistics (NBS)).

written immediately prior to the crisis conclude with an outlook on China's future.[6] These works, and many in the popular press, present a litany of threats facing the regime arising from nationalism, inequality, corruption, and the absence of political reform.[7] It is a widely held belief that growth is a necessary if precarious condition for political stability in China. Some go as far as Zhao, who writes that, "The state still bases its legitimacy on performance and is thus intrinsically unstable."[8] The party itself refers to the need to maintain rapid economic growth to stave off instability.[9] The cross-national analysis in chapter 3 shows that, in the post-World War II era, regimes experiencing economic growth do indeed tend to persist. Facing economic hard times, on the other hand, makes regimes more likely to fail. How did the Chinese regime manage to tame the dangerous winds of the Great Recession?

My principal claim is that the regime's successful maintenance of stability is partly due to two factors: its *hukou*-based management of urbanization and Keynesian stimulus package. These policies simultaneously structured, dispersed, and reduced the level of discontent in society, allowing the regime to avoid what might have become a revolutionary moment that could have challenged its rule. As in previous chapters, I acknowledge that other factors played a role in China's political stability: its status as a party regime, its military and policing prowess, its prior economic success, perhaps even the glory of the spectacle of the Beijing Olympics. Success has many fathers; I aim to demonstrate the importance of the *hukou* system and the stimulus, factors that could be overlooked in a complex multi-causal environment.

The policies and institutions of the regime managed the crisis in numerous ways. First, prior to the crisis, the *hukou* system made urbanization a relatively decentralized phenomenon, with urban clusters all over the country, as detailed in chapter 4. In a China without a *hukou*-molded city system, when the crisis hit, the regime would likely have faced fewer, larger cities whose street politics might have turned against it. Instead, the regime relied on the ballast provided by a massive urban population spread out in hundreds of cities to steady it against significant unrest bubbling up in a few locales. Second, the *hukou*-based incentives pushed migrants by the millions to leave the urban areas where they had been employed to return to the smaller cities of the interior and countryside. The *hukou* system both lowered the level of urban concentration in the country prior to the crisis and in the moment of crisis further dispersed the disaffected by the millions. Third, the regime then stimulated the economy with fiscal policies

[6] Chang 2001; Lam 2006; Shirk 2008; Pei 2008; Huang 2008. Also Perry 2008.

[7] Nationalism and nationalist protests present both political benefits and costs for the Chinese regime. See Weiss 2012, 2014.

[8] Zhao 2001a.

[9] e.g., Wen Jiabao's speech at the World Economic Forum in Dalian, September 2009 (Wen 2009).

and an expansion of bank loans that reduced levels of discontent by providing opportunities for employment. The geographic distribution of these policies— emergency loans to urban factories in the short term and large-scale investment in rural areas and the interior over the longer run—again points to the political fear of unrest in cities and the regime's continued efforts to influence individuals' and businesses' location decisions.

The Great Recession caused massive job losses and spikes in the numbers of labor disputes and unrest in China. The chapter begins by establishing that this episode was fraught with peril for the regime even with existing *hukou*-based policies. Without proactive government actions to stimulate demand, the collapse of order combined with the loss of money from abroad would have left millions more out of work and poorer. The robust response boosted the country's economic fortunes and decreased the likelihood of serious political turmoil. Urban-biased loans addressed concerns of instability in the short term, while more interior and rural-directed infrastructure projects continued the regime's long-term efforts to develop the western part of the country. At the height of the crisis, the regime retreated to loans tilted toward cities, reinforcing the claim that urban bias possesses short-term benefits that can make it attractive despite its long-term costs.

China Coming into the Crisis

China's path of export-oriented development in the 1980s was aided by policies such as the maintenance of a low value for the RMB and tax advantages.[10] The exchange rate regime has supported export-oriented development in two ways, both by keeping domestic wages down as a share of the final price of the product—denominated in an inflated foreign currency—and by reducing the purchasing power of Chinese consumers, thereby making the domestic market relatively unattractive. Exports took the lead in China's modern industrialization. With the sector employing 100 million workers in 2008, coastal areas came to dominate exports due to a combination of policy and geographic realities.[11] The Develop the West Campaign and other policies of the fiscal shift detailed in the previous chapter were a response to the increasing perception and reality

---

[10] Tong 2012, 101–4.

[11] Tong 2012; Yang 1990, 1991. There are debates as to whether China's recent economic growth is best described as "export-led" versus "investment-led" (see, for instance, Anderson 2007). Certainly when compared with some of its neighbors such as Singapore or Malaysia, the Chinese economy is more domestically oriented. Investment plays an even larger role in the stimulus and its immediate aftermath than it did beforehand. See also Gallagher 2005.

of a bifurcated China. These policies have attempted to control the differences over space between the regions, but have not removed them. China's coast has remained the economic vanguard of the country.

Millions of migrant laborers from inland provinces filled coastal factories and propelled the export economy forward.[12] However, in China, this migration had its peculiarities. Rural land in China remains collectively owned; migrants thus retain a connection to the countryside as they cannot sell their land rights and use that capital to settle in the cities of the coast.[13] As described in chapter 4, these "sojourning peasant transients"—the "floating population"— powered the factories driving the growth of the coastal provinces but were not treated as true citizens in their new localities.[14]

China's economic situation coming into 2008 was robust. By mid-year, its principal economic fear was an overheated economy and inflation.[15] Consumers faced rising prices; the consumer price index peaked at 8.7 percent in February and prices continued quickly rising through April 2008.[16] Even more distressing, inflation was growing in all sectors of the economy. The producer price index exceeded the level of consumer inflation and continued to move higher, hitting 10 percent in July 2008. The central government feared the rapid inflation implied a frothy economy and determined to try to return gradually to a more stable level of growth.

To "prevent overheating and control inflation," the regime used two main policy levers: increasing reserve requirements for banks and allowing significant appreciation of the Renminbi.[17] Large reserve requirements restrict growth in the money supply and reduce the amount of leverage in the economy by forcing banks to keep more funds in their vaults rather than loaning it out to fund additional investment. Policies were tightened, starting in November 2007 until June 2008.[18] Similarly, the Renminbi appreciated around 1 percent per month over the same timeframe of seven months.[19] This appreciation, unsurprisingly, hit the export sector hard. Chinese exporters pay input costs in yuan while the

---

[12] Naughton 2007, 130.

[13] Solinger 1995.

[14] Solinger 1999a.

[15] This narrative builds heavily from a series of pieces by Naughton in the *China Leadership Monitor* from 2008 to 2009, as well as his chapter in *The Global Recession and China's Political Economy* (Naughton 2008, 2009a, b, c, d, 2012).

[16] These percentages reflect annualized rates of inflation during a given month.

[17] The phrase was the regime's macroeconomic slogan announced in October 2007 (Naughton 2008).

[18] Including raises in the commercial bank reserve requirement twice that June, of 50 basis points each on June 15 and 25 (Naughton 2009a, 1).

[19] Naughton 2008.

goods produced are paid for in other currencies. Increasing the value of the yuan would reduce profits for firms by reducing the per item profit if prices abroad were not increased or harming sales if the prices were allowed to rise.[20] Tens of thousands of firms closed their doors, unable or unwilling to operate profitably with the revalued Renminbi.[21]

In July 2008, the macroeconomic slogan shifted to "preserving while controlling (*yi bao yi kong*)," referring to the goal of maintaining growth while limiting inflation. The slogan reflected fear of stagflation, that is, stagnant growth accompanied by high rates of inflation. At this time, the leaders in charge of economic policy implemented a relaxation of their general policy of tightening as a "mid-course correction, rather than a policy reversal," given concerns about the job losses occurring in the export sector.[22] These changes included pausing the appreciation of the RMB as well as adjusting the value-added tax rebate that exporters in selected sectors received.[23]

China's attention turned to Beijing's hosting of the summer Olympic Games in August 2008. Any trends in the economic figures from that month were discarded due to the exceptional circumstances. Many factories and construction sites in and around Beijing were ordered to close, in an attempt to improve air quality and decrease chances of instability flaring up during the Games.[24]

On 15 September, the investment bank Lehman Brothers went into bankruptcy.[25] Within days, the Treasury Secretary of the United States was literally on his knees begging Congressional leaders to support a bailout of Wall Street lest the global economy disappear overnight.[26] The Great Recession had begun. Before turning to how China was able to respond effectively to the crisis, an implicit assumption must be addressed: that China was not hit hard by the crisis. The speed and effectiveness of the Chinese system's containment and response to the crisis might lead one to imagine that China was not hurt by the downturn. Yet China was in fact affected.

---

[20] The appreciation of the yuan is primarily taking place in dollar terms. However, while the yuan was becoming more expensive to purchase for holders of dollars, the value of the dollar was sliding when compared to the euro.

[21] 新华网 2008; 长江商报 2008; Sina 2013.

[22] Naughton 2009a, 1.

[23] 新浪网 2008.

[24] e.g., Lim 2008. The possibility of disturbances from migrants or media depictions of the terrible work conditions laborers face in Beijing was also reduced by their dispersal back to their villages. Related is "sealing management" of villages, which entailed locking migrants into their villages at night. See China Digital Times 2010 for details.

[25] Mamudi 2008.

[26] For this particular moment, see Herszenhorn, Hulse, and Stolberg 2008.

Crisis Hits China

By the fall of 2008, the global financial crisis that would come to be called the Great Recession was at its most dire. Following the freezing of credit markets that September, growth reversed into free fall. China responded rapidly with a stimulus package that was formulated in November 2008 and began taking effect immediately. Even the stimulus initially only staunched the flow of losses. At this time, Chinese official economic data resembled nothing so much as an economy falling off a cliff.[27]

Figure 6.1 depicts the seriousness of the moment. It shows the patterns of two economic time series in China, exports and rail freight.[28] The decline of external demand for Chinese exports is obvious.[29] In September 2008, which marked the beginning of the rapid descent in export demand, China exported goods valued at a little over $136 billion. Two months later, the total was $22 billion less. In January 2009, only 4 months after exports peaked, the total was $90 billion, a drop of over one-third in 120 days. On average, in September 2008, a little over 4.5 billion dollars of goods were being shipped out of Chinese ports every day. By January 2009, that number had slipped below 3 billion dollars.[30] The figure shows that even after smoothing cyclical changes in economic activity, exports were in free fall for the second half of 2008, dropping to just over 60 percent of their previous high by early 2009. By any measure, losses on the order of a billion and a half dollars a day would be a substantial shock. To those employed in the export sector and those who had invested billions in factories making goods bound for export, these losses represented catastrophe.

[27] Of course, other possibilities could have existed. First, the economy could not have been harmed, in which case the effects of the stimulus would be indeterminate. The simple presence of a major policy response to the crisis, though, points against this possibility. Second, the crisis could have harmed the economy but the response was inadequate. In this scenario, the effects of the crisis would not be as time constrained. See section below on alternative explanations for a discussion of the reality of China's return to growth. There is much speculation and some evidence that GDP growth estimates were inflated in China during the depths of the crisis (e.g., Wallace, forthcoming).

[28] The numbers the six-month moving averages, normalized to their highest point to (1) smooth the Chinese New Year effect and (2) allow the two to be shown on the same scale.

[29] Data are from the Ministry of Commerce and measured in current US dollars. The solid line represents a six-month moving average of the export value. So the two series can be shown together, the maximum value of each is normalized to 100. The y-axis then represents that month's percent of the maximum six-month moving average of the series.

[30] Even factoring in the Chinese New Year annual business cycle effects, this represented a drastic move. The average difference between the January and February export totals and the previous November and December export totals for the past three years was 28.3 billion dollars, whereas for 2009, the difference was over 70 billion dollars. In 2008, by November and December, exports had already dropped over 20 billion dollars a month from their high in July.

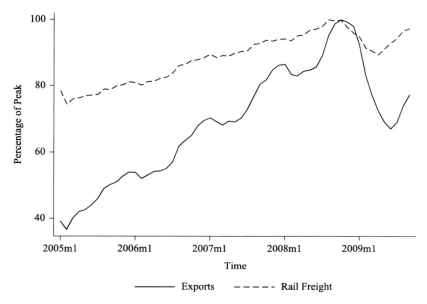

Figure 6.1 Exports and Rail Freight Collapse during the Great Recession. Note: Exports and Rail freight are normalized on a scale up to 100 for their peaks prior to the Great Recession. The figures shown are six month moving averages to smooth out seasonal variation.

A similar story emerges when looking at goods shipped within the borders of the PRC. The amount of freight traffic over rail is pictured as the dashed line.[31] Again, a long run of growth followed by a reversal dominates the series. Beginning around the fall of 2008, Chinese rail freight traffic contracts moved from strong growth to sharp decline. While the decline of internal freight traffic is not as stark as that of the exports, in an economy growing at 10 percent annually, to return to levels associated with two years prior is a substantial setback. Tens of millions of tons of goods were no longer moving around the country because they were no longer needed, whether to be processed by factories, consumed by households, or shipped outside its borders.

These trends demonstrate that the Chinese economy was negatively affected at the precise moment that the global financial crisis was coming to a head. While China's subsequent economic recovery may give the impression that it sailed smoothly through the crisis, contemporary accounts in the popular press also make clear that economic activity on the ground was seizing up as well.[32] Similar depictions of collapse can be found in Chinese monthly economic statistics from

---

[31] The choice to use the Chinese rail freight series came from the website seekingalpha.com, which used it to make a similar point, but as noted in the text almost any of the statistical monthly series displays the same pattern.

[32] Schuman 2008.

the fall of 2008. The economic shock hit China and did so through decreased demand for exports, which subsequently reduced domestic economic activity generally. Indeed, far from being unaffected, about 40 percent of the entire global population of those unemployed by the crisis were Chinese.[33]

The low demand for Chinese exports added to the difficulties many exporters faced due to the adjustments required by the yuan's appreciation vis-à-vis the dollar in 2008. The drop in exports in 2009 did not hit all Chinese provinces with the same intensity; export-producing factories were concentrated overwhelmingly along China's long coastline. Guangdong Province as of 2008 alone produced nearly 30 percent of China's exports.[34]

Figure 6.2 depicts the variation in export losses as a share of GDP and losses of industrial employment across China's provinces. Darker shades imply greater losses for both maps. Unsurprisingly, coastal provinces suffered the most from the sharp curtailing of demand for Chinese-produced goods in the rest of the world, as depicted in figure 6.2a using the share of export losses in 2009 as a share of 2008 GDP.[35] Industrial employment losses bear a remarkable resemblance, with the vast majority of the losses concentrated along the coast in areas that dominate the export sector, as shown in figure 6.2b.[36] Tong summarizes the geographic distribution of economic harm:

> In 2008, mainland China's top five most export-oriented provincial units were Guangdong, Fujian, Shanghai, Zhejiang, and Jiangsu, where exports amounted to 25–38 percent of industrial sales revenue. These regions were also among the worst performers in industrial activities for 2009. For example, while industrial employment declined

[33] International Food Policy Research Institute (IFPRI) 2009; Xinhua Net 2009; Chan 2010d, 660. The 40 percent figure is derived from an estimated global total of 50 million unemployed due to the Great Recession with 20 million of those in China. As we have seen, however, others have estimates within China that greatly exceed this figure, pointing to a larger global total and perhaps even greater share of those job losses occurring in China.

[34] 28.3 percent, from the 2008 data, *Zhongguo Tongji Nianjian* 2011.

[35] Xinjiang in China's far northwest also experienced a steep drop in exports as the natural resources that it exports dropped in price dramatically in 2009 compared to 2008.

[36] Again, darker shades reflect greater employment losses. The industrial employment data come from the National Bureau of Statistics' China Statistical Yearbook (http://www.stats.gov.cn), in particular the "Main Indicators of Industrial Enterprises above Designated Size (by Region)" data series, which captures firms with over 5 million yuan in revenue. Other employment estimates exist, but these are likely to be accurate as the state is more aware of the activities of large firms than it is of smaller firms. Indeed, as state-owned firms are overrepresented in the set of larger firms and are also more likely to be aided by the state through emergency loans (see below), these employment loss numbers reflect a small fraction of the total number of individuals who lost their jobs at some point during the crisis. The correlation between the export share of provincial GDP and the industrial employment losses in 2009 is 0.69.

(a)

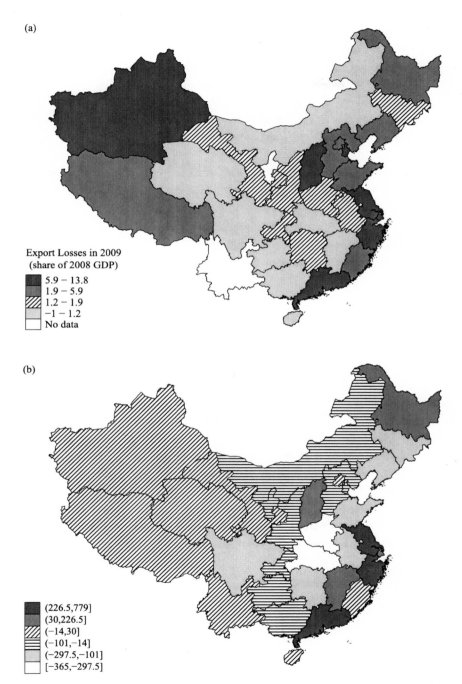

Export Losses in 2009
(share of 2008 GDP)

5.9 – 13.8
1.9 – 5.9
1.2 – 1.9
−1 – 1.2
No data

(b)

(226.5,779]
(30,226.5]
(−14,30]
(−101,−14]
(−297.5,−101]
[−365,−297.5]

Figure 6.2 Export and Industrial Employment Losses on China's Coast and Borders (a) 2009 Export Losses as a Share of 2008 GDP (b) Industrial Employment Losses in 2009

by 0.1 percent nationwide, that in Guangdong and the three Yangtze River delta provincial units declined significantly more (by 3.8 percent in Guangdong, 6.5 percent in Shanghai, 3.3 percent in Zhejiang and 7.1 percent in Jiangsu). In contrast, provinces with the best performance in industrial growth in 2009 were mostly inland, especially in central China (such as Inner Mongolia, Anhui, Sichuan, Hunan, Hubei, and Jilin), which are significantly less export-oriented.[37]

The managers and owners of these coastal factories responded to the collapse of demand as enterprises do around the globe: they slashed the size of their workforce.[38] *Nanfangdushibao* reported that 117 bosses had fled the export-production mecca of Dongguan, Guangdong in September and October of 2008, leaving 20,000 workers without their back wages.[39] In the fourth quarter of 2008, over 50,000 factories closed in Guangdong alone.[40]

Economic Crisis Sparks Instability

The economic crisis quickly sparked instability and represented a serious threat to the "harmonious society" that the Hu and Wen leadership had attempted to achieve. The collapse of factory orders led to millions being laid off, factories shuttering, bosses stealing away in the middle of the night, and a myriad of protests centered in China's factories and workshops. Tens of millions of Chinese lost their jobs during the 12 months of 2008. Kam Wing Chan suggests that this population was over 20 million.[41] Using their own survey in the wake of the crisis, Huang et al. estimated an even more terrifying figure: over 48 million laid-off Chinese.[42]

Workers responded en masse, although precise measurement of the number of incidents is spotty. Even more complex is assessing the extent to which overall social stability was shaken as regime officials at the local and national levels had

---

[37] Tong 2012, 103. N.b. Industrial Employment data.

[38] Branigan 2008.

[39] Nanfangdushibao 2008; Friedman 2012, 464.

[40] Chan 2010d, 665. The factory closure numbers vary from different sources based on different categories of firms being included or excluded in a given case. Chan here cites the Guangdong government. Additionally, this figure is only a raw figure, not an estimate of the additional number of firms that closed because of the crisis above the normal figure. Chan suggests that many firms disappear at the end of the year for purposes essentially amounting to tax evasion. Estimates for Guangdong vary from the 67,000 estimate from Chan 2010d to "only" 15,661 (Yangchengwanbao 2008; Friedman 2012).

[41] Chan 2010c.

[42] Huang et al. 2010.

incentives to mask the true level of discontent. One available metric is the number of participants in officially registered collective labor disputes, which nearly doubled from 271,704 cases in 2007 to 502,569 in 2008.[43]

The distribution of these labor disputes maps almost precisely onto the areas of the country that were hit the hardest by the reduction in exports. The provinces that experienced severe export losses during the crisis also saw increases in collective disputes.[44] These two factors correlate at a very high level, 0.74. In Guangdong alone, nearly 200,000 workers filed collective labor disputes in 2008, accounting for nearly 40 percent of the national total. In the prior three years, Guangdong had only held one-quarter of China's disputing workers.[45] The four provinces with the greatest increase in workers filing official complaints in 2008 were the industrial powerhouses of Guangdong, Zhejiang, Jiangsu, and Fujian. Alongside Guangdong's disputants increasing by over 135,000, each of these other three also saw over 10,000 more collective disputants than they had in 2007.[46]

Yet the crisis also led to an explosion in collective action outside of official channels. The boss of the largest dye factory in Shaoxing, Zhejiang ran off in October 2008, leaving behind more than 4,000 workers and debts in excess of $200 million.[47] Suddenly deprived of their livelihoods, these workers and millions like them reacted strongly to real and perceived injustices as the image of a world full of opportunities evaporated overnight. Scenes like that one played out hundreds of times during the fall of 2008.[48]

Workers directly challenged their lot, often using violence. Friedman describes the riot of Kaida workers in Dongguan, Guangdong province:

> In November 2008, the Hong Kong-owned Kaida toy factory was planning on terminating the contracts of several hundred of its workers. Management had made an offer on severance payments that workers were unsatisfied with, and which was likely below what they were

[43] China Labor Statistical Yearbooks, various years.

[44] As noted above, the number of collective disputants spiked in 2008 during the height of the crisis, whereas the number of employed dropped in 2009 (as the 2008 measure does not capture the full effect of the crisis). Data on collective labor disputants comes from the 2010 Labor Statistical Yearbook.

[45] The Labor Law change that had been put into practice also coincided with the Great Recession and likely increased the number of filings as well. Friedman argues that the number of disputes was affected by the crisis itself and legal changes (the labor contract law and labor dispute and mediation law, which "eliminated or greatly reduced the costs for workers to file a dispute") (Friedman 2012, 465).

[46] The pattern flipped in 2009, with the interior areas where migrants returned to having dramatic increases in disputants, particularly Chongqing, Hunan, and Jiangxi.

[47] Barboza 2009; Huang et al. 2010, 1. See also 中国劳工通讯 2009.

[48] Guo and Huang 2009. See also Sheridan 2009. Local governments scrambled to pay these back wages through every means possible to avoid further confrontations with the workers (Wong 2008).

legally entitled to. Unable to reach an agreement through informal
negotiations, several hundred workers rampaged through the factory,
smashing offices and other facilities. When the police turned up to try
to control the situation, the scope of the riot expanded. A reported 500
people engaged in property destruction and smashed several police
vehicles with as many as 2000 people observing.[49]

This was not a lone incident. Protests, riots, and other violent demonstrations
exploded in coastal provinces over the course of 2008.[50] In Jiaozuo, Henan,
workers from textile and cement factories disrupted traffic and blocked roads.[51]
Thousands protested in front of government offices in Dongguan when Smart
Union, a major toymaker, shut down operations in October.[52] Previously, such
direct action tactics were largely the domain of China's Manchurian rustbelt
workers in the north.[53] Migrant factory workers of China's coastal sunbelt turning to such unofficial expressions of outrage to register their discontent boded
poorly for the regime.

Thus, despite all of the efforts that the regime had put forward prior to
the crisis to spread urbanization around the country and buoy its political
stability, the country was still racked by outbreaks of protests, riots, and turmoil. These individual outbursts against particular factories or bosses were
beginning to connect and perhaps coalesce into something even more dangerous for the regime. Due to the financial crisis and other difficulties, the
Meifu Paper Products factory in Shenzhen, Guangdong, dismissed hundreds
of workers in November 2008.[54] Workers, who had not received wages for
three months, protested against the firm but also the city labor department
for failing to deliver on their promise of compensating workers. The protest attracted hundreds of local police, and the clash between the two sides
resulted in injuries to both police and protestors. The protestors started
throwing stones and eventually riot police with shields and helmets were
called in to end the demonstration. The dozen protest leaders were arrested
and, as often occurred, the city government has consequently agreed to pay
the amount they owe the workers.

[49] Friedman 2012, 466.
[50] Sheridan 2009.
[51] Radio Free Asia 2008a.
[52] Zhai and Leung 2008. See also 南方都市报 2008.
[53] Lee 2007.
[54] Radio Free Asia 2008b.

An even more explosive example of the dangers that erupted can be found in the connections between disputes amongst migrant workers in Guangdong and subsequent ethnic riots in Urumqi during 2009. After rumors of Han women being raped by Uyghur workers spread in the Early Light (Xuri) toy factory in Shaoguan, Guangdong, Han workers attacked the Uyghurs in their dormitory.[55] The violence spilled into the streets ending with an official casualty list of two Uyghurs dead and 118 others injured.[56] Local police "later arrested a bitter ex-employee of the factory who had ignited the fight by starting a rumor that 6 Uighur men had raped 2 Han women at the work site."[57] Yet this was not the end, as images depicting much greater violence with more killed, mostly Uyghurs, circulated.[58]

On 5 July, the violence spread to the Xinjiang Uyghur Autonomous Region on the far side of China. A thousand people marched to People's Square in Xinjiang's capital, Urumqi, calling for further investigation into the events in Guangdong, before the demonstration was put down.[59] Riots then broke out around the city, mainly in Han-dominated areas, with nearly 200 killed according to a State Council white paper.[60] Han counter-protests and riots spread on 7 July with a city leader speaking "sympathetically" with the crowds.[61] The stability in the region remains precarious despite the fact that the central government lavished funds to provide for social stability and further economic development in the region.[62] Uyghurs, numbering in the dozens to hundreds, remain

[55] Millward 2009. For more information on the Shaoguan incident in Guangdong that sparked the Urumqi riots, see Pomfret 2009; "Guangdong Toy Factory Brawl Leaves 2 Dead, 118 Injured" 2009. Watts (2009) of the *Guardian* provides more background.

[56] The others injured were of unspecified ethnicity (Millward 2009, 350).

[57] Wong 2009. But only Zhu, the spreader of the initial rumor, was arrested for a week after the incident (Millward 2009, 351).

[58] Millward 2009, 350.

[59] Millward 2009, citing Radio Free Asia 2009c. The Urumqi riots are sometimes referred to as the "7/5 incident" or "7/5" (Cliff 2012).

[60] "The most recent 'July 5' riot in Urumqi caused huge losses in lives and property of the people of various ethnic groups. By July 17, 2009, 197 people died (most being innocent victims) and over 1,700 were injured, with 331 shops and 1,325 motor vehicles destroyed or burned, and many public facilities were damaged" ("Full Text: Development and Progress in Xinjiang_English_Xinhua" 2013, cited by Millward 2009).

[61] Millward 2009, 354.

[62] Cliff 2012. Interestingly, both the initial incident in Shaoguan and the government response are related to migration policy. The initial Uyghurs working in Shaoguan ended up there because of government subsidies (Watts 2009), although it is unclear if the subsidies were given to the Uyghurs or to the factory owners for employing them. Cliff claims "the massive injection of funds into Xinjiang and the paired assistance program are intended to make the region attractive to Han and accelerate cultural change in Xinjiang. That means privileging Han people and Han ways of doing things" (Cliff 2012, 104).

"disappeared," and crackdowns persist, according to Amnesty International.[63] The incidents "seriously undermined the national unity, social harmony and stability" according to the China Institute of International Studies, a think tank associated with the Ministry of Foreign Affairs.[64]

All manner of acts of frustration, resistance, and violence emanated from the shock of the crisis. I argue the regime weathered the storm for three reasons: discontent that was engendered by the recession was structured, dispersed, and reduced to allow the regime to sail through relatively unscathed.[65] First, the status quo coming into the storm structured the political geography in favorable ways for the regime. In addition to the spread out city system, of critical importance was the structuring of individual migrants' beliefs about their position within the political and economic system, namely that migration was viewed overwhelmingly as a temporary economic phenomenon and not a permanent departure from the rural interior. Second, the *hukou* system and the geographic pattern of fiscal stimulus encouraged millions of individuals—specifically those individuals harmed by the crisis and so prone to inciting instability—to disperse from coastal urban centers to the smaller cities, towns, and villages of the interior. Third, the economic stimulus package offered a lifeline to businesses to keep running— reducing the number of workers left jobless by the crisis—and employment possibilities for the unemployed, typically through various government investment projects. The stimulus directly improved their economic prospects and also protected the regime's image of shepherding economic development successfully.

HOW DISCONTENT WAS STRUCTURED

China's system of migration restrictions contributed to its political stability throughout the economic crisis because it shaped people's lives in fundamental ways: most importantly, where they worked and what happened when they were laid off.[66]

First, as emphasized in chapters 3 and 4, China has very low levels of urban concentration. This structured discontent as the millions of laid-off workers were laid off in dozens to hundreds of cities, towns, and factories around the country rather than clustered in one of a handful of locales. Like gunpowder spread across a field and set alight, sparks may arise but not explode.

---

[63] Amnesty International 2012.

[64] *Guo ji wen ti yan jiu suo* (China Institute of International Studies) 2011, 322.

[65] As noted at the beginning of the chapter, my claim is not that these reasons are the whole story but merely the aspects emphasized in this book.

[66] Other policy choice and institutions were also important to China's ability to avoid instability due to the crisis. The *hukou* system is the focus because of its centrality in China's policy framework.

Second, the discontent tended to be channeled into siloed demonstrations.[67] The regime's pattern of prior behavior—cracking down on cross-coalition activities, but exercising comparative restraint against particularistic aggrieved groups—channeled individuals to follow those well-worn protest archetypes. That collective action was taking place at all, however, shows the extreme nature of the situation. While there is some evidence that such demonstrations were beginning to transgress the normal boundaries as seen above, such conventions insulated the regime in the immediate aftermath of factory closures.

Third, migrants were temporary, not permanent, residents of the localities in which they found themselves. This temporary status reduced their attachment to the communities they lived in and so lessened the chances of cross-cleavage alliances with workers or other groups in the communities in which they had worked.[68] When the migrants who staffed these factories were let go, they faced a stark set of choices. In some cities, as many as 80 percent of migrant workers live at their places of employment in dormitories and when laid-off, their income and housing could be cut off.[69] No welfare programs helped these migrants smooth their incomes as social services like unemployment benefits tend to be restricted to local *hukou* holders.[70] Official unemployment numbers increased only slightly, from 4.0 to 4.3 percent during the crisis, implying an addition of 600,000 unemployed urban *hukou* holders.[71] Yet the number of migrants who were laid off is orders of magnitudes larger, with estimates ranging from 20 to 48 million people.[72] This differential treatment further undermined potential working-class solidarity between migrants and non-migrant urban laborers.

HOW DISCONTENT WAS DISPERSED

The temporary status of migrants also had a second and even more critical effect: it induced migrants to return to the countryside when economic opportunities vanished in the cities. Without employment documents and income,

---

The pause in the appreciation of the RMB that began in the summer of 2008 and continued throughout the duration of the crisis also had stabilizing effects domestically.

[67] Along the lines of the "rightful resistance" arguments (O'Brien and Li 2006; Lorentzen 2010). See also Hurst 2009.

[68] Nelson 1976; Solinger 1995.

[69] For the estimates of dormitories housing 80 percent of workers, see Chan and Wang 2004, 638. As for a national total, different estimates put one-third to two-thirds of Chinese migrant workers living in dormitories owned and operated by their employers (Yusuf and Nabeshima 2008, 8) and (Miller 2012, 18).

[70] Chan 2010c, 359–60

[71] Chan 2010d, 667.

[72] e.g., Huang et al. 2010; Chan 2010d.

obtaining the permits required to stay outside of their *hukou* jurisdiction became an unaffordable option for millions of migrant workers. These discontented migrants dispersed to the countryside.

The *hukou* system shaped migrants' responses to the crisis, creating economic incentives for migrants to return to the smaller cities of the interior and countryside, scattering the jobless millions rather than leaving them massed in coastal megacities. When jobs and income-generating opportunities vanished in coastal factories, between 20 and 40 million migrant workers returned to their *hukou* jurisdiction rather than pay the costs to remain as temporary residents in urban areas.[73] The normal level of unemployment of migrants in urban areas is very small. Those unable to find work return to their hometowns as they are ineligible for urban social assistance.[74] Like an insurance policy, the political benefits for the regime of its *hukou* system of migration restrictions became obvious in times of trouble. The economic cost or premium for this insurance is the perpetuation of inefficiencies in labor and rural land markets.[75] I claim that migrants grudgingly dispersed from their coastal workplaces and that this dispersion lowered the chances of large-scale, regime-threatening collective action. Below, I establish (1) that migrants by the millions had already left coastal factory towns early in the fall of 2008, (2) that they did so reluctantly and were not happy to return to their hometowns and villages, (3) that wages dropped in coastal areas despite the exodus, further indicating the severe collapse in labor demand by employers in those locales, and (4) that dour expectations about the employment situation on the coast led to only the most employable to try their luck again as migrant laborers in coastal factories.

In late 2008 and early 2009, a wave of migrant workers left their urban, coastal places of employment and returned to the Chinese countryside.[76] The prominent Chinese news magazine *Caijing* surveyed migrants beginning in September 2008 and found that they (nearly 5 million) had already returned to their villages due to lack of economic opportunities.[77] Thousands of people were leaving Guangdong every day in the fall of 2008.[78]

---

[73] Huang et al. 2010.

[74] Chan 2010d, 667.

[75] Wang 2005.

[76] Chan (2010d, 668) refers to August 2008 propaganda calling for workers to return to the countryside.

[77] Source is Chang et al. 2009a, b.

[78] Hurst 2012. This figure comes from an interview with a senior official conducted by Hurst. Given the aggregate numbers of mass migration and Guangdong's share of the total migrant employment, this is likely a very conservative estimate. Likely tens of thousands of individuals were leaving Guangdong on a daily basis at the height of the employment crunch.

When Chen Xiwen, deputy director of the Central Rural Work Leading Group, announced that 20 million migrant workers stayed in their home villages following the Spring Festival holiday and did not venture back to the country's manufacturing zones, the magnitude of the displacement shocked many.[79] Unofficial estimates confirm or exceed this number.[80] These figures suggest that without the *hukou* system, 20 million migrants might have mobbed shuttered factories in coastal provinces, searching for work. These millions, looking for a roof over their heads and a way to earn a wage, could have together directed their anger against the regime, either its local or central manifestations.

These returnees made real concessions in leaving their coastal places of employment. Most clearly, this can be seen in their abandonment of pensions to which they had paid in for years. Migrants could close out social security accounts and receive back their own contributions of around 8 percent of wages, but local governments would keep the employer contribution component, which was much larger—20 percent of wages.[81]

Despite the loss of workers, wages were falling on the coast, as they were throughout China. The migrant hub of Shenzhen reduced its wage guidance for the first time in 11 years in 2009, to a level around 4 percent lower than it had been in 2008.[82] Based on survey data, wages fell on average by 7 percent in the South and declines exceeded 20 percent in the North.[83]

Many migrants chose not to try their luck again and look for work on the coast, and those that did tended to be the "best and brightest." This is consistent with the premise that migrants perceived a difficult job market following the Great Recession. Surveys of migrant workers in coastal areas found evidence that many did not return to the provinces where they had been employed.[84] The Sun-Yat Sen Center for Urban Studies surveyed nearly 3,000 migrants in Guangdong consistently over a number of time periods. In 2009, only 800 of those 3,000 were located in the province. Those that were found were the most educated and productive workers, signifying that migrants' expectations of employment opportunities had decreased. As such, the average qualifications of migrants improved, while less exemplary workers decided to stay in the countryside.[85]

[79] *People's Daily* 2009.
[80] Huang et al. 2010.
[81] Migrants would need to work in a particular city for at least 15 years for their accounts to vest and thus be able to keep their employer contributions as well (Chan 2010d, 666). On the details of the pension system of workers, Tian and Ma 2008; Chan 2010d, 666 n. 16.
[82] "Wages Fall for First Time in Decade" 2009, cited in Fix et al. 2009, 49.
[83] Huang et al. 2010, 6. They posit that this is primarily due to labor market fragmentation due to the *hukou* system. They also do find that more migrants leave the south than the north.
[84] Interview 2010010701.
[85] Interview 2010010701.

Migrants who had been living and working in coastal cities dispersed to their villages but also to cities in the interior, such as Zhuzhou in Hunan where migrants became the largest group of job-seekers as the crisis deepened.[86] This reverse migration continued despite the fact that wages were substantially lower in the interior.[87]

Why did millions of unemployed migrants choose not to return to coastal factories, nor to congregate in China's largest cities, but to scatter across a million villages, townships, and cities in China's interior? First, they had a place in the countryside. The inability to sell off one's rural land allocation due to the lack of land privatization became an asset rather than a liability for both migrants and the government. Land became, as a prominent scholar of Chinese urbanization put it, a "social safety net" for migrants: "if the state allowed the selling of rural land, it would be letting them sell their social security."[88] Migrant workers might not have had wages or government assistance checks, but they did have land allocated by their villages. With a roof over their head and land on which to grow food, at least they would not starve. Second, those who returned home for the Spring Festival holiday knew that without paying fees or locating new employment back along the coast, their urban prospects were tenuous at best. Rather than pay to travel to the coast in hopes of finding work, they chose to remain closer to home. At least two-thirds of the 25 million-strong population of "long-term" laid-off migrants returned to their villages, with more than half returning to agriculture and over 10 percent not looking for work outside the home.[89]

HOW DISCONTENT WAS REDUCED

The regime also instituted a massive Keynesian stimulus program to keep the economic dynamo of the country running. The shape of the stimulus benefited export firms on the coast in the short run and rural employment possibilities in the long run. Its principal purpose was to stabilize the political economy of China by giving jobs to the jobless and decreasing discontent. The geographic components of the stimulus are critical for understanding its effects on dispersion. China's prompt and aggressive counter-cyclical fiscal response directed state funds to projects around the country. The largest component of the fiscal stimulus targeted investment in high-speed rail, electricity grid development, and other transportation infrastructure.[90] The majority of this spending

---

[86] Hurst 2012, 121.
[87] Ibid., 123.
[88] Interview 2010010701.
[89] Huang et al. 2010, 8.
[90] Naughton 2009b.

and associated employment has been located in rural areas.[91] Financial stimulus in the form of loans to urban employers accompanied the rural spending. In this way, the geographic spread of the stimulus aided in the dispersal of the discontented.

An abrupt shift in migration patterns matched the timing and geographic focus of the stimulus. The stimulus package reduced the short-term number of unemployed workers. By doing so it also soaked up labor supply, keeping wages from collapsing further and allowing domestic consumers to continue to be able to afford products produced by their fellow citizens. The state stepped in to provide demand, filling in the gap caused by the collapse of external demand for goods produced in China. This short-term, Keynesian response, in both its size and direction, was critical in reducing potential discontent in China's coastal metropolises.

The economic stimulus package, announced in November 2008, was initially estimated at 4 trillion yuan, nearly US$600 billion.[92] This fiscal response was paired with a financial one, where banks were encouraged to provide loans to firms and local government investment vehicles to help them through the troubled waters. Although the broad strokes of China's response to the crisis have been well-established, the geographic distribution of stimulus funds has received far less attention.[93] Whereas one might have expected the government to direct aid to the coastal exporters who bore the brunt of the economic downturn, the Chinese central government instead sent much of its fiscal stimulus toward interior provinces to encourage employment there, fearing unrest both by the newly unemployed along the coast as well as by those who had already returned to their homes in the interior. The financial stimulus, on the other hand, was directed to urban employers and helped enterprises avoid bankruptcy to circumvent even larger urban unemployment problems.

China's economy began to suffer acutely from the crisis beginning in September 2008, at the same moment that the gears behind the global financial system ground to a halt. The central government did not receive the official September statistics from the bureaucracy until well into October, as collecting and analyzing the data is time intensive.[94] By early November, it became clear that China's economy had been hit by the economic crisis, and a meeting

[91] The stimulus continued pushing the interior's economic growth as had been a priority since the Jiang era Develop the West program.

[92] It is clear now that the actual size of government-directed funds greatly exceeds this 4 trillion figure. The massive increase in commercial loans that took place in China from 2008 to 2010 is in large part the banking system being directed by different levels of government to fund investment projects in order to keep the economic growth machinery running (World Bank 2012). Discussed below.

[93] Naughton 2009b.

[94] Orlik 2011.

of leading economic officials was held in Beijing.[95] From this meeting came the first announcement that the state planned to increase investment in the country and protect economic growth with a 4 trillion yuan economic stimulus package.

The 4 trillion figure was initially the only information offered about the program's size or structure. In addition to the public announcement, the meeting produced a private intra-Party document, Central Document 18. Although it has yet to be released, summaries have emerged and show that the central government sought to dramatically increase its own expenditures in the fourth quarter of 2008.[96] In particular, the central government planned to allocate an additional 100 billion yuan for investment in the fourth quarter, roughly 1.5 percent of national quarterly GDP. The speed of the government's response to the crisis was also crucial. After the effects of the downturn became apparent in mid-October, by 10 November the central government pledged to spend 100 billion yuan in 45 days. To put the resources to use in an effective manner required local governmental participation. Central Document 18 was released to local government party branches around 10 November. The next day, provincial governments met to discuss the policy and propose projects for central investment.[97]

Were the locations harmed by the crisis also where the center directed funds? The stark difference between the pair of maps depicting the coastal areas harmed by the crisis (figures 6.2a and 6.2b) and those showing the locales where fiscal stimulus was directed (figures 6.3a and 6.3b) requires a negative reply. Systematic data on programmatic spending by province for the stimulus are challenging to find. Data are currently available for one component of the stimulus package: local government bonds.[98] While the 1995 Budget Law forbid Chinese local governments from issuing public bonds, the stimulus package removed that barrier but allowed the center to determine the number of bonds that local governments could sell (figure 6.3a).[99]

Figure 6.3b shows the variation across provinces of investment, another proxy for fiscal stimulus funds. These maps show clearly that despite the fact that the global financial crisis hurt the coast (figure 6.2a and 6.2b), controlling for local GDP, the center preferred to direct resources to the interior (figure 6.3a and 6.3b). The contrast between the location of the economic harm and the spending by the regime to mitigate the downside political risks associated with that harm is striking.

---

[95] Xinhua 2008.

[96] Naughton 2009b.

[97] 大众日报 2008, cited by Naughton 2009b.

[98] The data for the map come from the Ministry of Finance and the National Bureau of Statistics. The depicted data is the ratio of official local debt to 2008 provincial GDP, in percentage terms.

[99] L. Liu and Chen 2005.

(a)

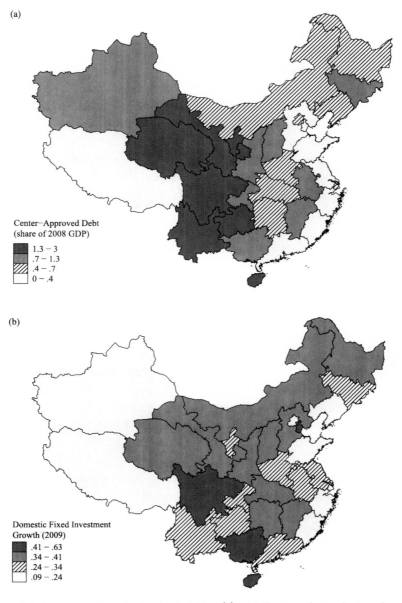

Center–Approved Debt
(share of 2008 GDP)

1.3 – 3
.7 – 1.3
.4 – .7
0 – .4

(b)

Domestic Fixed Investment
Growth (2009)

.41 – .63
.34 – .41
.24 – .34
.09 – .24

Figure 6.3 Location of Fiscal Stimulus in China (a) Distribution of Stimulus Funds—
Provincial Infrastructure Bonds (b) Domestic Fixed Investment Growth (2009).

Note: Fixed asset investment (FAI) increases dramatically across China due to the stimulus, but
regional patterns are stark. For the first half of 2009, "with FAI in eastern, central and western regions
increasing by 26.7%, 38.1% and 42.1% respectively" (Economist Intelligence Unit 2009).

While lauding the employment-generating projects of the stimulus package, experts cautioned that doing so might not be enough as job losses mounted in the export economy.

> While the number of jobs created by the massive infrastructure projects will be considerable, it is equally important to stem the decline arising from the export sectors, Cai Fang, a labor economics specialist with the Chinese Academy of Social Sciences in Beijing, said yesterday. "The stimulus projects for infrastructure nationwide will bring in a huge army of laborers and I'm sure a large number of migrant workers will return to construction sites for new work," said Cai, who is also a member of the Standing Committee of the National People's Congress.[100]

Following this line of advice, in addition to the fiscal stimulus, the regime also dramatically opened the flood gates in the financial sector and pushed banks to grant loans to companies to help them through the worst of the crisis. This financial stimulus was even larger than the 4 trillion RMB stimulus plan. Emergency loans to aid SMEs totaled some 6 trillion RMB.[101] The geographic distribution of these loans was tilted toward extant operations that were overwhelmingly in urban areas.

The stimulus' fiscal transfer of funds to interior provinces is consistent with the regime's overall strategy of shaping the geography of economic growth discussed in the previous chapter. The regime pursuing development in the interior of the country is consistent with many explanations: attempting to combat rising inequality at both the individual and regional levels by providing opportunities for employment in the interior, reducing the regime's perceived dependence on a small number of coastal economic zones for its GDP, and improving the chances of maintaining low-skill manufacturing jobs while allowing richer areas to move up the value chain.

China's construction of an "Industrial Transfer Zone" in the interior province of Anhui explicitly mentioned these reasons. The official Xinhua News Agency report announcing the zone begins: "China's government has approved plans to build its first national-level industrial transfer zone to encourage the relocation of low-end industries from coastal regions to inland areas."[102] Interviews revealed a similar story in a tentative agreement between the province he

---

[100] Li and Cui 2008.
[101] Friedman 2012, 467, citing *China Daily*; X. Wang 2009; "Exporters Get Sops to Fight Crisis— People's Daily Online" 2012. Although it is unclear if the 6 trillion figure is really correct: Caixin puts the total 2009 debt at only 5 trillion ("Nearly 5 Trillion Yuan Debt Issued in 2009" 2013).
[102] Xinhua 2010.

represents and the central government to implement an experimental policy regarding the transfer of various "illegal factories" to legal status.[103] The central government would forgive unpaid back taxes and wipe away prior illegal status if the factories underwent renovations in the next three years. Old factories that declined the opportunity to renovate would be destroyed, and the valuable land on which they stood would be used by new factories or other development projects. By destroying one-story factories and replacing them with more capital-intensive production facilities, the agreement would facilitate the movement of labor-intensive industries from this coastal province to interior locations akin to the Industrial Transfer Zone noted above.

In sum, the global financial crisis decimated demand for Chinese made goods and for the labor that produces them. Yet the sudden emergence of tens of millions of unemployed workers did not lead to the kind of large-scale urban protests that ousted dictators in Tunisia and Egypt in early 2011. Those tossed aside by factories shuttering in the wake of the crisis were not concentrated in the capital city or indeed in any large metropolis but were instead scattered across the country.

Complications

The argument offered here that China's ability to steer clear of disastrous possible outcomes coming out of the financial crisis is two-dimensional—namely, the *hukou* system and the stimulus package—is a reduced form of the very complex political and economic interplay at work. Two complications or caveats are required. One caveat that must be noted is the importance of center-regional conflicts in the moment of crisis. The second is added nuance regarding instability and danger to the regime. I take these in turn.

The phrase "the Chinese government" is overly simplistic as there are myriad different actors with different affiliations and interests encompassed by that term and as seen in the sub-national analysis in the previous chapters.[104] In particular and related to the situation at hand, the central government and the various provinces have conflicting interests when addressing the question of how to restructure the economy. These actors disagreed over the ways to deal

---

[103] I learned of this agreement before it became official and agreed to describe it anonymously until it is formally announced as government policy. "Illegal factories" in this case are those that were set up prior to the current approval process through early Reform era agreements with local governments.

[104] This is true also even of smaller pieces of that entity, such as "the center" or "the central government." As noted in chapter 2, Lee sees an inherent tension between local accumulation and central legitimation through law.

with the economic crisis as it was unfolding in 2008 in the areas dominated by export-oriented factories, namely the Pearl River Delta region of Guangdong and the Yangtze Delta Region in surrounding Shanghai. The general character of center-local interplay over the past five years is that described above: supporting the transfer of labor-intensive manufacturing to the interior. However, at the critical moments of the crisis, following through on this logic was deemed too extreme by the center and was postponed.

The provincial leader of Guangdong, Wang Yang, a Politburo member who was newly appointed to the province at the beginning of 2008, saw the collapse of many of the factories producing low value-added goods throughout 2008 as an opportunity rather than a calamity for the province. He came to popularize the slogan, "Empty the bird cage for new birds to settle down (*tenglong huanniao*)," expressing a desire to shift the type of economic activity in the province up the value chain. For Guangdong this would entail the Pearl River Delta region losing many of its labor-intensive factories (the old birds). That land would then be used by real estate projects or relatively capital-intensive factories.

In fact, the province for a few years prior to the crisis eagerly had been moving labor-intensive factories out of the Delta Region. In March 2005, the Guangdong government released Document 22, entitled "Joint Industrial Transfer Incentives for the Mountainous North, East and West Wings, and the Pearl River Delta."[105] The document envisioned the transfer of labor-intensive industry from the Pearl River Delta to the poorer northern and far eastern and western expanses of the province. This transfer would then allow for the redevelopment of the Pearl River Delta region to more productive uses.[106] This differs from the Develop the West Campaign in that rather than simply expand economic activity and investment in less developed areas, this policy attempted to change the nature of economic activity in the developed zones. By 2008, the province pledged to back this policy with 50 billion yuan over the next five years.[107]

At this point the desires of the provincial government and the central government began to diverge. Stress on low-margin manufacturers due to currency appreciation, combined with declining demand due to the financial crisis, led tens of thousands of factories to shut down and unknown numbers of others to

---

[105] 广东省人民政府 2005.

[106] While the language generally used to describe these more productive uses involves higher technology factories, one cannot avoid the suspicion that some of the land would become real estate developments, which in the current bubble environment allows for huge, immediate profits.

[107] "According to the strategy, from 2008-2012 the province will invest more than 50 billion Yuan to support the less developed regions in infrastructure construction, industry clusters transferring, key industry development and free working skill training. Especially, 500 million Yuan awards will be provided every year to encourage the enterprises to transfer to the less development regions" (Ouyang 2008). See also 杨春南 and 杨霞 2008.

approach that decision. Guangdong saw little problem in this, as many of these factories already were slated to be transferred elsewhere and occupied valuable land. In fact, the crisis could be seen as saving the provincial government of Guangdong significant resources. Rather than have to pay these low-end factory owners to move away or disband, the factories were disappearing on their own.

For years, the center supported developing the interior of the country in an effort to reduce regional inequality using fiscal policy, as detailed in chapter 5. Yet despite policy positions both before and after the crisis that encouraged SMEs to leave Guangdong and the coast, the center flinched when the crisis was at its worst. The central government in November 2008 examined the totality of the economy and was unsure how deep a drop in external demand for exports or employment for Chinese workers the global financial might occasion. Some, such as Zhou Tianyong, a Central Party School researcher senior adviser, predicted "mass-scale social turmoil" around the corner.[108] The head of the National Development and Reform commission, Zhang Ping, similarly suggested that "excessive bankruptcies and production cuts will lead to massive unemployment and stir social unrest."[109]

Immediately after announcing the national stimulus package, Wen Jiabao, the Chinese premier, traveled to the Pearl and Yangtze River Deltas with the message that SMEs must be supported in their coastal locations rather than allowing them to close in hopes that they would relocate to the interior.[110] Political triage required employment and the easiest way to ensure that workers would be employed at all would be to support their places of current employment in their current locales. Wen directed banks and local governments to throw money at the problem of SME bankruptcy to address the short-term risks. On November 26, 2008, Xu Zongheng, then mayor of Shenzhen, said that the city faced serious challenges and that he would lead efforts to "cut red tape, lower taxes, and reduce administrative fees for companies operating in the city."[111]

By 6 December, Wang Yang was singing the tune of the premier. Guangdong announced a program to aid SMEs with their "financing difficulties."[112] Yet even in this piece, Wang Yang's conflict is noted: "Predicting that next year would be one of the hardest for all businesses, Guangdong has decided to release at least 8.5 billion yuan in the next two years to speed up construction for planned SME relocations within the province, two years ahead of the original schedule." A few days later, *South China Morning Post* ran an article headlined: "Guangdong

---

[108] Moore 2008.
[109] BBC News 2008.
[110] Zhong 2008.
[111] Mitchell 2008.
[112] Zhai 2008.

Hi-Tech Policy Set to Continue."[113] However, the article also quotes a scholar who follows Wen Jiabao's prescription:

> Ding Li, an economist with the Guangdong Academy of Social Sciences, said one of the tough problems Guangdong enterprises were facing was a lack of resources to upgrade, an issue that could not be solved in a hurry. "You have to help [the labor-intensive enterprises] survive this crisis first, otherwise you just eliminate them from the market without any new companies available to fill the gap," Mr Ding said.[114]

Guangdong set up a loan guarantee program for SMEs hurt by the crisis and pushed firms to participate.[115] This guarantee program and others like it helped move banks to loan funds to SMEs rather than only to the large state-owned firms that have dominated the credit markets from banks for decades.

A third set of political actors, the governments of the interior provinces themselves, demonstrated concerns with the wave of migrants returning to their home villages. The local officials were unable to declare their aversion to taking back floods of jobless migrants even though these returning waves might inundate them and harm social stability.[116] Despite their desire to host these industries in the near future, the interior provinces understood supporting SMEs in their current coastal locales was a short-term delay in their transfer but key to avoiding hordes of unemployed arriving on their doorstep.

The situation in Hubei is illustrative. During October and November 2008, 300,000 rural migrants returned to the province from the coast and Hubei officials ordered local companies wanting to lay off their own workers to "seek approval for job cuts" in an attempt to avoid adding to the long lines of the unemployed.[117] Officials were very worried about social stability being affected by the return of migrants.[118]

Hubei was not unique in being concerned about the flood of disgruntled returnees. By 20 December, Henan was flooded with 3.37 million returnees.[119] Provincial officials estimated that a full 60 percent of these were due to the

---

[113] Guo 2008.

[114] Ibid.

[115] Lai 2009a, b. To be sure, the explosion of loans nationwide did flow to SOEs (Powell 2009; Ramzy 2009; Naughton 2009d), but even these SOEs are, of course, overwhelmingly urban enterprises (Garnaut 2009).

[116] cf. Fewsmith 2009. Cho (2009) contrasts with the Fewsmith take.

[117] See Cheng (2008) for more details.

[118] Chen 2008; Branigan 2009.

[119] Chang et al. 2009a, b.

crisis, implying an additional two million people coming back to the province without jobs.

Have returnees to the interior caused turmoil? Fewsmith argues that the wave of reverse migrants has not really increased difficulties in the country-side.[120] What the article that he cites reports, though, is that there has been an increase in complaints to local governments, but that this increase has been contained and controlled rather than explosive. The returnees are aggrieved, and their return to the countryside has been accompanied by rising frustration there. While adding to the burdens of local governments, this increase in small-scale discontent in the countryside demonstrates the national-level benefits to the Chinese regime of the *hukou* system's diffusion of unemployed migrants. Instead of thousands of unemployed and angry workers marching in coastal cities, bemoaning their fate and the state that has failed them, dozens of tiny disturbances vent discontent into the ether, barely visible from the next village over, let alone from Beijing.

Conclusion

How did the CCP and China's economy survive such a serious economic shock as the Great Recession without significant political instability? This chapter has argued that China's successful navigation of the turbulent waters of the past few years rests on two factors: a strong Keynesian fiscal stimulus package and a *hukou* system of managing urbanization. The former provided jobs directly and through cheap credit to local governments and firms, both large and small. The distribution of central stimulus funds, focusing on the interior of the country rather than the more directly affected coastal provinces, speaks to the regime's continuing determination to spread migrant populations widely throughout the country. The *hukou* system incentivized unemployed migrants to go back to their many villages rather than remain concentrated in coastal cities where organized, large-scale protests would be more likely to damage social stability. The regime's existing institutions and policy responses structured, dispersed, and reduced discontent arising from the Great Recession, allowing China to avoid the troubled waters that the global financial storm riled up.

The Chinese regime moved away from urban bias as its economic and political position strengthened (as detailed in chapter 5). This pro-rural stance can be seen as well in the stimulus, with the notable exception of emergency loans

[120] Fewsmith 2009.

to urban businesses as concerns peaked. The regime's urban-rural redistributive policy changes over time accord with the general argument of the book, but the question remains if the Chinese regime is unique in this regard. The next chapter returns to cross-national analysis to see where the Chinese case fits on the spectrum.

CHAPTER 7

Under Pressure

URBAN BIAS AND EXTERNAL FORCES

The Chinese regime has shaped the process of urbanization during its more than 60 years in power using a variety of measures: inducements to return to the countryside, preventive measures backed by force to keep farmers there, promotion of small cities over megalopolises, and a wide range of policies both extractive and supportive of agriculture. From taking food out of farmers' mouths to abolishing all agricultural taxes and replacing them with subsidies, the regime's redistributive policies along the urban-rural divide have varied dramatically over time. To describe this policy edifice as a single "deal with the devil" is a simplification, a model of reality rather than a full description.[1] Yet, this model can illuminate some aspects of authoritarian politics: threats that regimes face, their response to those threats, and the interactions between threat and response.

China's urban bias has changed over time, in its level and form. During the regime's early years, the economy produced little but agricultural goods, which were taxed heavily to support industrialization. The favored urban proletariat reaped the rewards of these policies. Farmers, understanding that they were on the short end of this arrangement, moved in droves to cities to try to receive their own iron rice bowls. Flush with revenue following the 1994 fiscal reform, Beijing increased its redistribution to the interior regions and rural areas. In doing so, the central government sought to reduce inequalities and ease the pressure on China's myriad cities. During the Great Recession of the late 2000s, the regime made emergency loans to coastal factories but also continued the longer

---

[1] Although, to be fair, it is unclear that one could portray anything but a simplification of such a multidimensional policy space that has varied so much over the different eras of the PRC.

term project of redirecting industrial protection away from the developed coast to the "backward" interior.

The cross-national analysis in the third chapter used a metric for urban bias— relative rate of assistance (RRA) to agriculture—to account for variation in regime survival. But what accounts for variation in urban bias across countries and over time? Who makes a deal with the devil? What kinds of deals are made in different countries at various times?

This chapter returns to the task of explaining variation in urban bias across non-democratic regimes. In broad terms, during moments of political or economic weakness, the Chinese regime relied on urban bias to pacify the cities. When it felt secure and financially fit, it moved away from urban bias. Feeding the unemployed in cities was a crucial part of stabilizing the country upon taking power. Directing investment funds to urban industry was the core of the regime's development strategy when it led an overwhelmingly poverty-stricken and agricultural economy. As the economy has grown in the reform era, the regime has shifted toward "feeding the countryside in turn." During the Great Recession, it temporarily pulled back from reducing urban bias—flooding urban factories with loans—but did so only because of the duress and depth of the recession.

What is harder to parse in China is the extent to which security and ability worked together or separately to encourage the regime to move away from urban bias. That is, did the regime move away from urban bias because its post-Tiananmen strong run gave it the confidence to worry about such long-run problems? Or was it a more budgetary or economic story, in which, the regime, once it had the funds to do so, moved away from urban bias? To separate resources and time horizons requires cross-national data.

Perfectly separating these political and economic effects on policy decisions is fundamentally impossible. A regime's political time horizons expand when its central coffers are filled due to economic growth. Similarly, a regime's economic situation depends in part on the investment decisions of individuals who consider the regime's prospects when they choose to sink their capital in one place rather than another. However, changes affecting the regime may more clearly operate through one channel rather than another. Isolating political and economic pressures on urban bias can improve our understanding of the levers affecting redistributive policy in nondemocracies.

Further complicating matters is that policies are not in constant flux. Inertia is a powerful force in the physical as well as the political world, keeping today's policies roughly the same as those in the past.[2] If policies remain constant over time, political

[2] This is not to critique inertia as problematic for citizens or rulers, only for researchers. Obviously, the fact that inertia dominates policy is informative along some dimensions. It could be the case that transaction costs to change policy are relatively high; that changing policy reinvigorates political

analysis of policy reduces to studies of its origins. Without shifts in policy, it is difficult to isolate the regime's strategy at work to remain in power.[3] Thus inertia allows the true politics at hand to be obscured and regimes to evade analysis. However, there are moments when inertia is taken off of the table by events.

When facing a crisis, policies that might have been acceptable in the past may fall from favor.[4] Most crises, however, are not particularly useful for social scientists as they arise from internal policy or political problems and thus the response to the crisis is, in truth, a response to these prior political situations. That is, the shift in post-crisis policy is often a function of the pre-crisis policy that precipitated the calamity in the first place. For example, China's shift away from urban bias after the Great Leap Forward had everything to do with the disastrous policies of the Leap itself that caused the Famine. The retreat away from Mao's Leap to more tractable and proto-capitalist agricultural policies happened because of the tragedy of the Leap and Mao's stepping back from power.

However, sometimes regimes are buffeted by factors beyond their control. Crises caused by external sources are relatively free from policy legacies. Exogenous shocks to regimes thus have two advantages for students of autocracies. First, identifying causal connections becomes possible; and second, they tend to be moments when regimes overcome policy inertia and shift policy, exposing some of their inner political dynamics.[5]

This hypothetical opportunity to assess the political choices of authoritarian regimes then requires difficult-to-acquire data along two dimensions: domestic policy in autocratic states and exogenous shocks. For the first dimension, the World Bank's agricultural distortions data are used to measure domestic redistributive policy. For the second dimension, two types of shocks are identified that might be expected to move redistributive policy: price shifts facing non-price setting commodity importers and civil wars in neighboring countries.

I argue that exogenous economic and political pressures enter the political calculus of dictators in ways that may change urban-rural redistribution. For

dissatisfaction with the regime even if the policy is an improvement; that the change could be viewed as a sign of weakness by enemies of the regime, foreign or domestic, and those enemies could push for further changes; that the regime is incompetent; that the crucial political situation is static despite changes in what outsiders might view as important political or economic variables, and so on.

[3] Or even if remaining in power is the goal. Many leaders are interested in looting and plunder; others care for a strong legacy; others fight ideological battles. The operative assumption in much of the work in economics on leaders in autocracies is that they are maximizing income, whereas political scientists are more likely to assume that holding on to office is the principal end of the policy decisions of a regime (Padro i Miquel 2004).

[4] It is even possible that the shift in policy might be suboptimal or even worse than the status quo but that the perception of inaction is more costly than standing still with a better policy.

[5] Of course, they are thus different from other internal crises and so one must be careful in inferring too much based on this particular type of crisis to the full set of crises.

example, exogenous economic shocks may occur when importers face oil price shifts. Oil price increases compel regimes under budget constraints to reallocate resources; even "maintaining the status quo" entails shifts in effective levels of taxation and subsidies from the prior period. Additionally, such price changes can lead to inflation and reduced consumption of other goods and services by both governments and private actors, creating or exacerbating extant grievances. In another example, political shocks to the time horizons of leaders may occur when neighboring countries face the outbreak of civil war.[6] Violence in the region may alter regime's expectations about the possibilities of violence domestically and necessitate changes in redistributive policy to respond to this change in perceived threats. To be sure, these external pressures do not dominate the political calculations of nondemocratic regimes. The research design uses these exogenous pressures not because of their relative importance for dictators' decisions but because of the clarity of their causal impact. If these external political forces consistently align with domestic changes in redistribution, then one can be confident of the direction of the causation. I find both economic and political shocks linked with regimes tilting their redistributive policy orientations toward cities. This cross-national finding is consistent with the patterns of China's redistributive policies described in the three prior chapters.

Threats and Urban–Rural Redistribution in Nondemocracies

Leaders have only a limited ability to foresee what patterns of threats are arrayed against them or even to know what threats have brought down rulers in other similar contexts. Every leader of a nondemocratic regime has a unique set of expectations about the variety of threats that he or she faces. Rebellious ethnic rivals in the periphery, well-connected leftist labor-intellectual organizers, party apparatchiks, well-armed militias, religious leaders, and ambitious colonels in the presidential guard are all different agents that might strike fear into the hearts of a leader. Even this list remains an abstraction: Mao did not fear just nameless apparatchiks, he feared that his rule was being usurped by Liu Shaoqi in particular, along with his capitalist roader friends. In addition to agents—known personally by the leader of the regime or not—other kinds of threats can make themselves apparent. Discontent in the countryside or on university campuses might create movements that can turn against the regime or be used by those known political actors to their advantage at the expense of the leader. Again, "the countryside" or "university campuses" are generic types standing in for more

---

[6] See Maves and Braithwaite (2013) for a related analysis.

specific locations, such as a politically active and charismatic astrophysics professor at Anhui Science and Technology University like Fang Lizhi who helped inflame the Tiananmen democracy movement in 1989.

Threats from individuals are likely to induce individual-level responses: denunciations, co-optations, ideological argumentation, and even to the extreme of assassinations. Challenges emanating from social groups can be addressed through both idea and interest-based actions. The analysis below focuses on how pressures coming from the outside of regimes can induce policy changes along the axis of cleavage at the heart of this book: the city vs. the countryside.

To evaluate the effects of resources and time horizons on urban bias, this chapter uses exogenous economic and political pressures to aid in causal identification. The rise and fall of oil prices places economic pressure on oil importers.[7] Political pressures on time horizons arise when civil wars emerge in neighboring countries.

Changes in global oil prices put pressure on oil-importing regimes to shift policy. Price shifts of major commodities can cause coffers to empty or overflow overnight. Negative revenue shocks occur when the oil price spikes; windfalls can occur when prices crash. Governments both purchase oil for consumption by the state and military and often act as a subsidizer of it, maintaining cheap oil for their populations. For example, in Egypt fuel subsidies cost more than those for bread.[8] Unless protected by government policy, private actors suffer from high oil prices. Inflation can result as the price increase trickles down through the economy. Relatedly, consumers and businesses might decrease their purchases of other goods while facing sticker shock from the fuel sector. Changes in key commodity prices act as exogenous pressure to the revenue and economic position of regimes.

One logical response to the budgetary pressure arising from higher oil prices would be to enact austerity policies with redistributive consequences that vary over space. Social spending that is tilted toward cities may be reduced and urban taxes increased to address basic budgetary concerns of regimes. The *austerity hypothesis* argues that exogenous negative economic shocks will reduce urban bias, all else equal. Rather than following this path, I argue that, for political reasons, regimes are likely to further tilt policy in the direction of cities. With limited resources, I expect regimes to engage in triage and focus on the potential for urban instability. Regimes facing a fiscal crunch due to increasing commodity prices move policy toward greater levels of urban favoritism. Alternatively, when

---

[7] The literature assessing the political economy of oil naturally focuses on oil exporters, arguing that regimes with easily accessible non-tax revenue can spur more social spending in general (Morrison 2009) but perhaps less spending during crises (Bueno de Mesquita and Smith 2010).

[8] Blaydes 2010.

oil prices decline, I expect regimes flush with resources to move their redistributive policy mixes away from urban bias toward a policy portfolio that is more balanced across different geographic areas. These expectations are captured in the *economic pressure hypothesis*.

> Economic pressure hypothesis: Regimes facing exogenous negative (positive) economic shocks will shift redistributive policy toward more (less) urban bias, all else equal.

To clarify, any pro-agricultural shift accompanying oil price increases would be counted as support for the austerity hypothesis; decreased support for agriculture under similar circumstances would support the economic pressure hypothesis.[9] When oil prices drop, the economic pressure hypothesis would expect a move away from urban bias, while the austerity hypothesis would expect more tilting toward cities.

A possible difficulty with oil prices serving as the measure of exogenous economic pressure comes from the possibility that the countryside is less dependent on oil than urban areas in the developing nondemocracies under consideration here. In this scenario, policies do not change; instead the costs of maintaining the status quo changes in favor of more spending in urban areas. I treat this scenario as a policy choice. Facing budget constraints, where do regimes allocate resources? Spending more on non-agricultural sectors when oil prices shift reflects the priorities of the regime, albeit by way of omission rather than commission.

Political crises could press regimes to reconsider redistributive policies along the urban-rural divide in manners similar to an economic crisis. Civil wars in nearby countries signal to regimes to consider this form of political threat. A possible interpretation is that nearby civil wars will be associated with a retreat from urban bias due to their link with rural insurgencies. Insurgency, a dominant technology in civil wars, is a phenomenon likely to take place in the rural periphery.[10] Stoking concerns of such a threat might induce the regime to decrease agricultural tax levels and increase spending in rural areas in a bid to assuage rural grievances before conflict may erupt. The *insurgency hypothesis* argues that exogenous political shocks in the form of civil wars in the region will shift redistributive policy toward less urban bias, all else equal.

---

[9] For instance, facing an oil price increase, an oil importer cuts back on agriculture. The measure used here, the relative rate of assistance to agriculture (see the data section below for more details), decreases, which is treated as increase in urban bias.

[10] Fearon and Laitin 2003. Insurgency's dominance as a civil war technology declines in the post-Cold War era but remains significant (Kalyvas and Balcells 2010).

However, I argue that nearby civil wars shorten a regime's time horizons and instead should be associated with increases in urban bias. Concerned with the possibility of contagion or spill-over effects, regimes focus on addressing potential short-term threats to their rule. By forcing regimes to consider their political mortality, choices might become skewed toward shoring up support in the short run and more accepting of long-term costs. Political crises are captured by civil wars breaking out in neighboring countries. As with the economic pressure hypothesis, a negative political shock induces a shift toward urban bias as seen in the *political pressure hypothesis*.

> Political pressure hypothesis: Regimes facing negative (positive) exogenous political shocks will shift redistributive policy toward more (less) urban bias, all else equal.

While the principal purpose of the chapter is to investigate these hypotheses, a number of additional factors might affect redistributive policy that should be accounted for. The developing world is biased against agriculture in its economic policies, yet rich countries tend to do the opposite and subsidize agricultural producers. This difference could be due to any number of factors: the small number of producers of food in rich countries compared with the large number of food consumers who have difficulty organizing; progressive inclinations in rich countries; maintenance of domestic food production as a luxury for the rich either in terms of preserving cultural heritage or as a security investment.[11] Following this pattern then, one might expect decreases in urban bias as nondemocratic countries increase their level of economic development. One may hypothesize that regimes with higher levels of development will have less urban-biased redistributive policies, all else equal. A final potential confounder for the analysis is a country's degree of democracy. While the scope of the analysis remains nondemocratic regimes, regimes with relatively greater levels of democracy possibly might be beholden to their rural majorities and thus, be less urban-biased.

Data

The first question for the analyst is the unit of observation. Given that the interest here is in cross-national comparisons of redistributive policy, the natural unit is the country-year in nondemocratic contexts. Metrics coding the regime type of country-years can be separated into two broad categories depending on

---

[11] Olson 1965; Varshney 1995.

their conception of democracy as a dichotomous or continuous variable.[12] As the claims of the chapter refer to nondemocratic rather than less democratic regimes, a dichotomous measure is preferred. The data used to limit the scope of the analysis to only nondemocratic country-years are from Cheibub and Gandhi, an update from the Przeworski et al. codings.[13] Regime types are coded as described above in chapter 3.

While urban bias has long been identified as critical to politics in these states, measurement has proven elusive until recently. Systematic and quantitative analyses attempting to explain urban bias levels (either as an independent or dependent variable) use proxies.[14] Black market premium, a measure of the extent to which a currency is overvalued, is the most common proxy.[15] These proxies have the advantage of being relatively easy to acquire but come at the cost of distance to the actual construct being proxied; as such I do not use them.

Instead, I again turn to the dataset on distortions to agricultural markets to proxy more directly for redistributive policy along the rural-urban divide here, as I did for the third chapter.[16] The relative rate of assistance to agriculture (RRA) shows not how much the policies of the state are assisting agriculture, but how much assistance is going to agriculture relative to other sectors of the economy.[17] The RRA and changes to it measures urban bias, the dependent variables in the analysis; as in chapter 3, I transform RRA so that an increase in the measure reflects an increase in urban bias.[18] Table 7.1 presents the list of countries under analysis; that is, those countries where RRA data was collected with at least one nondemocratic year during the period in question.

The principal independent variables are exogenous economic and political shocks. Economic shocks come from oil price shifts. Oil price data come from the St. Louis Federal Reserve's historical data series on the price of a reference

[12] Munck and Verkuilen 2002.

[13] Cheibub and Gandhi 2004; Przeworski et al. 2000. The results described below hold when the data is delimited by a less restrictive criterion, namely only those country-years with a Polity Democracy score above 7 are removed from the data.

[14] Ades and Glaeser 1995.

[15] The premium that one must pay in the black market for outside currencies with the domestic currency above the official over-valued rate. An over-valued currency has distributional implications that often align with urban bias in developing countries. Having one's domestic currency over-valued represents a tax on exporters and a subsidy to importers. As the economies of these states tend to be predominantly net exporters of agricultural (i.e., rural) goods and net importers of industrial (i.e., urban) goods, a high black market premium represents a pro-urban tilt in policy.

[16] Anderson and Valenzuela 2008.

[17] As the RRA measure requires additional information in order to be created, it is not surprising that it is available for a smaller set of the country-years under examination. As it happens, in the universe of country-years under examination in this study, these measures are highly correlated ($r > 0.9$).

[18] The clarifying transformation performed was to multiply the RRA by -100.

Table 7.1 **Country List**

Argentina	Ethiopia*	Nigeria	Taiwan
Bangladesh	Ghana	Pakistan*	Tanzania
Brazil	Indonesia	Philippines	Thailand
Cameroon	Kazakhstan*	Portugal	Turkey
Chile	Kenya	Russia	Uganda
China	Korea, South	Senegal	Vietnam
Cote d'Ivoire	Madagascar	South Africa	Zambia
Dominican Republic	Malaysia	Spain	Zimbabwe
Ecuador	Mexico*	Sri Lanka	
Egypt	Mozambique	Sudan	

Note: Ethiopia and Pakistan are divided into two country codes by the Quality of Government team based on their loss of territory (Ethiopia in 1992; Pakistan in 1971). All years for Mexico and Kazakhstan are dropped when examining oil importing country-years (tables 7.3 and 7.4). Other countries also have some years omitted in tables 7.3 and 7.4 due to data availability problems.

oil, West Texas Intermediate.[19] The data are monthly and transformed into average yearly prices and percent changes in price for the analysis in this chapter.[20] First, a continuous *Oil Price Change* measure represents pressure coming from that economic dimension that might influence geographic redistribution within a nondemocracy in a given country-year. Discrete metrics of *Oil Spike* (dramatic increases in the world price for oil) and *Oil Collapse* (dramatic decreases in the world price for oil) are also included, representing economic collapses and windfalls for these regimes.[21]

How oil price changes affect a given regime requires data on its status as a net producer or consumer of oil. I utilize estimates of oil rents within a state from the World Bank's Environmental Economics dataset to create a variable delineating regimes, with and without significant rents from petroleum, with a rule dividing the groups set at $100 per capita.[22] Only those states without these large rents were coded as potentially negatively affected by price increases. The *Import Share* is the share of energy use in a given country that comes from imports, with

---

[19] Data available at http://research.stlouisfed.org/fred2/series/OILPRICE.

[20] End year prices and price changes yield similar results.

[21] The Oil Spike variable takes on a value of one in all years where the average oil price change exceeds the median annual change (0.6 percent) plus one standard deviation of the average oil price change (30.1 percent) and zero otherwise. Seven years with RRA data meet this threshold. Oil Collapse is coded as one in years with 10 percent declines in the oil price and zero otherwise. Six collapses are coded in the data.

[22] World Bank Environmental Indicators; Dunning 2008. I follow Dunning and others in using the $100 per capita threshold.

data from the World Development Indicators. Those countries more reliant on imports receive more pressure on their economies and finances than do those less reliant on them.

The political pressure hypothesis and the alternative insurgency hypothesis use the number of civil wars in the region to account for urban bias. Region data come from the UN Statistical Bureau, specifically its "detailed" set which divides global territory into 22 regions.[23] Civil war data come from the UCDP dataset. *Regional Civil Wars* reflects the number of civil wars taking place in a region in a given year.[24]

The rest of the hypotheses use variables commonly found in the statistical analyses of social scientists. Levels of economic development are measured by GDP per capita. Urban population shares come from the World Bank Distortions to Agricultural Incentives project. The continuous scale democracy scores, within the set of dictatorship years, come from Polity 2.[25] Table 7.2 presents summary statistics for all of the variables used in the analysis.

Analysis

The analyses support both the economic and political pressure hypotheses. Oil Price Change consistently has positive and statistically significant coefficients, as expected in the economic pressure hypothesis. This gives strong support for the notion that negative economic shocks push policy away from agriculture and toward further urban bias. There are four tables that summarize the results, two for each of the economic and political pressure hypotheses. The first presents the basic results, and a second emphasizes the causal connections between the variables. For the economic pressure hypothesis, this is a dosage test: those countries who import more oil should be more seriously affected by price increases. For the political pressure hypothesis, I present a placebo test, where the possibility of random correlations is reduced by showing that different configurations of regional civil wars and urban bias that cannot be casually related are not correlated.

Table 7.3 shows that urban bias levels are higher, all else equal, when there are oil price increases. This result holds across numerous specifications: the presence

---

[23] http://unstats.un.org/unsd/methods/m49/m49regin.htm.

[24] The analyses that use this measure use changes in the number of civil wars rather than levels; countries that are currently experiencing civil wars are dropped from the analysis, although the results are robust to dropping only country-years where a civil war starts instead of all years where a country is experiencing a civil war.

[25] "Scale ranges from 0-10 where 0 is least democratic and 10 most democratic."

Table 7.2 **Summary Statistics for Analyses of Urban Bias and External Pressure**

Variable	Observations	Median	Mean	Standard Deviation	Min	Max
Urban Bias	914	22.69	22.23	31.90	−141.50	94.62
Δ Urban Bias	914	−0.44	−0.37	15.26	−100.00	157.26
Δ Oil Price	51	0.57	9.08	30.12	−46.23	167.85
Δ Regional Civil Wars	914	0	0.03	0.88	−3	4
Real GDP per Capita, Logged	914	7.54	7.64	0.85	5.81	9.63
Polity 2	914	−6	−3.66	5.00	−9	10
Year[a]	914	1982	1,982.22	11.98	1,957	2,004
Import Share	455	0.17	0.25	0.20	0.0003	0.83
Oil Price * Import Interaction	455	0.72	4.01	14.56	−32.33	134.35
Oil Price Spike	Occur in 1974, 1979, 1980, 1999, 2000, 2004, and 2005					
Oil Price Collapse	Occur in 1986, 1988, 1991, 1993, 1998, 2001					

[a] In tables 7.3 and 7.4, the linear time trend variable "Year" takes values from 2 to 49 rather than the year value to keep the estimated constants and other variables in similar orders of magnitude.

or absence of the lagged urban bias level, whether time effects are accounted for via a linear time trend (*Year*) or year fixed effects, and the inclusion of covariates (*Real GDP per capita* and *Polity Score*).

Interestingly, price increases drive the economic pressure hypothesis's support. Exogenous economic pressure affects urban bias levels but only negative shocks have the expected effect. Oil price drops do not lower levels of urban bias. These findings are consistent with oil price changes ratcheting up urban bias, as price increases yield more urban bias that subsequent price declines do not reverse. Such urban-biased subsidies might act in ways similar to social welfare programs in developed economies: once created, they are extremely difficult to roll back.[26]

The economic pressure hypothesis implies that changes in oil prices should cause regimes to change in urban bias. The previous analysis showed that country-years where oil prices increased were associated with higher levels of urban bias. Table 7.4 uses changes in urban bias as the dependent variable and

[26] Pierson 1996.

Table 7.3 **Urban Bias Levels Correspond with Oil Price Shocks**

DV: Urban Bias	Model 7.3.1	Model 7.3.2	Model 7.3.3	Model 7.3.4
Δ Oil Price	0.08***	0.07***		0.11***
	(0.02)	(0.02)		(0.03)
Oil Price Spike			2.96***	
			(0.91)	
Oil Price Collapse			2.32	
			(1.99)	
Real GDP per Capita, Logged				−5.24*
				(2.86)
Polity Score				−0.32**
				(0.12)
Year		−0.72***	−0.24***	
		(0.23)	(0.05)	
Lagged DV	0.79***		0.77***	0.76***
	(0.06)		(0.06)	(0.07)
Constant	0.97	42.69***	10.60***	36.35
	(4.30)	(5.85)	(2.09)	(22.04)
Observations	882	908	882	865
R-squared	0.68	0.14	0.64	0.68
Number of Countries	38	38	38	37
Year FE	YES	NO	NO	YES
Country FE	YES	YES	YES	YES

Robust standard errors in parentheses.
***$p < 0.01$, **$p < 0.05$, *$p < 0.1$.

lends further support to the hypothesis in two ways, showing that urban bias changes with changes in economic pressures and that this effect is more dramatic where the pressure is greatest.

First, changes in oil prices help account for changes in urban bias, and in the direction expected by the economic pressure hypothesis. The austerity hypothesis receives no support in the analyses here. The claim here is a modest one. A global increase in oil prices will affect oil importers but obviously is not the only factor that regimes consider when adjusting their mix of taxation and subsidies along the urban-rural divide.

Second, regimes that import a larger share of their energy should receive a larger dosage of the treatment of oil price increases. As such, they should be

Table 7.4 **Changes in Oil Prices Predict Changes in Urban Bias**

DV: Δ Urban Bias	Model 7.4.1	Model 7.4.2	Model 7.4.3
Δ Oil Price	0.03**		−0.02
	(0.01)		(0.02)
Oil Price Spike		1.92**	
		(0.81)	
Import Share			−0.77
			(7.44)
Import Share * Δ Oil Price			0.15**
			(0.08)
Year	−0.06***	−0.07***	−0.05
	(0.02)	(0.02)	(0.04)
Constant	0.39	0.73	0.61
	(0.44)	(0.46)	(2.37)
Observations	882	882	451
Number of Countries	38	38	30
Country FE	YES	YES	YES

Robust standard errors in parentheses.
***$p < 0.01$, **$p < 0.05$, *$p < 0.1$.

the ones becoming more biased toward their cities. Model 7.4.3 shows that the interaction term of oil price change and share of energy imports is positive as implied by the economic pressure hypothesis. Heavily treated states react with greater levels of policy shift than do those with lower levels of treatment.

The political pressure hypothesis argues that shortening of the time horizons of leaders may also cause regimes to shift to more urban bias as the prospect of long-term survival wanes. Table 7.5 summarizes a set of empirical tests of the hypothesis, finding consistent support.

Neighboring countries entering into (or concluding) civil wars change the assessments of domestic politicians to increase (or decrease) urban bias. Changes in the number of nearby civil wars are linked with changes in urban bias in the expected directions. An additional civil war started in a region increases urban bias by 0.1 standard deviations after controlling for country and year fixed effects. This result holds with the inclusion of covariates such as real GDP per capita and Polity 2 score as seen in Models 7.5.2 and 7.5.3.

As was the case with changes in oil prices, it is clear that nearby civil wars are not the principal sources of domestic redistributive policy, yet any systematic pattern between nearby civil wars and urban bias comes from the former causing

Table 7.5 **Changes in Nearby Civil Wars Linked to Changes in Urban Bias**

DV: Δ Urban Bias	Model 7.5.1	Model 7.5.2	Model 7.5.3
Δ Regional Civil Wars	1.57*	1.56*	1.54*
	(0.86)	(0.86)	(0.84)
Δ Real GDP per Capita, Logged		−6.88	−10.6
		(9.59)	(9.98)
Δ Polity 2 Score			−0.16
			(0.28)
Constant	−15.7***	−15.6***	−15.6***
	(4.94)	(5.09)	(5.15)
Observations	765	760	751
R-squared	0.109	0.109	0.110
Number of Countries	39	39	39
Year FE	YES	YES	YES
Country FE	YES	YES	YES

Robust standard errors in parentheses.
***$p < 0.01$, **$p < 0.05$, *$p < 0.1$.

the latter, rather than the other way around. The results support the expectation that regimes shift to urban bias where it is most critical—in cities—when time horizons are shortened.

One potential concern with this analysis is that some other factor might somehow be the source of both nearby civil wars and changes in urban bias, although what factor that might be is unclear. Table 7.6 presents the results of a placebo test to assist in ruling out that possibility. Placebo tests can help establish causality by showing that a non-treatment should have no effect on the outcomes in question.[27] The independent variable is the same as in Table 7.5. The only change has been in the dependent variable. In Table 7.5, I used contemporaneous urban bias policy change, which was increased in years with increases in civil wars in neighboring countries. Here in Table 7.6, I lag the dependent variable. Changes in civil wars today should not be able to affect urban bias changes in the previous year, as time moves forward. Causality in the reverse direction, on the

---

[27] In medicine, one is interested in the effect of the treatment absent the trappings of the treatment. Comparing the efficacy of a doctor in a white lab coat giving a patient a sugar pill versus a doctor in a white lab coat giving a patient the drug in question allows direct comparison of the drug versus the sugar pill controlling for the environment of treatment (Sekhon 2009).

Table 7.6 **Placebo—Urban Bias Changes Not Caused by Subsequent Civil Wars**

DV: Prior Change in Urban Bias	Placebo 7.6.1	Placebo 7.6.2	Placebo 7.6.3
Δ Regional Civil Wars	0.24	0.30	0.64
	(0.90)	(0.88)	(0.70)
Δ Real GDP per Capita, Logged		−14.0**	−9.05*
		(5.22)	(5.23)
Δ Polity 2 Score			−0.45
			(0.44)
Constant	−13.9***	−15.3***	−15.1***
	(3.95)	(4.74)	(4.60)
Observations	739	735	914
R-squared	0.111	0.114	0.099
Number of Countries	39	39	40
Year FE	YES	YES	YES
Country FE	YES	YES	YES

Note: Placebos 7.6.1 and 7.6.2 include only country-years where the home country in question is not coded as having its own civil war. Placebo 7.6.3 relaxes this restriction and only omits those cases where a civil war starts in the home country. Robust standard errors in parentheses.
***$p < 0.01$, **$p < 0.05$, *$p < 0.1$.

other hand, is possible chronologically but politically implausible—changes in the urban bias level causing civil wars in nearby countries.

The results summarized in Table 7.6 bear this out. The effect moves from accounting for urban bias changes to being unable to do so; the point estimate of the effect size for changes in the number of civil wars in the region drops to less than one-sixth its magnitude in Table 7.5 (0.24 vs. 1.57). While the treatment had the expected effect in the political pressure hypothesis, the placebo using a time-shifted dependent variable that could not possibly be caused by the independent variable shows no effect, furthering our confidence that the results here are not simply random correlations.

Discussion

The results point to exogenous changes in economic situations and political circumstances leading to changes in geographic redistributive policy in nondemocracies. In this section, I try to explain these patterns and describe the pieces of this puzzle that are not captured in the analysis.

The book's argument expects policy to be directed to the benefit of those who are able to act collectively during a political or economic crisis. Thus, those who could participate in an urban protest are likely to be beneficiaries of urban subsidies. Opponents in a civil war or insurgency, on the other hand, are unlikely to be bought off or remain bought off with side payments. Guerrillas and states broker peace deals with difficulty as states face a commitment problem once the rebels have disarmed.[28] Redistributing to potential insurgents follows a similar logic. The state would not like to subsidize a potential group of insurgents in time t only to find that the group used the funds to further arm itself and increase demands from the state in period $t + 1$ and into the future. Thus, even if conditions are ripe for rural insurgency, insurgents remain unlikely targets for redistributive policy. In a struggle being waged through armed, violent conflict, military materiel factors heavily in assessments of the probability of victory or subsequent bargaining. Protestors, however, are engaging fundamentally in ideological conflict where mass citizen support for the cause matters. Money can be converted into threats more easily in the arena of violence (i.e., rural uprisings) than in the arena of protests (i.e., urban uprisings). Second, a general subsidy to urbanites is unlikely to be wholly captured by opponents of the regime, whereas shifting resources to areas under insurgent control might fund the insurgency. Redistributive policy in the face of pressure—from political or economic sources—is likely to push towards shoring up regime support in cities.

The analysis above examines urban-rural redistribution, but other policy shifts to similar ends may be complementary or substitutive to these moves. First, leaders may promise transfers toward urban areas where protests are occurring but be removed prior to implementing such promises. In Tunisia, Ben Ali promised precisely this: redistribution toward unemployed college graduates that were behind much of the anti-regime protesting.[29] However, Ben Ali was ousted before being able to carry out this policy change. As such, the policy change did not happen.[30]

A second and related change consistent with the argument but not captured by the design is a cynical promise that goes unfulfilled. A regime facing a temporary threat may make grandiose promises in the hopes of defusing the situation while danger seems in the offing. When the revolutionary moment passes, this promise might be watered down or done away with altogether. Saudi Arabia's gargantuan preemptive buyoff of potential opponents in the wake of the oustings of Ben Ali and Mubarak served a political purpose at the time. Having emerged from the

---

[28] Fearon 1998.

[29] Schraeder and Redissi 2011.

[30] Here, if the country remained nondemocratic and failed to implement such a change, then its inclusion goes against the findings here. If the country transitions to democracy, it simply drops out of the data under analysis.

danger zone, the Saudi regime has stabilized to levels approaching its situation prior to the crisis, allowing it at least to contemplate walking back from those commitments.[31] Again, the promise of shifts in policy is consistent with the argument, although the lack of the need to follow through does go against the grain.

Third, the concessions in favor of urban over rural interests in a moment of economic or political crisis might take different forms than the policy changes reflected in the urban bias score. Increasing the political representation or institutional power of urban interests would be a buyoff of urban interests in a moment of crisis, yet the actual policy effects that such a change might entail (if subsequently implemented) would be seen only in the middle to long run, rather than in the immediate wake of the crisis. Such patterns of institutional change followed by policy shifts fundamentally are congruent with the argument but would actively weaken the statistical findings. That the results hold as they do despite this countervailing effect increases one's confidence in the overall argument.

Finally, the analysis here focuses on the important urban-rural dimension of political conflict in nondemocracies in the developing world; yet policy shifts might occur along other dimensions based on threats emanating from different cleavages in ways consistent with the broader argument. This analysis captures a small slice of the political strategies of regimes facing economic and political crises along a single dimension of potential conflict. Threats can and do emerge from a multitude of directions. Leadership of a nation-state affords a dictator a wide range of potential "goodies" to distribute to those who might be in a position to make demands. For instance, a leader may increase military spending, or make promises thereof, following a political crisis to reduce the probability of a military coup. As coups account for a plurality of nondemocratic regime transitions, increased military spending or other efforts to reduce the likelihood of such an eventuality—including perhaps making an agreement with a relevant regional or international superpower—could be smart decisions.

Similar behavior has been analyzed in various nondemocratic regimes. As noted in previous chapters, the Chinese central government directs resources to assuage the grievances of protestors and activists.[32] Simultaneously, lower level officials receive black marks for allowing such violations of social harmony to occur. Particular kinds of protest—"rightful resistance"—can become acceptable in a nondemocratic regime where center-local divides take center stage.[33] In Russia, Treisman suggests that local protests can lead central officials to direct

---

[31] For more details on the Saudi response to the Arab Spring from the perspective of 2013, see Wehrey 2013; Fattah 2013.

[32] Cai 2010.

[33] Lorentzen 2010; O'Brien and Li 2006.

resources to restive areas.[34] Of course, rewarding troublemakers who call attention to social ills can bring others out of the woodwork to such a degree that
overall regime stability is compromised. The Chinese regime tends to follow
a two-pronged strategy of arresting instigators and organizers while respond-
ing financially to the injustices that the instigators brought to light. The regime
simultaneously reduces tension and deters leading collective action.

Conclusion

The blossoming of work on nondemocratic regimes over the last decade has
improved our understanding of the determinants of regime survival. Political
science has seen a surge of interest in questions related to nondemocracies in
recent years. Multiple typologies of nondemocratic regimes have been shown
to account for variation in their durability, economic growth, probability of
democratization, inequality, and post-tenure fate of leaders.[35] Similarly, the presence of institutions—namely, elections and legislatures—aligns with long-lived
regimes and economic growth.[36] Yet, notably the bulk of this research assesses
outcomes of political choices rather than the policy choices themselves. While
we increasingly are able to know which regimes will endure and which will not,
less is known about the internal distributive politics of these regimes.

To identify causal patterns from the thicket of endogenous effects in a
regime's internal policies, this chapter uses pressures regimes face on redistributive policy arising from external forces. Oil prices and nearby civil wars affect the
political calculus of nondemocratic leaders, with both economic and political
pressures leading to policy shifts consistent with increases in urban bias during
troubled times. Yet this policy is no panacea; it is a deal with the devil, undercutting regimes by increasing urban concentration in the long run.

The economic and political forces nondemocratic regimes encounter come in
a myriad of forms, and accordingly these regimes respond in diverse ways using
all of the tools at their disposal. Repression and the threat of force ultimately lie
at the core of regime power in nondemocracies, but the evidence here shows
that regimes also adjust economic redistributive policy in the face of pressure.

China's changing levels of urban bias align with the global patterns of nondemocratic regimes presented here. The Chinese regime chose to tilt toward

---

[34] Treisman 1999. This pattern of behavior was predictable to such an extent that local leaders
inflamed passions and manufactured protests in order to grab additional central funds.

[35] e.g., Debs and Goemans 2010; Jennifer Gandhi 2008; Geddes 1999; Hadenius and Teorell
2007; Magaloni 2006; Wright 2008.

[36] e.g., Blaydes 2010; Boix 2003; Gandhi and Przeworski 2006; Lust-Okar 2005, 2006;
Wright 2008.

cities upon taking power when it was solidifying its rule—as described in chapter 4—and during tough times, such as the Great Recession, as discussed in the previous chapter. It moved away from urban bias when its resources and time horizons expanded, as described in chapter 5. The Chinese regime has tacked back and forth in its urban bias—and through its migration-restricting *hukou* system—found a loophole to the Faustian bargain of urban bias. These policy choices have allowed it to manage its urbanization in ways that aid the regime's survival by mitigating the risk of urban unrest.

CHAPTER 8

Conclusion

The Arab Spring saw numerous nondemocratic regimes collapse. Protests by the people in cities around North Africa and the Middle East destroyed the political bases of these regimes. Yet China's long-lived CCP-led regime coasted through this storm with barely a whisper of discontent rattling in the winds. The Chinese regime shared many characteristics with those that were ousted—particularly Mubarak's NDP-led Egyptian regime. Beijing, like Cairo, is a massive city that is the seat of a historic empire. Cairo, however, like most large capital cities in developing countries, was plagued with cankerous slums, while Beijing was without such large clusters of the urban poor in nonstate spaces.

The book argues that the shape of Chinese urbanization and city structure are part of the story of the regime's longevity. The management of urbanization that has taken place in the PRC during the CCP's rule has shaped the lives of its citizens and the political fate of the regime. Cities are dangerous due to the ability of their citizens to act collectively in massive numbers at a moment's notice and at the political and economic heart of the regime. As such, regimes treat their urbanites—these members of the industrial and cultural vanguard—well. Such lavish treatment has costs, and those costs are overwhelmingly placed on the backs of those in the rural agricultural sector.

The political argument for urban bias is compelling, but it has unintended consequences, like so many initially appealing policies. In this case, tilting policies to favored large cities may aid in appeasing restive urbanites today but increases their number over time as farmers escape the yoke of the peasant burden to enjoy the fruits of urban subsidies. The second-order effect of inducing urban concentration undercuts the purpose of urban bias and creates cities that are ever larger and more difficult to govern. The Faustian bargain of urban bias is too appealing to dictators who know that they only have one shot at power. The downside costs spiraling into the future are insignificant when compared with the more pressing need to pacify potential protestors in the here and now.

The cross-national analysis in chapter 3 shows support for three basic contentions of the argument. First, since 1950, authoritarian regimes leading countries with high levels of urban concentration do not endure when compared with those without such dominant megalopolises to govern. Second, urban bias induces urban concentration over time, suggesting that spreading the spoils of rural taxes in cities does indeed induce individuals to move to favored cities. Third, the Faustian bargain of urban bias helps regimes endure today but aids in their destruction over time.

The Chinese CCP-led regime has managed urbanization by "grasping for stones" to keep from falling into the raging waters of history that flow below it. The regime pushed for strong industrialization as early as the 1950s but found farmers flocked to cities, unwilling to bear the load of the country's drive to become a manufacturing power. The regime maintained policies benefiting urban workers but stopped movement into cities by way of migration restrictions—its *hukou* system—finding a loophole in the Faustian bargain. The fourth chapter detailed the *hukou* system's rise, its disastrous consequences during the Great Leap Forward, and its various reforms. One reason why China has prospered during the past 30 years has been a willingness to allow farmers to escape the drudgery and poverty of the countryside and move to urban factories. The fifth chapter explored China's reduction of agricultural taxation and increased spending in the rural interior. Yet even in China's moves away from urban bias, there is evidence of consideration of the effect on urban instability. Fiscal transfers to rural counties are in part determined by the economic situation in nearby urban areas. Transfers to rural areas are consistent with attempts to mitigate potential migration to troubled cities and thereby reduce concerns for instability by improving conditions in the surrounding rural counties.

The political utility of China's stubborn maintenance of the *hukou* system and collective ownership of rural land was evident during the Great Recession of 2008-9. As described in chapter 6, tens of millions of migrants lost their jobs in factories and dispersed to their rural interior homelands. Rural land acted successfully as a safety net. The regime's massive stimulus program—financial and fiscal—cranked into high gear within a few months of the depth of the crisis in the fall of 2008. The Great Recession sparked discontent within China, but China's *hukou* system and stimulus structured, dispersed, and reduced that discontent to limit the possibility of serious political turmoil.

The Chinese regime has shifted away from urban bias since the late 1990s as its economy has prospered, illustrating that increased resources make it easier for governments to extricate themselves from the Faustian bargain. However, even China has fallen back on urban bias during the Great Recession, extending massive loans to urban businesses at the height of the crisis. Cross-national data similarly show that other authoritarian regimes increase urban bias in tough times. In budgetary affairs, this focus on the short-term often entails increasing levels of urban bias, as demonstrated in chapter 7, insulating regimes from potential tumult.

Four broader conclusions can be drawn from the argument and evidence of the book. Next, I discuss the utility of China as a case that can improve general understanding of nondemocratic politics and the idea that the Internet will displace cities as the communal forum in the years to come. Finally, I turn to future expectations of urbanization and regime survival in China.

First, the study of nondemocracies has been focused on revolutions and democratization. While both fascinating and significant, political accounts directed at these foci do not perfectly fit the patterns and narratives of regime survival that underlie this work. Revolution is a rare cause of regimes being overthrown, and democracy is a rare outcome at the end of a nondemocratic regime's reign. Although threats of revolution and democratization motivate politics in nondemocracies, a nondemocratic regime is replaced in most cases under more prosaic terms by another nondemocratic regime, without being directly ousted from power at the hand of a mass revolution or through a vote.

Second, the political power of the masses can be felt even absent collective action. Elites have long been the center of attention in the study of nondemocratic regimes and rightly so. However, this perspective underplays the importance of threats and instances of collective action on elites and intra-elite interactions. The elephant in the room may not need to stir to make its presence felt. Even more, engorged cities and impenetrable slums inhibit the ability of regimes to observe and understand the lives of their citizens. Without insight into the lives of their population, regimes are less able to anticipate incipient threats and nip them in the bud before they flower into social movements.

Third, political phenomena occur over time and policies that resolve problem X today may create problem Y next year. Second-order effects and the long-term implications of political decisions have received relatively scant attention by social scientists. While such an analysis may unwind previously accepted general laws, it also speaks to a maturing field of knowledge; understanding first-order effects is a necessary step to understanding the full ramifications of policies, but it is insufficient. The first-order political logic of urban bias is significant, but so too are its ancillary effects, which undercut its primary purposes.

Fourth, the argument calls for disaggregating modernization. Countries over time have been exposed to changes in the different aspects of modernization—economic development, industrialization, education, urbanization, and specialization, among others. These different factors can have political effects that point in opposite directions. China's experience of industrializing while managing urbanization is but one example of the utility of examining the effects of different components of modernization separately rather than as a whole, since there is no universal modernizing pathway that all countries experience.

China as Appropriate Case Study

Does studying China help shed light on the broader political dynamics of urbanization, redistribution, and nondemocratic regime survival? This book makes the case for a positive reply by iterating between Chinese and cross-national analyses. The arguments are congruent and supported across these different levels of analysis. The limits of the political utility of urban bias are exposed in a long-lived regime such as China's, which instituted its *hukou* system to manage urban inflows before cities were overrun with unemployed migrants. In a regime that collapses quickly, the long-term costs of urban bias may never appear.

The CCP-led PRC is an outlier along many dimensions. Of these, the immense population of China, today usually given as 1.3 billion people, stands out.[1] China now has over half of its population living in urban areas, totaling nearly 700 million individuals. Obviously, the logistics and even comprehension of such numbers is anything but trivial. For the analyses here, one concern is the measure of urban concentration. Beijing is a very large city—around 20 million people as of 2012—but because of China's massive urban population, Beijing's share of the urban population is miniscule and near the bottom of the table of nondemocratic regimes. It is implausible that Beijing could hold anywhere near the median level of urban concentration found in the post-World War II dataset used in chapter 3 (35 percent) or indeed even half of that amount, as the lower figure would still imply a city of over 100 million people. Yet looking within China's urbanization policies, it is clear that the regime has had concerns similar to those present in smaller countries. Beijing's population has been the most controlled in the country since the founding of the PRC and is likely to continue to be into the future. Party elites laid bare the calculus behind this concern during the Great Leap Forward's darkest days: Beijing's citizens needed to be fed, even if that meant starving farmers.

In terms of comparing the Chinese regime to regimes in other countries, there are three serious differences that need to be addressed. These principal ways in which the CCP differs from many other nondemocratic regimes is that it is a

---

[1] The 2010 Census figure for 1 November 2010 is 1,339,724,852 people, which is 39 million more than the 1.3 billion number usually given. While in context this seems a reasonable rounding decision, when examined from a different perspective, say that of the population of states of the United States, it would place it at the top of the heap, with the "rounding error" having millions more people than California (36.8 million).

party-led regime, it is communist, and its governing capacity is seen as greater than that of other dictatorships.[2] While there are differences between the Chinese case and other authoritarian regimes, I do not believe that these concerns invalidate the applicability of facts and insights garnered in the Chinese case to other countries. In all three ways, I believe the objections to be overstated and that China is more comparable to other regimes than is often assumed. In particular, factors that distinguish China are seen as dichotomous when they actually are arrayed along a spectrum.

The "partyness" of the Chinese regime makes it part of the largest category of nondemocratic regimes at the start of the twenty-first century and does not disqualify extrapolation from this case.[3] Party regimes in autocracies, often referred to as Single Party or Hegemonic Party regimes, differ from other types of nondemocracies because a political party rules rather than an individual, family, military junta, or religious leader. Dictators often have a nominal party attached to their political movement, especially in the increasingly common set of dictatorships with elections.[4] Discriminating between parties that are simply names without any sort of reach and genuine parties is nontrivial.[5] Political parties should be load-bearing, not ornamental; they need to be credible "power-sharing arrangements with their ruling coalitions" to have force.[6] To return to the question of case selection then, the objection that the CCP regime in China is different because it is a party regime seems to view parties as a dichotomous variable, whereas in many ways the variation looks continuous. The Chinese regime is likely viewed as on one edge of this spectrum in 2013, but its position has varied over time as the personal political influence of Deng Xiaoping and especially Mao Zedong trumped the institutions of the party at a number of key junctures in the past 60 years. So the "partyness" of China does not separate it so dramatically from other dictatorships as to make a comparison uninformative.

The second potential objection to using the CCP-led regime as a case study is the second 'C' in CCP, that is, its status not only as a party regime but as a Communist Party regime. Some have argued that left-wing dictatorships come to power through different means, face different challenges, and have different

---

[2] It should be noted that in the cross-national regressions, some of these regime characteristics are controlled for and thus do not affect the analysis of the variables in question.

[3] Magaloni 2006.

[4] Ibid.

[5] A prominent coding of autocratic regime types is offered in Geddes 1999. Hadenius and Teorrell 2007; Magaloni 2006; and Cheibub and Gandhi 2008 all put forward alternative codings as well. Chapter 3 discusses this subject in more depth. A new dataset is also available (Geddes, Wright, and Frantz 2012).

[6] Magaloni 2006, 1. Credibility can be a function of the institutional features of the autocracy, such as having a legislature or elections, especially multiparty elections (Gandhi 2008; Magaloni 2006).

supporters than do other—namely, right-wing—dictatorships.[7] Again, those who take this position treat the divide as dichotomous, with China falling on the left-wing side and as such imply that China should not be compared with right-wing dictatorships. The use of the terms naming this divide, left and right, follows a traditional conceptualization of a unidimensional political spectrum with relatively redistributionist, progressive policies on the left and regressive, anti-redistributionist policies on the right. However, the dimension is just that, a continuum where policies, parties, and regimes can be placed at any point, not simply in one of two bins. The anti-colonial leader of a revolutionary movement who after taking power exploits the nation's wealth by placing it in his own bank accounts is difficult to characterize as left or right wing. If he then plays the populist and seizes the property of the rich and divvies it up to the poor, a binary choice has difficulty capturing the complexity of such behavior.

The curious case of the CCP itself points to the importance of examining policy shifts that may be obscured by regime type labels and classifications. How left-wing, party-dominant and communist has China really been? In addition to Mao personally pre-empting party decisions or letting loose a popular movement attacking the party during the Cultural Revolution, the Reform era policies so associated with China's economic growth are difficult to square with communist ideals.[8] In the past decade the party has allowed capitalists to become members.[9] Some observers see the party as replacing the proletariat as its political base with the capitalist and entrepreneurial class to hold down the poor classes in pursuit of profits and stability.[10] In terms of the coalitional elements or policies pursued, a separate boxes approach to authoritarian regime ideology is too simplistic to capture the real world variation in policies and changes over time, as the CCP's experience suggests.

The third critique of the CCP being generalizable to other dictatorships is the CCP's ability to control events within its borders. A common perception is that China's state capacity is off the charts, but this again falls short of portraying the multifaceted reality. First, the CCP's ability to affect change within its territory or control the lives of its citizens has vacillated wildly in different directions during its reign over the PRC. From initial problems of implementation following victory in 1949, to the massive collective mobilization of the Great Leap Forward, to the attacks on the party apparatus during the Cultural Revolution, to the party's general stepping back from the tactical operations of

[7] Boix 2003.

[8] Or, for that matter, Communist ideals. China's Reform era policies are in conflict both with the ideological tenets of communism and with the prior political strategies of Communist parties.

[9] Dickson 2003.

[10] Chen 2002, 2003.

the economy of the Reform era, it is clear that the influence and presence of the party in the daily lives of the Chinese people has waxed and waned over time. Second, all dictatorships have some control over their territories; this capacity varies cross-sectionally as well as diachronically in the cross-national analyses. In a state with lower levels of capacity, the policy options might be different due to capacity constraints, but the choices that are made will likely be with similar motivating concerns and goals. The examination of changes in urban bias across countries over time in chapter 7 lends further credence to this conclusion. Going further, this analysis is a call for scholars to examine policies as well as institutions, even in opaque, nondemocratic contexts.

Studying China has numerous advantages. The "China Model" or "Beijing Consensus" is increasingly viewed as an alternative to the Western liberal order.[11] The extent to which the CCP's leadership is becoming a model for other dictatorships makes further investigations here doubly fruitful. If Beijing's policies are implemented abroad, their political and economic effects have already been examined. If these policies are not implemented or are implemented but yield outcomes different than in China, then these results too benefit from the prior study of the Chinese case.

Twitter as a City

The Chinese regime's Internet censorship apparatus is one domain where other nondemocratic regimes have attempted to emulate China. This book persists with the age old tradition of considering a city only those physical places where many people live near each other. Yet, increasingly, our lives involve staring at glowing screens, our interactions mediated by the Internet. China's most prominent dissident artist, Ai Weiwei, remarked in August 2012 for Foreign Policy's "Cities Issue" that "Twitter is my city, my favorite city."[12] He continued:

> I can talk to anybody I want to. And anybody who wants to talk to me will get my response. They know me better than their relatives or my relatives. There's so much imagination there; a lot of times it's just like poetry. You just read one sentence, and you sense this kind of breeze or a kind of look. It's amazing.[13]

[11] e.g., Ramo 2004; Halper 2010; Chan, Lee, and Chan 2008.
[12] Landreth 2012.
[13] Ibid.

Yet despite Ai's enthusiasm, the comparison has limits. Cities are areas where people coalesce in proximity to one another to share ideas, make and sell goods and services to each other, to commune. Cities radiate energy, possibility, and power. In salons, community halls, and parks, people in cities can come together to exchange ideas in private conversations and march out afterwards in public fashion.

In some ways, Twitter—or the Internet more broadly—recreates the information sharing that can happen in cities, and in fact can be substantially more efficient about the spreading of news than any kind of rumors floating in the air of a city. Facts can be checked and verified or debunked instantaneously online. Of course, dubious claims can spread with equal speed.

The community online is tied together by interest rather than simply by geographic proximity. The China specialists around the world that I communicate with over email list-servs, blogs, or Twitter share more of my interests than the people slinging dough at Pizza House across the street. Ai, though, has connected the real and the Internet world's both during his response to the Sichuan Earthquake and in creating a festival at his condemned Shanghai studio.[14]

Referring to the Internet as a single entity, though, is problematic as increasingly the Chinese Internet is becoming something separate and distinct from what is used in the rest of the world. Access to Twitter, for instance, is blocked inside of the country and only accessible via technologies that circumvent the Great Firewall of China. Twitter is not alone; Wikipedia, Facebook, various blogging services, and many Western media outlets routinely cannot be accessed directly from devices in the mainland. In addition to limiting exposure to foreign sites, Chinese Internet controls censor domestic news media and user posts online. Thousands of government employees, along with censors hired by firms themselves to remain in the good graces of the regime, filter, delete, and constrain the content of discussions occurring over the Chinese Internet. Calls for collective action are particularly quick to be eliminated by the "net nannies."[15]

Even absent such controls, it is easy to overstate the political power of Twitter or the Internet to overthrow dictators. Shame can move electorates and democratically elected officials often respond to shame by abdicating (for instance, Elliot Spitzer's resignation as governor of New York in 2008), but the conversation eventually turns and leaders that do not resign tend to endure after their crises blow over.[16]

[14] Although in the latter case, he was unable to attend himself due to being detained.

[15] King, Pan, and Roberts 2013.

[16] Note that in the United States, these crises are almost exclusively sexual in nature, presumably due to the mix of interest in the public and the media in reporting. Financial scandals disappear much quicker if they are reported on at all.

Dictators, though, have no shame. In today's world, democracy is thought of as a norm.[17] Dictators do not allow their own populations the right to participate in the selection of their leaders. What could shame such a person or regime? Pushing leaders out of office requires more than shame. It requires individuals motivated enough to risk condemnation, violence, imprisonment, torture, and death to jointly rage against the government, against the dictator. The Internet can foment that rage, aid in organizing and directing it to the maximum of its capacity, and share it with the world. As such, the Internet is powerful and can undermine dictators, but the real power to end tyranny still lives in the space of streets and sidewalks, of guns and tanks, of people. People marching, occupying, protesting together, and risking everything have to be able to change the minds of well-equipped military officers and grunts to not open fire. That is the moment when a real city takes back power from the dictator.

Much was made of the causal powers of Twitter and Facebook on fomenting or organizing the protests of the Arab Spring. Yet, such analyses may dwell on the novel rather than the important.[18] Twitter had never been used in this way before and so describing how it connected protestors is fascinating. Undiscovered territory is catnip to journalists, but the new is not always the most essential. People in the streets and the military's unwillingness to shoot them lay at the heart of the regime's political unwinding during the Arab Spring. The political economy of urban grievances is more central to the regime's downfall than the technological tools that the aggrieved used to communicate. Social science, too, can fall into such traps of the novel over the core political facts. Policies vary by geography and can alter the political geography of a country in turn. These interactions matter for nondemocratic regimes: for both their survival and the lives of the citizens over which they rule.

Looking Forward

For the past six decades, the Chinese regime has managed urbanization. It has done so in different ways during different eras. Cities and the regulation of their growth have always been important components to the regime's strategy. Looking forward, this will continue to be so. Yet, increasingly it appears to be the case that the regime's other priorities, namely promoting consumption-led growth and moving up the value chain in the industrial sector, are coming into conflict with the flat urban hierarchy and promotion of small cities that have characterized it

[17] Sen 1999.
[18] See Morozov (2011) for an expanded take against Internet-centrism and cyber-utopianism.

for so long. This debate can be seen in the use of two different Chinese terms for what is called "urbanization" in English: *chengzhenhua* (城镇化) and *chengshihua* (城市化).[19] The former, *chengzhenhua*, implies an urbanization of towns or a "townization" much as the regime has promoted throughout the Reform era. The latter, *chengshihua*, is the urbanization of cities and is associated with the growth of China's leading megacities and provincial capitals.

Urban concentration's advantages are said to arise from two sources: a transition to consumption-led growth and a desire to move higher up the value chain in production. The Great Recession and China's response to it illustrated to the regime that it both needed to and could shift its economy toward more of a domestic focus. International buyers disappeared overnight, leaving the regime to try to hold the pieces together. The regime's success in accomplishing this task showed that domestic demand could serve as the catalyst for growth. As China has grown, the rest of the world has taken what has been made in China. But as China becomes an ever larger share of the global economy, the rest of the world is not enough. The Chinese consumer would need to supplement lackluster growth in foreign demand.

At the same time, the stimulus funded substantial investment and moved China even further into an investment-led economy. Some of these investments were white elephants, wasted resources that could have been better utilized, but the bulk of the funds went to infrastructural and other construction projects that will serve some economic purpose if not necessarily turn an economic profit for the parties making the investment.[20] Yet, as Miller puts it, "China's economy. . . can digest a few white elephants," since on average 20 million people move to cities and need housing every year.[21] The rush of investments increases the capital stock in the country and makes the need to transition to a consumption-led economy plainer. With few roads left to build, how does the regime chart a new domestic, consumption-led economic trajectory?

Individuals residing in cities consume more goods and services than do individuals residing in the countryside. As such, some suggest that transitioning more people into cities will spur demand for the accoutrements of urban life. Urbanization means not only new apartments to be built, but also for those apartments to be designed, furnished, decorated, and cleaned. The individuals in them will need to be fed and will do so through market-based means rather than non-market activity on the farm. By promoting urbanization, the regime

[19] Via Bill Bishop's Sinocism ("The Sinocism China Newsletter for 03.04.13" 2013). Referencing "李克强论城镇化" 2013.

[20] These economic purposes are in addition to their political ones, employing the unemployed during the moment of potential rebellion.

[21] Miller 2012, 123.

believes that it can induce consumption. Yet moving an impoverished farmer to a city will not necessarily increase his or her consumption. Cai Fang argues that only with *hukou* reform will urban consumption increase, while Miller believes that even this necessary step would be insufficient, arguing that increased incomes combined with declining savings rates are necessary as well.[22]

Despite economic incentives to increase urbanization, the regime continues to shape the contours of migration to China's first tier cities, illustrating continuing fears of "Latin Americanization"—slums, crime, and instability in megacities. Large cities are historically engines of economic growth. Developing China's megacities may also promote the research and development, innovation, and creativity that will spark China's race to the technological frontier and to expand that frontier's bounds. The efforts undertaken to expand their limits are limited, however. Beijing, Shanghai, and other major metropolises are encouraged to grow in size but mostly by expanding their population of desirable migrants. Localities have increasingly set up point-based systems that allow access to social services and *hukou* to migrants that bring with them a combination of skills, experience, and money.[23] It is not the case that China's first tier cities are throwing their gates open to all who desire to live within them.

While there has been some discussion about moving away from the promotion of smaller cities, serious actions changing the regime's decades-long policy of managing urbanization have yet to be revealed. The Party's 12th Five Year Plan, which runs from 2011 to 2015, as well as statements of the new Premier Li Keqiang, point to an increased willingness to consider arguments about the advantages that come from allowing the largest cities in China to grow to even greater dimensions.[24] However, previous experiences with discussions of *hukou* reform have disappointed many, suggesting that the regime is unlikely to quickly or easily remove obstacles to urban concentration.

Fundamentally, the regime is deciding between different possible futures, attempting to plan for policies that give itself and the individuals who constitute it the best chances to continue to rule. Reforms to privatize land and abolish the *hukou* system in one fell swoop are unlikely. The regime seeks to avoid abrupt discontinuities, instead preferring experimentation and policies that have track records of success from local experiments.

The joint sessions of the National People's Congress and the Chinese People's Political Consultative Conference, also known as the Two Conferences (*liang hui*), are a key event in the annual Chinese political calendar. They are also

---

[22] Cai Fang is interviewed in Miller 2012, 159; Miller's view is on p. 157.

[23] Miller 2012, among others.

[24] Miller 2012, 3. See also the 12th Five Year Plan ("中国第十二个五年规划纲要 (全文)-搜狐新闻," 2013).

a Chinese Groundhog Day, the continual repetition of the same story endlessly with no real changes occurring or even on the horizon.[25]

When I heard word in February and early March 2006 that serious reform was in the offing, I was excited by the prospects of observing how a changed policy would affect the growth of China's cities. Yet in that year, as in every other that has come since, major reform at the national level has been left to the future. Long-range planning calls for the equalization of social services across the rural-urban divide and the end of discrimination against rural migrants in cities, but the prospects of implementation remain hazy.

Kam Wing Chan and Will Buckingham published an article in the *China Quarterly* entitled "Is China Abolishing the *Hukou* System?" in 2008. Their answer was no. Yet they demonstrate that both the domestic and foreign media constantly talk about the end of the system as either already having happened or just around the corner:

> The most ironic piece we discovered—and perhaps the one most telling of the prognosis for the latest round of *hukou* reforms—was an announcement by Shenzhen, China's largest and most famous city of migrants, that called for tightening of admission of migrants' children to local public schools on the same day the *New York Times*' eye-catching story on abolition of the *hukou* hit the streets.[26]

Their evidence consists of material from the 2005 version of Groundhog Day, but the story in the main persists. In 2010, 13 prominent Chinese newspapers jointly published an editorial calling for reform.[27] That it was quickly removed from the websites of these newspapers speaks to the fate of actual reforms. Indeed, the *Economic Observer Online*'s deputy editor-in-chief, Zhang Hong, was also removed.[28] Almost every winter similar stories emerge about a transition away from the migration restrictions of the *hukou* system. Almost every time, half measures and excuses proliferate while reform remains off the table.

A plausible path forward on *hukou* reform could emerge from China's desire to increase consumption. Boosting consumption would require migrants to move to cities and become urban citizens with higher incomes and access to the social safety net. That in turn may help convince them to spend today rather than save for the future.[29] One can see movement in this direction with the 2008 Land

[25] Referencing the 1993 Bill Murray film.
[26] Chan and Buckingham 2008.
[27] See Chan 2010a; Chinese Law Prof Blog 2010, for more details.
[28] Miller 2012, 43.
[29] Ibid., 157. Miller cites Cai Fang on this point as well, p. 159.

Reform Law, that, while not as sweeping as initially intended due to the Great Recession, remained significant.[30] Within weeks of the passage of this law, both Chengdu and Chongqing opened rural property exchanges.[31] These exchanges created what came to be called the *dipiao* or land credit system, which operated similar to carbon credit markets. Farmers with rights to rural construction land could sell their land use rights to others interested in using land elsewhere. Building on a new greenfield site in these locales required an equivalent land credit, which developers could purchase from farmers that had reduced their land use footprints by moving to more dense housing in the countryside—that is, rural apartment blocks rising up amongst rice or wheat fields.[32] By consolidating their rural construction land and converting it to farm land, farmers were able to trade the land on which their homes had existed in peripheral areas to builders interested in developing areas closer to important cities while the regime maintained a certain amount of aggregate farmland.

Yet by coming closer to disconnecting the farmer from the land, these reforms ate away at the only social security system that those born in China's countryside retain.[33] These concerns as well as more basic ones about abuses by local governments led the national authorities to halt trading in these exchanges just two weeks after they had opened.[34] The financial cost of expanding the urban safety net to migrants is immense, estimated at over 67,000 RMB ($10,000) per capita for 10 million migrants in the already highly indebted city of Chongqing alone.[35] Even without including pensions or any social security payments, the expense is enormous. Expanding "social housing" to provide low rents to the newly urbanized and those in need of cheap housing was also a component of the 12th Five Year Plan, with between 20 and 36 million units coming on line by 2015.[36]

Separating the *hukou* system from the social safety net has been suggested as another alternative.[37] Yet even with changes in terminology, such as "unified residents' systems" supposedly abolishing rural and urban *hukou* status and now present in nearly half of Chinese provinces, little substantively has changed for migrants to the largest cities—they remain unable to access social services.[38] It remains the case that the hurdles to acquire local *hukou* are higher in larger

---

[30] Ibid., 69. Miller cites Li Cheng about the importance of this reform.

[31] Ibid., 70.

[32] Ibid., 76.

[33] Ibid., 81. Miller cites Hu Jing in the New Left Review.

[34] Ibid., 78.

[35] Ibid., 56. Miller cites Victor Shih's assessment that Chongqing has over 1T RMB in debt.

[36] Ibid., 22. The official number is 36, but only 20 million or so are estimated to be normal housing and not university dorms, military encampments, and the like.

[37] See, for instance, World Bank 2012.

[38] Miller 2012, 37–38.

cities, even in the relatively pro-mega-city 12th Year Plan.[39] The extraordinary lengths to which the Beijing *hukou* is protected and coveted can be seen in the regulations regarding transferring one's *hukou* to Beijing following marrying a local Beijinger, which is allowed, but only after a full 10 years have elapsed to show that the marriage is a true one.[40]

Three puzzles motivated this book: China's long-lasting regime, its lack of slums, and its recent move away from urban bias. China has protected urbanites with subsidies and social services, while keeping migrants either in the countryside or as temporary rather than permanent residents through its *hukou* system. The regime has increasingly directed funds to rural and interior locales in a bid to improve their economic prospects and reduce the divisions within the country. As the regime looks to continue its economic growth, it is hoping that redistributive policies such as generous social service provision in the countryside can allow it to continue to urbanize without slums. These choices have helped account for the CCP's survival. As China's management of urbanization evolves, the regime steps into untrodden ground, making decisions that are simultaneously perilous and promising.

[39] Ibid., 39.
[40] Ibid.

BIBLIOGRAPHY

Achen, Christopher. H. 2002. "Toward a New Political Methodology: Microfoundations and ART." *Annual Review of Political Science* 5(1): 423–50.

Ades, Alberto, and Edward L. Glaeser. 1995. "Trade and Circuses: Explaining Urban Giants." *Quarterly Journal of Economics* 110: 195–227.

Al Jazeera. 2011. "Ben Ali Gets Refuge in Saudi Arabia—Middle East—Al Jazeera English." 16 January. http://www.aljazeera.com/news/middleeast/2011/01/201111652129710582.html.

Amnesty International. 2012. "Amnesty International | Urumqi Riots Three Years on—Crackdown on Uighurs Grows Bolder." *Amnesty International*. 4 July. http://www. amnesty.org/en/for-media/press-releases/urumqi-riots-three-years-crackdown-uighurs -grows-bolder-2012-07-04.

Anderson, Benedict R. O'G. 1991. *Imagined Communities: Reflections on the Origin and Spread of Nationalism*. Rev. and extended. London: Verso.

Anderson, Jonathan. 2007. "Is China Export-Led?" UBS Investment Research—Asian Focus. http://www.allroadsleadtochina.com/reports/prc_270907.pdf.

Anderson, Kym, and Ernesto Valenzuela. 2008. "Estimates of Global Distortions to Agricultural Incentives, 1955 to 2007". World Bank. Washington, DC.

——. 2012. "Distortions to Agricultural Incentives." Trade and International Integration, 9 April. http://go.worldbank.org/5XY7A7LH40.

Anderson, Kym, M. Kurzweil, W. J. Martin, D. Sandri, and E. Valenzuela. 2008. "Methodology for Measuring Distortions to Agricultural Incentives." Agricultural Distortions Working Paper. http://siteresources.worldbank.org/INTTRADERESEARCH/Resources/544824-1146153362267/AgDistortionsMethodology_Rev0108.pdf.

Arendt, Hannah. 1958. "Totalitarian Imperialism: Reflections on the Hungarian Revolution." *Journal of Politics* 20(1): 5–43.

Au, Chun-Chung, and J. Vernon Henderson. 2006. "How Migration Restrictions Limit Agglomeration and Productivity in China." *Journal of Development Economics* 80(2): 350–88.

Avelino, George, David S. Brown, and Wendy Hunter. 2005. "The Effects of Capital Mobility, Trade Openness, and Democracy on Social Spending in Latin America, 1980–1999." *American Journal of Political Science* 49(3): 625–41.

Bachman, David M. 1991. *Bureaucracy, Economy, and Leadership in China: The Institutional Origins of the Great Leap Forward*. Cambridge: Cambridge University Press.

Bandelj, Nina, and Dorothy J. Solinger, eds. 2012. *Socialism Vanquished, Socialism Challenged: Eastern Europe and China, 1989-2009*. New York: Oxford University Press.

Banister, Judith. 1987. *China's Changing Population*. Stanford, CA: Stanford University Press.

Banks, Arthur S. 2011. "Cross-National Time-Series Data Archive, 1815-[2011]." Abacus. http://abacus.library.ubc.ca/handle/10573/42657.

Baranovitch, Nimrod. 2003. "From the Margins to the Centre: The Uyghur Challenge in Beijing." *China Quarterly* 175: 726–50.

Barboza, David. 2009. "A Textile Capital of China Is Hobbled by a Downturn Gone Global." *The New York Times*, 28 February, sec. Business / World Business. http://www.nytimes.com/2009/02/28/business/worldbusiness/28textile.html.

Bates, Robert H. 1981. *Markets and States in Tropical Africa: The Political Basis of Agricultural Policies*. Berkeley and Los Angeles: University of California Press.

BBC News. 2008. "China 'Faces Mass Social Unrest.'" *BBC*, 5 December, sec. Asia-Pacific. http://news.bbc.co.uk/2/hi/7766921.stm.

Beissinger, Mark R. 2007. "Structure and Example in Modular Political Phenomena: The Diffusion of Bulldozer/Rose/Orange/Tulip Revolutions." *Perspectives on Politics* 5(2): 259–76.

Beja, Jean P., and Michel Bonnin. 1995. "The Destruction of the Village." *China Perspectives* 2: 21–5.

Bergsten, C. Fred, Charles Freeman, Nicholas R. Lardy, and Derek J. Mitchell. 2008. *China's Rise: Challenges and Opportunities*. Washington, DC: Peterson Institute.

Bernstein, Thomas P. 1977. *Up to the Mountains and Down to the Villages: The Transfer of Youth from Urban to Rural China*. New Haven: Yale University Press.

——. 1984. "Stalinism, Famine, and Chinese Peasants." *Theory and Society* 13(3) (May): 339–77.

Bernstein, Thomas P., and Xiaobo Lü. 2000. "Taxation without Representation: Peasants, the Central and the Local States in Reform China." *China Quarterly* 163 (September): 742–63.

——. 2002. *Taxation without Representation in Rural China*. Cambridge: Cambridge University Press.

Bienen, Henry, and Nicolas van de Walle. 1989. "Time and Power in Africa." *American Political Science Review* 83(1): 19–34.

Blaydes, Lisa. 2010. *Elections and Distributive Politics in Mubarak's Egypt*. Cambridge: Cambridge University Press.

Blaydes, Lisa, and Mark Andreas Kayser. 2011. "Counting Calories: Democracy and Distribution in the Developing World." *International Studies Quarterly* 55(4) (December): 887–908.

Boix, C. 2003. *Democracy and Redistribution*. Cambridge: Cambridge University Press.

Box-Steffensmeier, Janet M., and Bradford S. Jones. 1997. "Time Is of the Essence: Event History Models in Political Science." *American Journal of Political Science* 41(4): 1414–61.

——. 2004. *Event History Modeling: A Guide for Social Scientists*. Cambridge: Cambridge University Press.

Brandt, Loren, Jikun Huang, Guo Li, and Scott Rozelle. 2002. "Land Rights in Rural China: Facts, Fictions and Issues." *China Journal* 47: 67–97.

Branigan, Tania. 2008. "Chill Winds Blow through China's Manufacturing Heartland." *The Guardian*, 31 October. http://www.guardian.co.uk/business/2008/oct/31/china-manufacturing.

——. 2009. "China Fears Riots Will Spread as Boom Goes Sour." *The Observer*, 24 January. http://www.guardian.co.uk/world/2009/jan/25/china-globaleconomy.

Brown, David S., and Wendy Hunter. 2004. "Democracy and Human Capital Formation." *Comparative Political Studies* 37(7): 842–64.

Bueno de Mesquita, Bruce, and Alastair Smith. 2010. "Leader Survival, Revolutions, and the Nature of Government Finance." *American Journal of Political Science* 54(4) (October): 936–50.

Bueno de Mesquita, Bruce, Alastair Smith, Randolph M. Siverson, and James D. Morrow. 2003. *The Logic of Political Survival*. Cambridge, MA: MIT Press.

Cai, Fang, and Meiyan Wang, eds. 2008. *Reports on China's Population and Labor* [中国人口与劳动问题报告]. Beijing: Shehui Kexue Wenxian Chubanshe.

Cai, Hongbin, and Daniel Treisman. 2006. "Did Government Decentralization Cause China's Economic Miracle?" *World Politics* 58(4): 505.

Cai, Yongshun. 2002. "The Resistance of Chinese Laid-off Workers in the Reform Period." *China Quarterly* 170: 327–44.

———. 2006. *State and Laid-Off Workers in Reform China: The Silence and Collective Action of the Retrenched*. New York: Routledge.

———. 2010. *Collective Resistance in China: Why Popular Protests Succeed or Fail*. Stanford, CA: Stanford University Press.

Chan, Anita, and Hong-zen Wang. 2004. "The Impact of the State on Workers' Conditions: Comparing Taiwanese Factories in China and Vietnam." *Pacific Affairs* 77(4): 629–46.

Chan, Kam Wing. 1994. *Cities with Invisible Walls: Reinterpreting Urbanization in Post-1949 China*. New York: Oxford University Press.

———. 2009. "The Chinese Hukou System at 50." *Eurasian Geography and Economics* 50(2): 197–221.

———. 2010a. "Making Real Hukou Reform in China." *East Asia Forum*. 3 March. http://www.eastasiaforum.org/2010/03/03/making-real-hukou-reform-in-china/.

———. 2010b. "Fundamentals of China's Urbanization and Policy." *The China Review* 10(1): 63–94.

———. 2010c. "The Household Registration System and Migrant Labor in China: Notes on a Debate." *Population and Development Review* 36(2): 357–64.

———. 2010d. "The Global Financial Crisis and Migrant Workers in China: 'There Is No Future as a Labourer; Returning to the Village Has No Meaning.'" *International Journal of Urban and Regional Research* 34(3): 659–77.

Chan, Kam Wing, and Will Buckingham. 2008. "Is China Abolishing the Hukou System?" *China Quarterly* 195: 582–606.

Chan, Kam Wing, and Li Zhang. 1999. "The Hukou System and Rural-Urban Migration in China: Processes and Changes." *China Quarterly* 160: 818–55.

Chan, Lai-Ha, Pak K. Lee, and Gerald Chan. 2008. "Rethinking Global Governance: A China Model in the Making?" *Contemporary Politics* 14(1): 3–19.

Chandra, Kanchan. 2006. "What Is Ethnic Identity and Does It Matter?" *Annual Review of Political Science* 9(1): 397–424.

Chang, Gordon G. 2001. *The Coming Collapse of China*. New York: Random House.

Chang, Hongxiao, Bo Ren, Hai Deng, Qiong Zhou, Weiao Li, Peng Li, and Yanling Zhang. 2009a. "农民工失业调查." *Caijing*, 19 January. http://magazine.caijing.com.cn/2009-01-17/110066604.html.

———. 2009b. "A Precarious Festival for China's Migrants." *Caijing*, 19 January. http://english.caijing.com.cn/2009-01-23/110051086.html.

Cheibub, José A., and Jennifer Gandhi. 2004. "Classifying Political Regimes: A Six-Fold Measure of Democracies and Dictatorships." APSA Paper.

Cheibub, José. A., Jennifer Gandhi, and James R. Vreeland. 2010. "Democracy and Dictatorship Revisited." *Public Choice* 143(1): 67–101.

Chen, An. 2002. "Capitalist Development, Entrepreneurial Class, and Democratization in China." *Political Science Quarterly* 117(3): 401–22.

———. 2003. "Rising-Class Politics and Its Impact on China's Path to Democracy." *Democratization* 10(2): 141–62.

———. 2008. "The 1994 Tax Reform and Its Impact on China's Rural Fiscal Structure." *Modern China* 34(3): 303–43.

Chen, Stephen. 2008. "Mass Influx of Migrants Triggers Job Fears Inland." *South China Morning Post*, 19 December. http://www.scmp.com/article/664351/mass-influx-migrants-triggers-job-fears-inland.

Cheng, Tiejun, and Mark Selden. 1994. "The Origins and Social Consequences of China's Hukou System." *China Quarterly* 139: 644–68.

Cheng, Yunjie. 2008. "Government Reacts to Return of Rural Migrants." *Xinhua*, 19 November, sec. China Focus. http://www.chinadaily.com.cn/china/2008-11/19/content_7219957.htm.

Cheung, Jennifer. 2013. "The Long Uphill Struggle for Migrant Schools in Beijing Continues." *China Labour Bulletin*. http://www.clb.org.hk/en/node/110095.

China Digital Times. 2010. "Sealed Management—China Digital Times (CDT)." 5 October. http://chinadigitaltimes.net/china/sealed-management/.

"China to Launch 10 Key Projects in Western Regions." 2008. *China Daily.* 22 June. http://www.chinadaily.com.cn/bizchina/2008-06/22/content_6784587.htm.

Chinese Law Prof Blog. 2010. "The Famous Hukou Editorial." *Chinese Law Prof Blog.* 26 March. http://lawprofessors.typepad.com/china_law_prof_blog/2010/03/the-famous-hukou-editorial.html.

Cho, Mun Young. 2009. "Forced Flexibility: A Migrant Woman's Struggle for Settlement." *.China Journal* 61: 51–76.

Christiansen, Flemming. 2009. "Food Security, Urbanization and Social Stability in China." *Journal of Agrarian Change* 9(4): 548–75.

Cingranelli, David L., and David L. Richards. 2008. "The Cingranelli-Richards (CIRI) Human Rights Data Project Coding Manual. Version 2008.3.13."

———. 2011. "CIRI Human Rights Data Project." http://www.humanrightsdata.org.

Cliff, Thomas. 2012. "The Partnership of Stability in Xinjiang: State–Society Interactions Following the July 2009 Unrest." *China Journal* 68: 79–105.

Cole, James H. 1986. *Shaohsing: Competition and Cooperation in Nineteenth-Century China.* Tucson: University of Arizona Press.

Conquest, Robert. 1986. *The Harvest of Sorrow: Soviet Collectivization and the Terror-Famine.* New York: Oxford University Press.

Cox, Gary W., and Mathew D. McCubbins. 1986. "Electoral Politics as a Redistributive Game." *Journal of Politics* 48(2): 370–89.

Dahl, Robert. 1971. *Polyarchy.* New Haven: Yale University Press.

Davies, Robert W. 1980. *The Socialist Offensive: The Collectivisation of Soviet Agriculture, 1929-1930.* Cambridge, MA: Harvard University Press.

Davies, R. W., and Stephen G. Wheatcroft. 2004. *The Years of Hunger: Soviet Agriculture, 1931-1933.* New York: Palgrave Macmillan.

Davin, Delia. 1999. *Internal Migration in Contemporary China.* New York: St. Martin's Press.

Davis, James C., and J. Vernon Henderson. 2003. "Evidence on the Political Economy of the Urbanization Process." *Journal of Urban Economics* 53(1): 98–125.

DeLong, J. Bradford, and Andrei Shleifer. 1993. "Princes and Merchants: European City Growth before the Industrial Revolution." National Bureau of Economic Research. http://www.nber.org/papers/w4274.

Debs, Alexandre, and H. E. Goemans. 2010. "Regime Type, the Fate of Leaders, and War." *American Political Science Review* 104(3): 430–45.

Deininger, Klaus, and Songqing Jin. 2005. "The Potential of Land Rental Markets in the Process of Economic Development: Evidence from China." *Journal of Development Economics* 78(1): 241–70.

Diamond, Larry. 2003. "Can the Whole World Become Democratic? Democracy, Development, and International Policies." Center for the Study of Democracy. http://escholarship.org/uc/item/7bv4b2w1.pdf.

Diaz-Cayeros, Alberto, Beatriz Magaloni, and Barry Weingast. 2003. "Tragic Brilliance: Equilibrium Hegemony and Democratization in Mexico." *Working Paper.*

Dickson, Bruce J. 2003. *Red Capitalists in China: The Party, Private Entrepreneurs, and Prospects for Political Change.* Cambridge: Cambridge University Press.

———. 2011. "No 'Jasmine' for China." *Current History.* http://www.viet-studies.info/kinhte/China_NoJasmine_Current%20History.PDF.

Dikötter, Frank. 2010. *Mao's Great Famine: The History of China's Most Devastating Catastrophe, 1958-1962.* New York: Walker & Company.

Dittmer, Lowell. 1978. "Bases of Power in Chinese Politics: A Theory and an Analysis of the Fall of the 'Gang of Four.'" *World Politics* 31(1): 26–60.

Drazen, A. 2001. *The Political Business Cycle after 25 Years.* Cambridge, MA: MIT Press.

Dunning, Thad. 2008. *Crude Democracy: Natural Resource Wealth and Political Regimes.* Cambridge: Cambridge University Press.

Dutton, Michael Robert. 1992. *Policing and Punishment in China: From Patriarchy to "the People."* Cambridge: Cambridge University Press.

Economist Intelligence Unit. 2009. "China's Stimulus Package: A Six-Month Report Card."

Emerson, John Philip. 1982. *The Labor Force of China, 1957-80.* Washington, DC: U.S. Government Printing Office.

Escribà-Folch, Abel, and Joseph Wright. 2010. "Dealing with Tyranny: International Sanctions and the Survival of Authoritarian Rulers." *International Studies Quarterly* 54(2): 335–59.

"Exporters Get Sops to Fight Crisis—People's Daily Online." 2012. http://english.people.com.cn/90001/6674319.html.

Fattah, Zainab. 2013. "Saudi King Gifting Land Undercuts Homebuilding Promises." *Bloomberg.* 25 March. http://www.bloomberg.com/news/2013-03-24/saudi-king-gifting-land-und ercuts-homebuilding-promises.html.

Fearon, James D. 1998. "Commitment Problems and the Spread of Ethnic Conflict." In *The International Spread of Ethnic Conflict: Fear, Diffusion, and Escalation,* edited by David A. Lake and Donald S. Rothchild. Princeton: Princeton University Press.

——. 2000. "Why Use Elections to Allocate Power?" Unpublished manuscript.

Fearon, James D., and David Laitin. 2003. "Ethnicity, Insurgency, and Civil War." *American Political Science Review* 91(1): 75–90.

Fei, Xiaotong. 1986a. *Jiangcun jing ji: Zhongguo nong min de sheng huo.* Nanjing: Jiangsu ren min chu ban she: Jiangsu sheng xin hua shu dian fa xing.

——, ed. 1986b. *Xiao cheng zhen, xin kai tuo.* Nanjing: Jiangsu ren min chu ban she : Jiangsu sheng xin hua shu dian fa xing.

Feler, Leo, and J. Vernon Henderson. 2011. "Exclusionary Policies in Urban Development: Under-Servicing Migrant Households in Brazilian Cities." *Journal of Urban Economics* 69(3) (May): 253–72.

Fewsmith, Joseph. 2009. "Social Order in the Wake of Economic Crisis." *China Leadership Monitor.* 28. http://www.hoover.org/publications/clm/issues/44613342.html.

Fitzpatrick, Sheila. 1983. *The Russian Revolution.* New York: Oxford University Press.

——. 1994. *Stalin's Peasants: Resistance and Survival in the Russian Village after Collectivization.* New York: Oxford University Press.

——. 1999. *Everyday Stalinism: Ordinary Life in Extraordinary Times: Soviet Russia in the 1930s.* New York: Oxford University Press.

Fix, Michael, Demetrios G. Papademetriou, Jeanne Batalova, Aaron Terrazas, Serena Yi-Ying Lin, and Michelle Mittelstadt. 2009. "Migration and the Global Recession." *Migration Policy Institute, Commissioned by the BBC, September.* http://www.migrationpolicy.org/pubs/MPI-BBCreport-Sept09.pdf.

Fock, Achim, and Christine Wong. 2008. "Financing Rural Development for a Harmonious Society in China: Recent Reforms in Public Finance and Their Prospects". SSRN Scholarly Paper ID 1233069. Rochester, NY: Social Science Research Network. http://papers.ssrn.com/abstract=1233069.

Frangeul, Frédéric. 2011. "D'où Vient La 'Révolution Du Jasmin'?" *Europe1.fr—International.* 17 January. http://www.europe1.fr/International/D-ou-vient-la-revolution-du-jasmin-375743/.

Friedman, Eli. 2012. "Getting Through the Hard Times Together? Chinese Workers and Unions Respond to the Economic Crisis." *Journal of Industrial Relations* 54(4) (September): 459–75.

Friedrich, Carl. 1954. "The Unique Character of Totalitarian Society." In *Totalitarianism,* edited by Carl Friedrich: Cambridge, MA: Harvard University Press.

Friedrich, Carl, and Zbigniew Brzezinski. 1956. *Totalitarian Dictatorship and Autocracy.* Cambridge, MA: Harvard University Press.

Fuma, Susumu. 1993. "Late Ming Urban Reform and the Popular Uprising in Hangzhou." In *Cities of Jiangnan in Late Imperial China*, edited by Linda Cooke Johnson. Albany: State University of New York Press.

Fung, Ho-lup. 2001. "The Making and Melting of the 'Iron Rice Bowl' in China 1949 to 1995." *Social Policy & Administration* 35(3): 258–73.

Gallagher, Mary Elizabeth. 2005. *Contagious Capitalism: Globalization and the Politics of Labor in China*. Princeton: Princeton University Press.

Gandhi, Jennifer. 2008. *Political Institutions under Dictatorship*. Cambridge: Cambridge University Press.

Gandhi, Jennifer, and Adam Przeworski. 2006. "Cooperation, Cooptation, and Rebellion under Dictatorships." *Economics & Politics* 18(1): 1–26.

Gardner, Bruce L. 2002. *American Agriculture in the Twentieth Century: How It Flourished and What It Cost*. Cambridge, MA: Harvard University Press.

Garnaut, John. 2009. "Small Is Beautiful for China's Bank Boss." *The Age*, 27 April. http://www.theage.com.au/business/small-is-beautiful-for-chinas-bank-boss-20090426-ajea.html.

Geddes, Barbara. 1999a. "Authoritarian Breakdown: Empirical Test of a Game Theoretic Argument." *APSA Paper*.

———. 1999b. "What Do We Know about Democratization after Twenty Years." *Annual Review of Political Science* 2: 115–44.

Geddes, Barbara, Joseph Wright, and Erica Frantz. 2012. "New Data on Autocratic Regimes." Unpublished manuscript. http://dictators.la.psu.edu.

Gilboy, George J., and Eric Heginbotham. 2004. "The Latin Americanization of China?" *Current History* 103: 256–61.

Giles, John, Albert Park, and Juwei Zhang. 2005. "What Is China's True Unemployment Rate?" *China Economic Review* 16(2): 149–70.

Göbel, Christian, and Lynette Ong. 2012. "Social Unrest in China." *Long Briefing, Europe China Research and Academic Network (ECRAN)*. http://papers.ssrn.com/sol3/papers.cfm?abstract_id=2173073.

Goemans, H. E., Kristian S. Gleditsch, and Giacomo Chiozza. 2009. "Introducing Archigos: A Dataset of Political Leaders." *Journal of Peace Research* 46(2) (March): 269–83.

Goldstone, Jack A. 1995. "The Coming Chinese Collapse." *Foreign Policy* 99 (July): 35–53.

Goodman, David S. G. 2004. "The Campaign to "Open up the West": National, Provincial-level and Local Perspectives." *China Quarterly* 178: 317–34.

Goodman, David S. G., and Gerald Segal, eds. 1995. *China Deconstructs: Politics, Trade and Regionalism*. New York: Routledge.

Gottschang, Thomas R. 1987. "Economic Change, Disasters, and Migration: The Historical Case of Manchuria." *Economic Development and Cultural Change* 35(3) (April): 461–90.

Gu, Yanwu. 2012. "人聚-文摘报-光明网." http://epaper.gmw.cn/wzb/html/2011-05/12/nw.D110000wzb_20110512_3-06.htm.

"Guangdong Toy Factory Brawl Leaves 2 Dead, 118 Injured." 2009. *China.org.cn*. 27 June. http://www.china.org.cn/china/news/2009-06/27/content_18023576.htm.

Guldin, Gregory Eliyu. 2001. *What's a Peasant to Do?: Village Becoming Town in Southern China*. Boulder, CO: Westview Press.

Guo, Al. 2008. "Guangdong Hi-Tech Policy Set to Continue." *South China Morning Post*. 11 December. http://www.scmp.com/article/663350/guangdong-hi-tech-policy-set-continue.

Guo ji wen ti yan jiu suo (China Institute of International Studies). 2011. *CIIS Blue Book on International Situation and China's Foreign Affairs 2009/2010*. Beijing: World Affairs Press.

Guo, Jianqiang, and Min Huang. 2009. "论金融危机背景下我国群体性事件的防治." *Qiushi* (9): 70–73.

Guo, Qiang. 2006. " 'Temporary Residence Permit System Illegal.' " *China Daily*, 27 December. http://www.chinadaily.com.cn/china/2006-12/27/content_769202.htm.

Guowuyuan nongcun shuifeigaige gongzuo xiaozu. 2001. "Nong cun shui fei gai ge gong zuo shou ce." http://catalog.hathitrust.org/api/volumes/oclc/56545134.html.

Hadenius, Axel, and Jan Teorell. 2007. "Pathways from Authoritarianism." *Journal of Democracy* 18(1): 143.

Halper, Stefan A. 2010. *The Beijing Consensus: How China's Authoritarian Model Will Dominate the Twenty-First Century*. New York: Basic Books.

Hamrin, Carol Lee. 1984. "Competing 'Policy Packages' in Post-Mao China." *Asian Survey* 24(5) (May): 487–518.

Han, Jianwei, and Motohiro Monshima. 1992. "Labor System Reform in China and Its Unexpected Consequences." *Economic and Industrial Democracy* 13(2) (May): 233–61.

Han, Suk-Jung. 2004. "The Problem of Sovereignty: Manchukuo, 1932-1937." *Positions: East Asia Cultures Critique* 12(2): 457–78.

Hand, Keith J. 2006. "Using Law for a Righteous Purpose: The Sun Zhigang Incident and Evolving Forms of Citizen Action in the People's Republic of China." *Columbia Journal of Transnational Law*. 45: 114-195.

Harding, Harry. 1997. "The Chinese State in Crisis, 1966-69." In *The Politics of China: The Eras of Mao and Deng*, edited by Roderick MacFarquhar, 2nd ed. Cambridge: Cambridge University Press.

Harris, John R., and Michael P. Todaro. 1970. "Migration, Unemployment and Development: A Two-Sector Analysis." *American Economic Review* 60(1): 126–40.

Harttgen, Kenneth, Stephan Klasen, and Sebastian Vollmer. 2012. "An African Growth Miracle? Or: What Do Asset Indices Tell Us about Trends in Economic Performance?" Courant Research Centre PEG. http://www.iariw.org/papers/2011/harttgenpaper.pdf.

He, Xin Frank. 2003. "Sporadic Law Enforcement Campaigns as a Means of Social Control: A Case Study from a Rural-Urban Migrant Enclave in Beijing." *Columbia Journal of Asian Law* 17: 121.

Heilmann, Sebastian, and Elizabeth J. Perry, eds. 2011. *Mao's Invisible Hand: The Political Foundations of Adaptive Governance in China*. Cambridge, MA: Harvard University Asia Center.

Henderson, J. Vernon. 2003. "The Urbanization Process and Economic Growth: The So-What Question." *Journal of Economic Growth* 8(1): 47–71.

Herbst, Jeffrey. 2000. *States and Power in Africa*. Princeton: Princeton University Press.

Herd, Richard. 2010. "A Pause in the Growth of Inequality in China?" OECD Publishing. http://ideas.repec.org/p/oec/ecoaaa/748-en.html.

Hershkovitz, Linda. 1993. "Tiananmen Square and the Politics of Place." *Political Geography* 12(5) (September): 395–420.

Herszenhorn, David M., Carl Hulse, and Sheryl Gay Stolberg. 2008. "Talks Implode During a Day of Chaos; Fate of Bailout Plan Remains Unresolved." *New York Times*, 26 September, sec. Business. http://www.nytimes.com/2008/09/26/business/26bailout.html.

Hirschman, Albert O. 1970. *Exit, Voice, and Loyalty Responses to Decline in Firms, Organizations, and States*. Cambridge, MA: Harvard University Press.

Hobsbawm, Eric J. 1973. *Revolutionaries: Contemporary Essays*. New York: Pantheon Books.

Hofmann, Paul. 1975. "President of Peru Ousted in Coup Led by the Military." *New York Times*, 30 August.

Holbig, Heike. 2004. "The Emergence of the Campaign to Open Up the West: Ideological Formation, Central Decision-Making and the Role of the Provinces." *China Quarterly* 178: 335–57.

Howe, Christopher. 1971. *Employment and Economic Growth in Urban China, 1949-1957*. Cambridge: Cambridge University Press.

Hu, Chi-hsi. 1980. "Mao, Lin Biao and the Fifth Encirclement Campaign." *China Quarterly* 82 (June): 250–80.

Huang, Jikun, Huayong Zhi, Zhurong Huang, Scott Rozelle, and John Giles. 2010. "The Impact of the Global Financial Crisis on off-Farm Employment and Earnings in Rural China." *World Development* 39(5): 797–807.

Huang, Yasheng. 2008. *Capitalism with Chinese Characteristics: Entrepreneurship and the State.* Cambridge: Cambridge University Press.

Human Rights in China. 1999. *Not Welcome at the Party: Behind the "Clean-up" of China's Cities: A Report on Administrative Detention Under "Custody and Repatriation": Press Release, 29 September 1999, Full Report.* New York: Human Rights in China. http://www.hrichina.org/sites/default/files/publication_pdfs/c-r_99.pdf.

———. 2011. "Jasmine Organizers Call for Rallies Every Sunday." *Human Rights in China* 中国人权. 22 February. http://www.hrichina.org/content/4895.

Hung, Wu. 1991. "Tiananmen Square: A Political History of Monuments." *Representations* 35 (July): 84–117.

———. 2005. *Remaking Beijing: Tiananmen Square and the Creation of a Political Space.* Chicago: University of Chicago Press.

Huntington, Samuel P. 1968. *Political Order in Changing Societies.* New Haven: Yale University Press.

Hurst, William. 2009. *The Chinese Worker after Socialism.* Cambridge: Cambridge University Press.

———. 2012. "Slowdown in the World's Workshop?: Chinese Labor and the Global Recession." In *The Global Recession and China's Political Economy,* edited by Dali L. Yang. New York: Palgrave Macmillan.

International Food Policy Research Institute (IFPRI). 2009. "Wanted: Good Jobs for Fighting Poverty." *IFPRI Forum.* http://www.ifpri.org/sites/default/files/publications/if25_0.pdf.

Jerven, Morten. 2010. "Accounting for the African Growth Miracle: The Official Evidence— Botswana 1965–1995." *Journal of Southern African Studies* 36(1): 73–94.

Jiang, Chengcheng. 2011. "In Beijing, Students in Limbo After Migrant Schools Closed." *Time,* 14 September. http://www.time.com/time/world/article/0,8599,2093175,00.html#ixzz28xliu8p.

Jiang, Yarong, and David Ashley. 2000. *Mao's Children in the New China : Voices from the Red Guard Generation.* London: Routledge.

Jiang, Zemin. 2010. *Selected Works of Jiang Zemin.* Beijing: Foreign Languages Press.

Jin, Chongji, ed. 1998. *Zhou Enlai Zhuan.* Vol. 4. 4 vols. Beijing: Zhong yang wen xian chu ban she.

Johnson, D. Gale. 1997. "Agriculture and the Wealth of Nations." *American Economic Review* 87(2): 1–12.

Johnston, Bruce F., and John W. Mellor. 1961. "The Role of Agriculture in Economic Development." *American Economic Review* 51(4): 566–93.

Juvenal. 1999. *Sixteen Satires.* Translated by Peter Green. 3rd ed. London: Penguin Classics.

Kalyvas, Stathis N. 1999. "The Decay and Breakdown of Communist One-Party Systems." *Annual Review of Political Science* 2: 323-43.

———. 2004. "The Urban Bias in Research on Civil Wars." *Security Studies* 13(3): 160–90.

———. 2006. *The Logic of Violence in Civil War.* Cambridge: Cambridge University Press.

Kalyvas, Stathis N., and Laia Balcells. 2010. "International System and Technologies of Rebellion: How the End of the Cold War Shaped Internal Conflict." *American Political Science Review* 104(3): 415–29.

Kasara, Kimuli. 2007. "Tax Me If You Can: Ethnic Geography, Democracy, and the Taxation of Agriculture in Africa." *American Political Science Review* 101(1): 159–72.

Kau, Michael Y. M, and John K. Leung. 1986. *The Writings of Mao Zedong: 1949-1976.* New York: ME Sharpe.

Kaufman, Robert R. 2009. "The Political Effects of Inequality in Latin America: Some Inconvenient Facts." *Comparative Politics* 41(3) (April): 359–79.

Kaufman, Robert R., and Alex Segura-Ubiergo. 2001. "Globalization, Domestic Politics, and Social Spending in Latin America." *World Politics* 53(4): 553–87.

Kennedy, John James. 2007. "From the Tax-for-Fee Reform to the Abolition of Agricultural Taxes: The Impact on Township Governments in North-West China." *China Quarterly* 189: 43.

King, Gary, Jennifer Pan, and Margaret E. Roberts. 2013. "How Censorship in China Allows Government Criticism but Silences Collective Expression." *American Political Science Review* 107(2): 326–43.

Knight, John, and Lina Song. 1999. *The Rural-Urban Divide Economic Disparities and Interactions in China*. Oxford: Oxford University Press.

Koshizawa, Akira. 1978. "China's Urban Planning: Toward Development Without Urbanization." *Developing Economies* 16(1): 3–33.

Krugman, Paul. 1991. *Geography and Trade*. Cambridge, MA: MIT Press.

Kung, James Kai-Sing, and Shuo Chen. 2011. "The Tragedy of the Nomenklatura: Career Incentives and Political Radicalism during China's Great Leap Famine." *American Political Science Review* 105(1) (February): 27–45.

Kuran, Timur. 1991. "Now Out of Never: The Element of Surprise in the East European Revolution of 1989." *World Politics* 44(1): 7–48.

Lai, Chloe. 2009a. "Small Companies Can Start Getting Loans." *South China Morning Post*, 15 February. http://www.scmp.com/article/670074/small-companies-can-start-getting-loans.

———. 2009b. "Banks Join Easy-Credit Scheme for Small Firms." *South China Morning Post*, 19 February. http://www.scmp.com/article/670441/banks-join-easy-credit-scheme-small-firms.

Laitin, David. 1998. *Identity in Formation*. Ithaca, NY: Cornell University Press.

Lake, David, and Matthew Baum. 2001. "The Invisible Hand of Democracy." *Comparative Political Studies* 34(6): 587–621.

Lam, Willy Wo-Lap. 2006. *Chinese Politics in the Hu Jintao Era: New Leaders, New Challenges*. Armonk, NY: M. E. Sharpe.

Landreth, Jonathan. 2012. "'Twitter Is My City': An Exclusive Interview with Ai Weiwei." *Foreign Policy*, October. http://www.foreignpolicy.com/articles/2012/08/13/twitter_is_my_city?page=full.

Landry, Pierre F. 2008. *Decentralized Authoritarianism in China: The Communist Party's Control of Local Elites in the Post-Mao Era*. Cambridge: Cambridge University Press.

Lee, Ching Kwan. 1999. "From Organized Dependence to Disorganized Despotism: Changing Labour Regimes in Chinese Factories." *China Quarterly* 157: 44–71.

———. 2007. *Against the Law: Labor Protests in China's Rustbelt and Sunbelt*. Berkeley and Los Angeles: University of California Press.

Lee, James. 1978. "Migration and Expansion in Chinese History." In *Human Migration: Patterns and Politics*, edited by William H. McNeill and Ruth S. Adams. Bloomington: Indiana University Press.

Levitsky, Steven, and Lucan A. Way. 2010. *Competitive Authoritarianism: Hybrid Regimes after the Cold War*. Cambridge: Cambridge University Press.

———. 2012. "Beyond Patronage: Violent Struggle, Ruling Party Cohesion, and Authoritarian Durability." *Perspectives on Politics* 10(4): 869–89.

Lewis, John W. 1966. "Political Aspects of Mobility in China's Urban Development." *American Political Science Review* 60(4) (December): 899–912.

Lewis, Michael. 2012. "Obama's Way." *Vanity Fair*, 5 October. http://www.vanityfair.com/politics/2012/10/michael-lewis-profile-barack-obama.

Lewis, W. Arthur. 1954. "Economic Development with Unlimited Supplies of Labour." *Manchester School* 22(2): 139–91.

———. 1963. "Economic Development with Unlimited Supplies of Labor." In *The Economics of Underdevelopment*, edited by A. N. Agarwala. New York: Oxford University Press.

Li, Changping. 2002. *Wo xiang zong li shuo shi hua*. Beijing: Guang ming ri bao chu ban she.

Li, Choh-Ming. 1962. *The Statistical System of Communist China*. Berkeley and Los Angeles: University of California Press.

Li, Jing, and Xiaohuo Cui. 2008. "Creating Jobs for Migrant Workers Top Govt Agenda." *China Daily*, 14 November. http://www.chinadaily.com.cn/bizchina/2008-11/14/content_7204190.htm.

Li, Peng. 2010. "Nearly 5 Trillion Yuan Debt Issued in 2009 -." *Caixin.* 4 February. http://english. caixin.com/2010-02-04/100115296.html.

Li, Weiguang, ed. 2000. *Ruhe Jisuan He Jiaona Nongmuye Shui* [How to calculate and pay agricultural (and poultry) tax)]. Beijing: Renmin daxue chubanshe.

Liang, Heng, and Judith Shapiro. 1983. *Son of the Revolution.* New York: Knopf.

Lieberthal, Kenneth. 2004. *Governing China.* 2nd ed. New York: W. W. Norton.

Lim, Louisa. 2008. "Some Economies Suffer As Beijing Cleans Up Air: NPR." *All Things Considered.* http://www.npr.org/templates/story/story.php?storyId=93803287.

Lin, Justin Yifu. 1988. "The Household Responsibility System in China's Agricultural Reform: A Theoretical and Empirical Study." *Economic Development and Cultural Change* 36(3) (April): S199–S224.

——. 1992. "Rural Reforms and Agricultural Growth in China." *American Economic Review* 82(1) (March): 34–51.

Lin, Justin Yifu, and Dennis Tao Yang. 2000. "Food Availability, Entitlements and the Chinese Famine of 1959-61." *Economic Journal* 110(460): 136–58.

Lin, Justin Yifu, Fang Cai, and Zhou Li. 1998. "Competition, Policy Burdens, and State-Owned Enterprise Reform." *American Economic Review* 88(2): 422–27.

Linz, Juan J. 2000. *Totalitarian and Authoritarian Regimes.* Boulder, CO: Lynne Rienner Publishers.

Linz, Juan J., and Alfred C. Stepan. 1996. *Problems of Democratic Transition and Consolidation: Southern Europe, South America, and Post-Communist Europe.* Baltimore: Johns Hopkins University Press.

Lipset, Seymour M. 1959. "Some Social Requisites of Democracy: Economic Development and Political Legitimacy." *American Political Science Review* 53(1): 69–105.

Lipton, Michael. 1977. *Why Poor People Stay Poor: Urban Bias in World Development.* Cambridge, MA: Harvard University Press.

Liu, Alan P. L. 1992. "Symbols and Repression at Tiananmen Square, April-June 1989." *Political Psychology* 13(1) (March): 45–60.

Liu, Ligang, and Shaoqiang. Chen. 2005. "Should Chinese Local Governments Be Allowed to Issue Bonds?" *China & World Economy*: 47–64.

Liu, Xiaoli, and Wei Liang. 1997. "Zhejiangcun: Social and Spatial Implications of Informal Urbanization on the Periphery of Beijing." *Cities* 14(2) (April): 95–108.

Loewe, Michael, and Edward L. Shaughnessy. 1999. *The Cambridge History of Ancient China: From the Origins of Civilization to 221 BC.* Cambridge: Cambridge University Press.

Lohmann, Susanne. 1994. "The Dynamics of Informational Cascades: The Monday Demonstrations in Leipzig, East Germany, 1989-91." *World Politics* 47(1): 42–101.

Lorentzen, Peter L. 2013. "Regularizing Rioting: Permitting Public Protest in an Authoritarian Regime." *Quarterly Journal of Political Science* 8(2): 127–158.

Lu, Mai., and Calla Weimer. 2005. "An End to China's Agriculture Tax." *China: An International Journal* 3(2): 320–30.

Lü, Xiaobo. 1997. "The Politics of Peasant Burden in Reform China." *Journal of Peasant Studies* 25(1): 113–38.

Lust-Okar, Ellen. 2005. *Structuring Conflict in the Arab World: Incumbents, Opponents, and Institutions.* Cambridge: Cambridge University Press.

——. 2006. "Elections under Authoritarianism: Preliminary Lessons from Jordan." *Democratization* 13(3): 456–71.

Lynch, Marc. 2012. *The Arab Uprising: The Unfinished Revolutions of the New Middle East.* New York: Public Affairs.

Magaloni, Beatriz. 2006. *Voting for Autocracy: Hegemonic Party Survival and Its Demise in Mexico.* New York: Cambridge University Press.

Malesky, Edmund, and Paul Schuler. 2010. "Nodding or Needling: Analyzing Delegate Responsiveness in an Authoritarian Parliament." *American Political Science Review* 104(3): 482–502.

Malik, Lubna, and Lynn T. White. 2008. "Contemporary China: A Book List." Unpublished manuscript.

Mallee, Hein. 1995. "China's Household Registration System under Reform." *Development and Change* 26(1): 1–29.

Mamudi, Sam. 2008. "Lehman Folds with Record $613 Billion Debt." *MarketWatch*. 15 September. http://www.marketwatch.com/story/lehman-folds-with-record-613-billion-debt.

Manion, Melanie. 2004. *Corruption by Design: Building Clean Government in Mainland China and Hong Kong*. Cambridge, MA: Harvard University Press.

Mao, Sabrina, and Maxim Duncan. 2011. "Closure of Migrant Children Schools in China Sparks Anguish." *Reuters*, 18 August. http://www.reuters.com/article/2011/08/18/us-china-migrant-schools-idUSTRE77H10I20110818.

Mao, Zedong. 1968. "In Camera Statements of Mao Tse-Tung." *Chinese Law and Government* 1(4): 3–103.

Masoud, Tarek. 2011. "The Road to (and From) Liberation Square." *Journal of Democracy* 22(3): 20–34.

Maves, Jessica, and Alex Braithwaite. 2013. "Autocratic Institutions and Civil Conflict Contagion." *Journal of Politics* 75(2): 478–90.

Meltzer, Allan H., and Scott F. Richard. 1981. "A Rational Theory of the Size of Government." *Journal of Political Economy* 89(5): 914–27.

Mertha, Andrew C. 2005. "China's Soft Centralization: Shifting Tiao/Kuai Authority Relations." *China Quarterly* 184: 791–810.

Meyer, Jeffrey F. 1991. *The Dragons of Tiananmen: Beijing as a Sacred City*. Columbia: University of South Carolina Press.

Miller, Tom. 2012. *China's Urban Billion: The Story behind the Biggest Migration in Human History*. New York: Zed Books.

Millward, James A. 2009. "Introduction: Does the 2009 Urumchi Violence Mark a Turning Point?" *Central Asian Survey* 28(4): 347–60.

Ministry of Finance. 2005. "Report on the Implementation of the Central and Local Budgets for 2004 and on the Draft Central and Local Budgets for 2005." 5 March. http://english.gov.cn/official/2005-07/29/content_18176.htm.

Mitchell, Tom. 2008. "Shenzhen Factories Shed 50,000." *Financial Times*, 26 November. http://www.ft.com/intl/cms/s/0/f98f7c46-bc09-11dd-80e9-0000779fd18c.html#axzz2S3BkYnpK.

Mitter, Rana. 2004. *A Bitter Revolution : China's Struggle with the Modern World*. Oxford: Oxford University Press.

Moore, Malcolm. 2008. "2008: A Testing Year for China." *Telegraph.co.uk*, 16 December, sec. worldnews. http://www.telegraph.co.uk/news/worldnews/asia/china/3797002/2008-Chinas-character-test-in-messy-year.html.

Morrison, Kevin M. 2009. "Oil, Nontax Revenue, and the Redistributional Foundations of Regime Stability." *International Organization* 63(1): 107–38.

Mosher, Arthur Theodore. 1966. *Getting Agriculture Moving; Essentials for Development and Modernization*. New York: Published for the Agricultural Development Council by Praeger.

Mulligan, Casey B, Xavier Sala-i-Martin, and Ricard Gil. 2003. "Do Democracies Have Different Public Policies than Nondemocracies?" National Bureau of Economic Research. http://www.nber.org/papers/w10040.

Mumford, Lewis. 1961. *The City in History: Its Origins, Its Transformations, and Its Prospects*. New York: Harcourt.

Munck, Gerardo L., and Jay Verkuilen. 2002. "Conceptualizing and Measuring Democracy: Evaluating Alternative Indices." *Comparative Political Studies* 35(1): 5–34.

Myoe, Maung Aung. 2006. "The Road to Naypyitaw: Making Sense of the Myanmar Government's Decision to Move Its Capital." *SSRN eLibrary*, 1 November. http://papers.ssrn.com/sol3/papers.cfm?abstract_id=1317156.

Nanfangdushibao. 2008. "东莞两月117家欠薪企业逃匿 近2万人受影响." 南方都市报, 19 November. http://news.hexun.com/2008-11-19/111406330.html.

Nathan, Andrew J. 2001. "The Tiananmen Papers." *Foreign Affairs* 80(1) (January): 2–48.

National Bureau of Statistics (NBS), China. www.stats.gov.cn.

National Commission on Terrorist Attacks. 2004. *The 9/11 Commission Report: Final Report of the National Commission on Terrorist Attacks upon the United States.* 1st ed. New York: W. W. Norton & Company.

Naughton, Barry. 1992a. "Implications of the State Monopoly over Industry and Its Relaxation." *Modern China* 18(1) (January): 14–41.

———. 1992b. "Hierarchy and the Bargaining Economy: Government and Enterprise in the Reform Process." In *Bureaucracy, Politics, and Decision Making in Post-Mao China*, edited by Kenneth G. Lieberthal and David M. Lampton. Berkeley and Los Angeles: University of California Press.

———. 1995. "China's Macroeconomy in Transition." *China Quarterly* 144: 1083–1104.

———. 2004. "The Western Development Program." In *Holding China Together: Diversity and National Integration in the Post-Deng Era*, edited by Barry Naughton and Dali Yang, 253–96. Cambridge: Cambridge University Press. http://site.ebrary.com/id/10131677.

———. 2007. *The Chinese Economy.* Cambridge, MA: MIT Press.

———. 2008. "A New Team Faces Unprecedented Economic Challenges." *China Leadership Monitor* 26. http://www.hoover.org/publications/clm/issues/27770769.html.

———. 2009a. "The Scramble to Maintain Growth." *China Leadership Monitor* 27: 1–11.

———. 2009b. "Understanding the Chinese Stimulus Package." *China Leadership Monitor* 28. http://www.hoover.org/publications/clm/issues/44613157.html.

———. 2009c. "China's Emergence from Economic Crisis." *China Leadership Monitor* 29. http://www.hoover.org/publications/clm/issues/52971317.html.

———. 2009d. "Loans, Firms, and Steel: Is the State Advancing at the Expense of the Private Sector?" *China Leadership Monitor* 30. http://www.hoover.org/publications/clm/issues/70535412.html.

———. 2012. "China's Response to the Global Crisis, and the Lessons Learned." In *The Global Recession and China's Political Economy*, edited by Dali L. Yang. New York: Palgrave Macmillan.

Naughton, Barry, and Dali Yang, ed. 2004. *Holding China Together: Diversity and National Integration in the Post-Deng Era.* Cambridge: Cambridge University Press..

Nelson, Joan M. 1976. "Sojourners versus New Urbanites: Causes and Consequences of Temporary versus Permanent Cityward Migration in Developing Countries." *Economic Development and Cultural Change* 24(4) (July): 721–57.

Nordhaus, William D. 1975. "The Political Business Cycle." *Review of Economic Studies* 42(2): 169–90.

O'Brien, Kevin J., and Lianjiang Li. 2006. *Rightful Resistance in Rural China.* Cambridge: Cambridge University Press.

Oakes, Tim. 2004. "Building a Southern Dynamo: Guizhou and State Power." *China Quarterly* 178: 467–87.

OECD. 1999. *China in the Global Economy Agriculture in China and OECD Countries Past Policies and Future Challenges (OECD Proceedings): Past Policies and Future Challenges (OECD Proceedings).* OECD Publishing.

Oi, Jean C. 1989. *State and Peasant in Contemporary China: The Political Economy of Village Government.* Berkeley and Los Angeles: University of California Press.

———. 1999. *Rural China Takes off: Institutional Foundations of Economic Reform.* Berkeley and Los Angeles: University of California Press.

———. 2005. "Patterns of Corporate Restructuring in China: Political Constraints on Privatization." *China Journal* 53 (January): 115–36.

Oi, Jean C., and Shukai Zhao. 2007. "Fiscal Crisis in China's Townships: Causes and Consequences." In *Grassroots Political Reform in Contemporary China*, edited by Elizabeth J. Perry and Merle Goldman. Cambridge, MA: Harvard University Press.

Oksenberg, Michel, and James Tong. 1991. "The Evolution of Central-Provincial Fiscal Relations in China, 1971-1984: The Formal System." *China Quarterly* 125: 1–32.

Olson, Mancur. 1965. *The Logic of Collective Action: Public Goods and the Theory of Groups.* Cambridge, MA: Harvard University Press.

Ong, Lynette H. 2012. "Between Developmental and Clientelist States: Local State-Business Relationships in China." *Comparative Politics* 44(2): 191–209.

Orlik, Thomas. 2011. *Understanding China's Economic Indicators: Translating the Data into Investment Opportunities.* 1st ed. Upper Saddle River, NJ: FT Press Science.

Ouyang, Yan. 2008. "Guangdong Adopts 50 Billion to Boost Labor and Industry Transfer-China—Guangdong." *Newsgd.com.* 2 June. http://www.newsgd.com/specials/list/gdheadline/gdheadlines/content/2008-06/02/content_4421874.htm.

Padro i Miquel, Gerard. 2004. "The Control of Politicians in Divided Societies: The Politics of Fear." *Working Paper.*

Page, Jeremy. 2011. "What's He Doing Here? U.S. China Envoy Huntsman in Hot Water Over Protest Cameo—China Real Time Report—WSJ." 23 February. http://blogs.wsj.com/chinarealtime/2011/02/23/china-ambassador-huntsman-unusual-jasmine-protest-cameo/tab/print/.

Pan, Yihong. 2002. "An Examination of the Goals of the Rustication Program in the People's Republic of China." *Journal of Contemporary China* 11(31): 361–79.

Park, Albert. 2008. "Rural-Urban Inequality in China." In *China Urbanizes: Consequences, Strategies and Policies,* edited by Shahid Yusuf and Tony Saich. Washington, DC: World Bank Publications.

Park, Albert, Scott Rozelle, Christine Wong, and Changqing Ren. 1996. "Distributional Consequences of Reforming Local Public Finance in China." *China Quarterly* 147(1): 751–78.

Patel, David. 2013. "Roundabouts and Revolutions: Public Squares, Coordination, and the Diffusion of the Arab Uprisings." Manuscript.

Pei, Minxin. 2008. *China's Trapped Transition: The Limits of Developmental Autocracy.* Cambridge, MA: Harvard University Press.

Peking Review. 1976. "Twelve Million School Graduates Settle in the Countryside." *Peking Review,* January 9.

People's Daily. 2009. "Chen Xiwen: Financial Crisis Claims Jobs and Sends about 20 Million Migrant Workers Home." 3 February. http://english.peopledaily.com.cn/90001/90776/90882/6584511.html.

Pepinsky, Thomas B. 2007. "Autocracy, Elections, and Fiscal Policy: Evidence from Malaysia." *Studies in Comparative International Development (SCID)* 42(1): 136–63.

——. 2009. *Economic Crises and the Breakdown of Authoritarian Regimes: Indonesia and Malaysia in Comparative Perspective.* New York: Cambridge University Press.

Perry, Elizabeth J. 2002. *Challenging the Mandate of Heaven: Social Protest and State Power in China.* Armonk, NY: M. E. Sharpe.

——. 2008. "Chinese Conceptions of 'Rights': From Mencius to Mao- and Now." *Perspectives on Politics* 6(1: 37–50.

Perry, Elizabeth J., and Xun Li. 1997. *Proletarian Power: Shanghai in the Cultural Revolution.* Boulder, CO: Westview Press.

Pierson, Paul. 1996. "The New Politics of the Welfare State." *World Politics* 48(2): 143–79.

Policzer, Pablo. 2009. *The Rise and Fall of Repression in Chile.* 1st ed. Notre Dame, IN: University of Notre Dame Press.

Pomfret, James. 2009. "Ethnic Tensions Spark Brawl at China Factory-Report." *Reuters,* 27 June. http://www.reuters.com/article/2009/06/27/idUSHKG364598.

Powell, Bill. 2009. "China's Banks Become the Government's Foot Soldiers." *Time,* 23 March. http://www.time.com/time/world/article/0,8599,1887078,00.html.

"Probe into Death in Custody Leaves Many Stones Unturned | South China Morning Post." 2013. http://www.scmp.com/article/415436/probe-death-custody-leaves-many-stones-unturned.

Pryor, Frederic L. 1992. *The Red and the Green: The Rise and Fall of Collectivized Agriculture in Marxist Regimes*. Princeton: Princeton University Press.

Przeworski, Adam, Michael E. Alvarez, Jose Antonio Cheibub, and Fernando Limongi. 2000. *Democracy and Development: Political Institutions and Well-Being in the World, 1950-1990*. Cambridge: Cambridge University Press.

Putterman, L. 1993. *Continuity and Change in China's Rural Development: Collective and Reform Eras in Perspective*. New York: Oxford University Press.

"Q&A: Tunisia Crisis." 2011. *BBC*, 19 January 19, sec. Africa. http://www.bbc.co.uk/news/world-africa-12157599.

"Quarterly Chronicle and Documentation." 1989. *The China Quarterly* 120: 893–946.

Radio Free Asia. 2008a. "河南焦作市周一连续发生两起工人集体堵路抗议事件." 7 October. http://www.rfa.org/mandarin/yataibaodao/dulu-10072008135605.html.

—— 2008b. "深圳纸厂劳工示威与警冲突 劳动仲裁不保赔偿." 13 November. http://www.rfa.org/mandarin/yataibaodao/shenzhen-11132008090741.html.

Ramo, Joshua Cooper. 2004. *The Beijing Consensus*. London: Foreign Policy Centre.

Ramzy, Austin. 2009. "In China's Lending Boom, Small Businesses Go Begging." *Time*, 15 July. http://www.time.com/time/world/article/0,8599,1910514,00.html.

Rao, J. Mohan. 1986. "Agriculture in Recent Development Theory." *Journal of Development Economics* 22(1) (June): 41–86.

Ravallion, Martin, and Shaohua Chen. 2007. "China's (uneven) Progress against Poverty." *Journal of Development Economics* 82(1): 1–42.

Riskin, Carl. 1994. "Chinese Rural Poverty: Marginalized or Dispersed?" *American Economic Review* 84(2): 281–84.

Roberts, Dexter. 2000. "China's Wealth Gap." *Business Week*, 8 May. http://www.businessweek.com/2000/00_19/b3680011.htm.

Ross, Michael L. 2006. "Is Democracy Good for the Poor?" *American Journal of Political Science* 50(4): 860–74.

——. 2012. *The Oil Curse: How Petroleum Wealth Shapes the Development of Nations*. Princeton: Princeton University Press.

Rousseau, Jean-Jacques. 1997. *Rousseau: "The Social Contract" and Other Later Political Writings*. Cambridge: Cambridge University Press.

Rudra, N., and S. Haggard. 2005. "Globalization, Democracy, and Effective Welfare Spending in the Developing World." *Comparative Political Studies* 38(9): 1015–49.

Ryssdal, Kai, and Djavad Salehi-Isfahani. 2009. "Effect of Iran's Politics on Its Economy." *Marketplace.org*. 30 June. http://ssl.marketplace.org/topics/world/effect-irans-politics-its-economy.

Salehyan, Idean, and Cullen Hendrix. 2011. "Social Conflict in Africa Database (SCAD)." www.scaddata.org.

Schapiro, Leonard, and John W. Lewis. 1969. "The Roles of the Monolithic Party under the Totalitarian Leader." *China Quarterly* 40: 39–64.

Scharping, Thomas, and Kam Wing Chan. 1987. "Urbanization in China since 1949." *China Quarterly* 109: 101–9.

Schedler, Andreas. 2012. "The Measurer's Dilemma Coordination Failures in Cross-National Political Data Collection." *Comparative Political Studies* 45(2) (February): 237–66.

Schraeder, Peter J., and Hamadi Redissi. 2011. "Ben Ali's Fall." *Journal of Democracy* 22(3): 5–19.

Schultz, Theodore W. 1978a. "On Economics and Politics of Agriculture." *Bulletin of the American Academy of Arts and Sciences* 32(2): 10–31.

——, ed. 1978b. *Distortions of Agricultural Incentives*. Bloomington: Indiana University Press.

Schuman, Michael. 2008. "China's Booming Car Market Shifts into Reverse." *Time*, 11 December. http://www.time.com/time/world/article/0,8599,1865811,00.html.

Schurmann, Franz. 1966. *Ideology and Organization in Communist China*. Berkeley and Los Angeles: University of California Press.

Scott, James C. 1998. *Seeing Like a State: How Certain Schemes to Improve the Human Condition Have Failed*. New Haven: Yale University Press.

——. 2010. *The Art of Not Being Governed: An Anarchist History of Upland Southeast Asia*. New Haven: Yale University Press.

"Seeking Answers to a Death in Detention | South China Morning Post." 2013. http://www.scmp. com/article/414190/seeking-answers-death-detention.

Sekhon, Jasjeet S. 2009. "Opiates for the Matches: Matching Methods for Causal Inference." *Annual Review of Political Science* 12: 487–508.

Selden, Mark. 1993. *The Political Economy of Chinese Development*. Armonk, NY: M. E. Sharpe.

Sen, Amartya Kumar. 1999. "Democracy as a Universal Value." *Journal of Democracy* 10(3): 3–17.

Shambaugh, David. 1993. "Deng Xiaoping: The Politician." *China Quarterly* 135 (September): 457–90.

Shenzhen Daily. 2009. "Wages Fall for First Time in Decade." *ShenZhen Government Online*. 22 July. http://english.sz.gov.cn/ln/200907/t20090723_1154681.htm.

Sheridan, Michael. 2009. "Violent Unrest Rocks China as Crisis Hits—Times Online." *The Sunday Times*, 1 February. http://business.timesonline.co.uk/tol/business/economics/article5627687.ece.

Shih, Victor, and Zhang Qi. 2007. "Who Receives Subsidies? A Look at the County Level in Two Time Periods." In *Paying for Progress in China*, edited by Vivienne Shue and Christine Wong. London: Routledge.

Shirk, Susan L. 1993. *The Political Logic of Economic Reform in China*. California Series on Social Choice and Political Economy. Berkeley and Los Angeles: University of California Press.

——. 2008. *China: Fragile Superpower*. New York: Oxford University Press.

Shue, Vivienne. 2002. "Global Imaginings, the State's Quest for Hegemony, and the Pursuit of Phantom Freedom in China." In *Globalization and Democratization in Asia: The Construction of Identity*, edited by Kristina Jonsson and Catarina Kinnvall. New York: Routledge.

Siegel, David A. 2009. "Social Networks and Collective Action." *American Journal of Political Science* 53(1) (January): 122–38.

Sina. 2013. "中小企业应对经济降温_财经_新浪网." http://finance.sina.com.cn/focus1/zxqydjw/index.shtml.

Skilling, H. Gordon. 1966. "Interest Groups and Communist Politics." *World Politics* 18(3): 435–51.

Slater, Dan. 2010. *Ordering Power: Contentious Politics and Authoritarian Leviathans in Southeast Asia*. Cambridge: Cambridge University Press.

Smith, Graeme. 2009. "Political Machinations in a Rural County." *China Journal* 62: 29–59.

Solinger, Dorothy. 1995. "The Floating Population in the Cities: Chances for Assimilation?" In *Urban Spaces in Contemporary China: The Potential for Autonomy and Community in Post-Mao China*, edited by Deborah S. Davis, Richard Kraus, Barry Naughton, and Elizabeth J. Perry. Cambridge: Cambridge University Press.

——. 1999a. *Contesting Citizenship in Urban China: Peasant Migrants, the State, and the Logic of the Market*. Berkeley and Los Angeles: University of California Press.

——. 1999b. "China's Floating Population." In *The Paradox of China's Post-Mao Reforms*, edited by Merle Goldman and Roderick MacFarquhar. Cambridge, MA: Harvard University Press.

——. 2001. "Research Report: Why We Cannot Count the 'Unemployed.'" *China Quarterly* 167: 671.

Soong, Ronald. 2006. "Statistics of Mass Incidents." *EastSouthWestNorth*. 15 November. http://www.zonaeuropa.com/20061115_1.htm.

Spence, Jonathan D. 1999. *The Search for Modern China*. 2nd ed. New York: W. W. Norton & Company.

Staniland, Paul. 2010. "Cities on Fire: Social Mobilization, State Policy, and Urban Insurgency." *Comparative Political Studies* 43(12) (December): 1623–49.

Stasavage, David. 2005. "Democracy and Education Spending in Africa." *American Journal of Political Science* 49(2): 343–58.

State Council. 1997. "国务院批转公安部小城镇户籍管理制度改革试点方案." http://www.people.com.cn/item/flfgk/gwyfg/1997/112901199705.html.

Stavis, Benedict. 1978. *The Politics of Agricultural Mechanization in China*. Ithaca, NY: Cornell University Press.

Steiner, H. Arthur. 1950. "Chinese Communist Urban Policy." *American Political Science Review* 44(1) (March): 47–63.

Stokes, Susan C. 2005. "Perverse Accountability: A Formal Model of Machine Politics with Evidence from Argentina." *American Political Science Review* 99(3): 315–25.

Strand, David. 1995. "Conclusion: Historical Perspectives." In *Urban Spaces in Contemporary China: The Potential for Autonomy and Community in Post-Mao China*, edited by Deborah S. Davis, Richard Kraus, Barry Naughton, and Elizabeth J. Perry. Cambridge: Cambridge University Press.

Svolik, Milan W. 2012. *The Politics of Authoritarian Rule*. Cambridge: Cambridge University Press.

Taylor, Lance. 1983. *Structuralist Macroeconomics: Applicable Models for the Third World*. New York: Basic Books.

Teiwes, Frederick C. 1995. "Mao Texts and the Mao of the 1950s." *Australian Journal of Chinese Affairs* 33 (January): 127–49.

"The Sinocism China Newsletter for 03.04.13." 2013. *The Sinocism China Newsletter*. https://sinocism.com/?p=8683.

Thornton, Patricia M. 2010. "From Liberating Production to Unleashing Consumption: Mapping Landscapes of Power in Beijing." *Political Geography* 29(6): 302–10.

Thurston, Anne. 1987. *Enemies of the People*. New York: Knopf.

——. 1990. "Urban Violence during the Cultural Revolution: Who Is to Blame." In *Violence in China : Essays in Culture and Counterculture*, edited by Jonathan Neaman Lipman and Stevan Harrell. Albany: State University of New York Press.

Tian, Bingxin. 2003. *China's No. 1 Document (Zhongguo Diyi Zhengjian)*. Huizhou: Guangdong People's Press.

Tian, Ye, and Jipeng Ma. 2008. "民工'退保潮' 考验中国社保体制." *ACFTU Worker's News*. February 28. http://acftu.people.com.cn/GB/6934125.html.

Tibaijuka, Anna. 2005. "Report of the Fact-Finding Mission to Zimbabwe to Assess the Scope and Impact of Operation Murambatsvina."

Tien, H. Yuan. 1973. *China's Population Struggle: Demographic Decisions of the People's Republic, 1949–1969*. Columbus: Ohio State University Press.

Tiewes, Frederick C. 1997. "The Establishment and Consolidation of the New Regime, 1949-1957." In *The Politics of China: The Eras of Mao and Deng*, edited by Roderick MacFarquhar, 2nd ed. Cambridge: Cambridge University Press.

Tilly, Charles. 1978. *From Mobilization to Revolution*. Reading, MA: Addison-Wesley Pub. Co.

Timmer, C. Peter. 1988. "The Agricultural Transformation." In *Handbook of Development Economics*, Vol. 1, edited by Hollis Burnley Chenery, T. N. Srinivasan, and Jere Richard Behrman. New York: Elsevier.

——. 2005. "Agriculture and pro-Poor Growth: An Asian Perspective." *Available at SSRN 984256*. http://papers.ssrn.com/sol3/papers.cfm?abstract_id=984256.

Tobler, Waldo R. 1970. "A Computer Movie Simulating Urban Growth in the Detroit Region." *Economic Geography* 46: 234–40.

Tong, Sarah Y. 2012. "Global Crisis and China's Trade Adjustment." In *The Global Recession and China's Political Economy*, edited by Dali L. Yang. New York: Palgrave Macmillan.

Torpey, John. 1997. "Revolutions and Freedom of Movement: An Analysis of Passport Controls in the French, Russian, and Chinese Revolutions." *Theory and Society* 26(6): 837–68.

Treisman, Daniel. 1999. *After the Deluge Regional Crises and Political Consolidation in Russia*. Ann Arbor: University of Michigan Press.

Tsai, Lily L. 2007. *Accountability Without Democracy: Solidary Groups and Public Goods Provision in Rural China*. Cambridge: Cambridge University Press.

Tucker, Robert C. 1961. "Towards a Comparative Politics of Movement-Regimes." *American Political Science Review* 55(2): 281–89.

Twitchett, Denis, and Michael Loewe, eds. 1986. *The Cambridge History of China*. Vol. 1, *The Ch'in and Han Empires, 221 BC-AD 220*. 1st ed. Cambridge: Cambridge University Press.
UN DESA. 2010. "World Urbanization Prospects. The 2009 Revision." Population Division, United Nations Department of Economic and Social Affairs (UN DESA), New York, NY, USA.
UN Habitat. 2012. *State of the World's Cities 2012-2013*. New York: Routledge.
Unger, Jonathan. 2002. *The Transformation of Rural China*. Armonk, NY: M. E. Sharpe.
Urdal, Henrik. 2008. "Urban Social Disturbance in Asia and Africa: Report on a New Dataset, PRIO Papers."
Varshney, Ashutosh, ed. 1993. *Beyond Urban Bias*. Portland, OR: Frank Cass.
——. 1995. *Democracy, Development, and the Countryside: Urban-Rural Struggles in India*. Cambridge: Cambridge University Press.
Vogel, Ezra. 1971. "Preserving Order in the Cities." In *The City in Communist China*, edited by John Wilson Lewis and Jerome Alan Cohen. Stanford, CA: Stanford University Press.
Voice of America. 2011. "Tunisian Government: 14 Killed as Rioting Continues." *VOA*. 8 January. http://www.voanews.com/content/article-11-killed-in-tunisia-protests-113162684/133295.html.
Walder, Andrew G. 2002. "Beijing Red Guard Factionalism: Social Interpretations Reconsidered." *Journal of Asian Studies* 61(2): 437–71.
——. 2009. *Fractured Rebellion: The Beijing Red Guard Movement*. Cambridge, MA: Harvard University Press.
Wallace, Jeremy L. 2013. "Cities, Redistribution, and Authoritarian Regime Survival." *Journal of Politics* 75(3): 632–45.
——. "Juking the Stats? Authoritarian Information Problems in China." *British Journal of Political Science*. Forthcoming.
Wang, Dazhong, ed. 2006. 透视流动人口中的犯罪现象 (*Toushi Liudong Renkou Zhongde Fanzui Xianxiang*). Beijing: Zhongguo Renmin Gongan Daxue Chubanshe (People's Public Security University Press).
Wang, Fei-Ling. 2005. *Organizing through Division and Exclusion: China's Hukou System*. Stanford, CA: Stanford University Press.
Wang, Gabe T., and Xiaobo Hu. 1999. "Small Town Development and Rural Urbanization in China." *Journal of Contemporary Asia* 29(1): 76–94.
Wang, Meiyan, and Fang Cai. 2008. "Experiences and Perspectives of Hukou System Reform (户籍制度改革的历程与展望)." In *Reports on China's Population and Labor* (中国人口与劳动问题报告), edited by Fang Cai. Beijing: Shehui Kexue Wenxian Chubanshe.
Wang, Shaoguang. 2004. "For National Unity: The Political Logic of Fiscal Transfer in China." In *Nationalism, Democracy and National Integration in China*, edited by Leong Liew and Wang Shaoguang. London: RoutledgeCurzon.
Wang, Xu. 2009. "Exporters Get Sops to Fight Crisis." *China Daily*, June 9. http://www.chinadaily.com.cn/china/2009-06/09/content_8261379.htm.
Wang, Zhuoqiong, and Liming Zhou. 2006. "Hukou Blamed for Compensation Discrepancy." *China Daily*, January 27.
Watts, Jonathan. 2009. "Old Suspicions Magnified Mistrust into Ethnic Riots in Urumqi." *The Guardian*, 10 July. http://www.guardian.co.uk/world/2009/jul/10/china-riots-uighurs-han-urumqi.
Wedeen, Lisa. 2013. "Ideology and Humor in Dark Times: Notes from Syria." *Critical Inquiry* 39 (Summer 2013): 841–73.
Weeks, Jessica L. 2008. "Autocratic Audience Costs: Regime Type and Signaling Resolve." *International Organization* 62(1): 35–64.
Wehrey, Frederic. 2013. "Eastern Promises." *Carnegie Endowment for International Peace*. 12 February. http://carnegieendowment.org/sada/2013/02/12/eastern-promises/ffn3.
Weingast, Barry R., Yingyi Qian, and Gabriella Montinola. 1995. "Federalism, Chinese Style: The Political Basis for Economic Success in China." *World Politics* 48(1): 50–81.

Weiss, Jessica C. 2013. "Authoritarian Signaling, Mass Audiences, and Nationalist Protest in China." *International Organization* 67(1): 1–35.

———. 2014. *Powerful Patriots: Nationalist Protest in China's Foreign Relations.* New York: Oxford University Press.

Wemheuer, Felix. 2014. *Famine Politics in Maoist China and the Soviet Union.* New Haven: Yale University Press.

Wen, Jiabao. 2004. "Excerpts from the Report on the Work of the Government by Chinese Premier Wen Jiabao, 5 March 2004." *China Report* 40(3) (August): 331–43.

———. 2006. "Government Work Report." In *Delivered at the National People's Congress Meeting.* Vol. 5.

———. 2009. "Full Text of Chinese Premier Wen Jiabao's Speech at 2009 Summer Davos in Dalian." 11 September. http://english.gov.cn/2009-09/11/content_1414917.htm.

Wen, Tiejun. 2006. "The Three Rural Problems Local Reasoning." "三农"问题的本土化思路. http://www.eeo.com.cn/observer/eeo_special/2006/09/08/44963.shtml.

White, Lynn T. 1978. *Careers in Shanghai: The Social Guidance of Personal Energies in a Developing Chinese City, 1949-1966.* Berkeley and Los Angeles: University of California Press.

———. 2009. "Chinese Political Studies: Overview of the State of the Field." *Journal of Chinese Political Science* 14(3) (September): 229–51.

Whiting, Susan H. 2000. *Power and Wealth in Rural China: The Political Economy of Institutional Change.* Cambridge: Cambridge University Press.

Wines, Michael. 2005. "In Zimbabwe, Homeless Belie Leader's Claim." *New York Times,* 13 November, sec. International / Africa. http://www.nytimes.com/2005/11/13/international/africa/13zimbabwe.html.

Wong, Christine. 1991. "Central–Local Relations in an Era of Fiscal Decline: The Paradox of Fiscal Decentralization in Post-Mao China." *China Quarterly* 128: 691–715.

———. 2002. "China: National Development and Sub-National Finance". The World Bank.

———. 2005. *Can China Change Development Paradigm for the 21st Century? Fiscal Policy Options for Hu Jintao and Wen Jiabao after Two Decades of Muddling through.* Unpublished manuscript.

Wong, Christine, Christopher John Heady, and Wing Thye Woo. 1995. *Fiscal Management and Economic Reform in the People's Republic of China.* New York: Oxford University Press.

Wong, Edward. 2008. "Factories Shut, China Workers Are Suffering." *New York Times,* 14 November. http://www.nytimes.com/2008/11/14/world/asia/14china.html?hp=&pagewanted=all.

———. 2009. "Riots in Western China Amid Ethnic Tension." *New York Times,* 6 July, sec. International / Asia Pacific. http://www.nytimes.com/2009/07/06/world/asia/06china.html.

Wong, Jan. 1996. *Red China Blues.* Sydney: Doubleday.

Wong, Kam C. 2009. *Chinese Policing: History and Reform.* New York: Peter Lang Publishing.

Wong, Roy Bin. 1997. *China Transformed Historical Change and the Limits of European Experience.* Ithaca, NY: Cornell University Press.

World Bank. 2012. *China 2030: Building a Modern Harmonious and Creative High Income Society.* Washington, DC: World Bank Publications.

Wright, J. 2008. "Do Authoritarian Institutions Constrain? How Legislatures Impact Economic Growth and Foreign Aid Effectiveness." *American Journal of Political Science* 52(2): 322–43.

Wright, Joseph. 2011. "Electoral Spending Cycles in Dictatorships." Unpublished manuscript.

Wu, Yu-Shan. 1994. *Comparative Economic Transformations: Mainland China, Hungary, the Soviet Union, and Taiwan.* Stanford, CA: Stanford University Press.

Xiao, J. 2002. "Rural Economic Situation in the First Half of 2002 and Outlook for the Whole Year." *China Development Review* 4(4): 47–60.

Xinhua. 2005. "China to Promote Rural Cooperative Medical System", 11 August.

———. 2008. "温家宝主持国务院常务会　确定扩大内需十项措施_高层动态_新华网." 9 November. http://news.xinhuanet.com/newscenter/2008-11/09/content_10331258_1.htm.

———. 2009. "Development and Progress in Xinjiang." 21 September. http://news.xinhuanet.com/english/2009-09/21/content_12090477_8.htm.

———. 2010. "China to Set up First National Industrial Transfer Zone." *China Daily*, 22 January. http://www.chinadaily.com.cn/business/2010-01/22/content_9363376.htm.

Xinhua Net. 2009. "联合国报告预计到2010年全球失业人口达5千万人." 28 May. http://www.china.com.cn/news/txt/2009-05/28/content_17847417.htm.

Xinjingbao. 2010. "市人大建议缩减低端劳动力." *Xinjingbao*, August 3.

Xu, Feng. 2008. "Gated Communities and Migrant Enclaves: The Conundrum for Building 'harmonious Community/shequ.'" *Journal of Contemporary China* 17(57): 633–51.

Xu, Yingfeng. 1999. "Agricultural Productivity in China." *China Economic Review* 10(2): 108–21.

Yan, Yuanyuan, Linxiu Zhang, H. Holly Wang, and Scott Rozelle. 2006. *Insuring Rural China's Health? An Empirical Analysis of China's New Cooperative Medical System*. Unpublished manuscript.

Yang, Dali. 1990. "Patterns of China's Regional Development Strategy." *China Quarterly* 122: 230–57.

———. 1991. "China Adjusts to the World Economy: The Political Economy of China's Coastal Development Strategy." *Pacific Affairs* 64(1): 42–64.

———. 2001. "Rationalizing the Chinese State: The Political Economy of Government Reform." In *Remaking the Chinese State: Strategies, Society, and Security*, edited by Jianmin Zhao and Bruce J. Dickson. London: Routledge.

———. 2002. "China in 2001: Economic Liberalization and Its Political Discontents." *Asian Survey* 42(1) (February): 14–28.

———. 2004a. "Economic Transformation and State Rebuilding in China." In *Holding China Together Diversity and National Integration in the Post-Deng Era*, edited by Barry Naughton and Dali Yang. Cambridge: Cambridge University Press.

———.2004b. *Remaking the Chinese Leviathan: Market Transition and the Politics of Governance in China*. Stanford, CA: Stanford University Press.

Yang, Fenglu. 2002. "Housing Registration System Reform: Cost & Benefits (户籍制度改革: 成本与收益)." *Economist (经济学家)* (2).

Yang, Jisheng. 2012. *Tombstone: The Great Chinese Famine, 1958-1962*. Edited by Edward Friedman, Stacy Mosher, and Jian Guo. Translated by Stacy Mosher and Jian Guo. New York: Farrar, Straus and Giroux.

Yang, Rae. 1998. *Spider Eaters: A Memoir*. Reprint. Berkeley and Los Angeles: University of California Press.

Yangchengwanbao. 2008. "广东15661家中小企业倒闭　称未出现'倒闭潮'-搜狐财经." 羊城晚报, 17 December. http://business.sohu.com/20081217/n261268992.shtml.

Yep, Ray. 2004. "Can 'Tax-for-Fee' Reform Reduce Rural Tension in China? The Process, Progress, and Limitations." *China Quarterly* 177: 42–70.

Young, Alwyn. 2010. "The African Growth Miracle." Manuscript. http://citeseerx.ist.psu.edu/viewdoc/summary?doi=10.1.1.186.3146.

Yüeh, Tai-yün, and Carolyn Wakeman. 1985. *To the Storm: The Odyssey of a Revolutionary Chinese Woman*. Berkeley and Los Angeles: University of California Press.

Yusuf, Shahid, and Kaoru Nabeshima. 2008. "Optimizing Urban Development." In *China Urbanizes: Consequences, Strategies and Policies*, edited by Shahid Yusuf and Tony Saich. Washington, DC: World Bank Publications.

Zeldin, Wendy. 2003. "CHINA-Forced Detention and Repatriation System Abolished." *World Law Bulletin*, July. http://www.fas.org/sgp/othergov/wlb/200307.pdf.

Zhai, Ivan. 2008. "Guangdong Targets SMEs in 10b Yuan Programme." *South China Morning Post*, 6 December. http://www.scmp.com/article/662820/guangdong-targets-smes-10b-yuan-programme.

Zhai, Ivan, and Paggie Leung. 2008. "Workers Seeking Back Pay Keep up Protest against Toymaker." *South China Morning Post*, 18 October. http://www.scmp.com/article/656713/workers-seeking-back-pay-keep-protest-against-toymaker.

Zhang, Liang, Andrew J. Nathan, and Perry Link, eds. 2002. *The Tiananmen Papers*. New York: PublicAffairs.

Zhang, Linxiu, Renfu Luo, Chengfang Liu, and Scott Rozelle. 2006. "Investing in Rural China: Tracking China's Commitment to Modernization." *Chinese Economy* 39(4): 57–84.

Zhang, Xing Quan. 1997. "Chinese Housing Policy 1949-1978: The Development of a Welfare System." *Planning Perspectives* 12(4): 433–55.

Zhao, Dingxin. 2001a. "China's Prolonged Stability and Political Future: Same Political System, Different Policies and Methods." *Journal of Contemporary China* 10(28): 427–44.

———. 2001b. *The Power of Tiananmen: State-Society Relations and the 1989 Beijing Student Movement*. Chicago: University of Chicago Press.

Zhao, Gang. 1986. *Man and Land in Chinese History: An Economic Analysis*. Stanford, CA: Stanford University Press.

Zhong, Wu. 2008. "Regions Won't Dance to Beijing's Tune." *Asia Times Online*, 26 November. http://www.atimes.com/atimes/China/JK26Ad01.html.

Zhongguo Tongji Nianjian (China Statistical Yearbook). Various Years. Beijing: Zhongguo Tongji Chubanshe.

Zipf, George Kingsley. 1941. *National Unity and Disunity. The Nation as a Bio-Social Organism*. Principia Press.

———. 1949. *Human Behavior and the Principle of Least Effort: An Introduction to Human Ecology*. Addison-Wesley Publishing.

Zweig, David. 1986. "Prosperity and Conflict in Post-Mao Rural China." *China Quarterly* 105 (March): 1–18.

中华人民共和国国务院.　　1983.　　"劳动人事部关于积极试行劳动合同制的通知." 中华人民共和国国务院公报 (6): 213–15.

中国劳工通讯. 2009. "中国工人运动观察报告 (2007–2008)."

"中国第十二个五年规划纲要 (全文)-搜狐新闻." 2013. http://news.sohu.com/20110316/n279851018.shtml.

中国西部开发网. 2013. "Develop the West Campaign Map." http://www.chinawest.gov.cn/web/Column1.asp?ColumnId=6.

"中華人民共和國戶口登記條例."　　1958.　　http://www.wanfangdata.com/wf/~laws/GJFL/1001AB/g100000690.htm.

刘建民, and 欧阳煌. 2000. "费改税: 农村公共分配关系改革的突破口." 农业经济问题 21(2): 34–39.

南方都市报.　　2008.　　"东莞玩具业面临寒冬　　樟木头最大玩具厂合俊玩具倒闭." *Nanfangdushibao*, 16 October. http://news.southcn.com/dishi/zsj/content/2008-10/16/content_4649902.htm.

博讯新闻. 2011. "中国茉莉花集会组织者致全国人民公开信." 博讯新闻（临时网站）. 22 February. http://www.boxunblog.com/2011/02/blog-post_7256.html.

大众日报.　　2008.　　"姜大明: 加快推进事关山东长远发展的项目建设." 大众日报, 12 November. http://www.gov.cn/gzdt/2008-11/12/content_1146573.htm.

"崔永元等致信教育部长 呼吁保留农民工子弟校-搜狐教育." 2013. http://learning.sohu.com/20120727/n349165431.shtml.

广东省人民政府.　　2005.　　"关于我省山区及东西两翼与珠江三角洲联手推进产业转移的意见（试行）." 广东省人民政府.　7　March.　http://zwgk.gd.gov.cn/006939748/200909/t20090915_8897.html.

广州日报.　　2008.　　"前5月珠三角近一半出口鞋企因汇率变化退出市场_产经动态_新浪财经_新浪网." *Sina Finance*. 30 June. http://finance.sina.com.cn/chanjing/b/20080630/08245035968.shtml.

新浪网 2008. "解读宏观调控政策新举措_后深意" 12 August. http://finance.sina.com.cn/review/20080812/14575191792.shtml.

新华网. 2008. "央行调增地方商行信贷规模10%救急中小企业." 5 August. http://finance.sina.com.cn/g/20080805/03405166413.shtml.

朱守银. 1998. "农业税费制度改革试验研究报告." 管理世界 2: 48.

"李克强论城镇化." 2013. http://www.21cbh.com/HTML/2013-3-2/5MNjUxXzYzMDE 5MA.html.

杨春南, and 杨霞. 2008. "广东决定用500亿元推动产业和劳动力'双转移.'" 新华网. 29 May. http://news.xinhuanet.com/newscenter/2008-05/29/content_8278993.htm.

"江苏省突发公共事件总体应急预案." 2006. *Www.gov.cn.* March 22. http://www.gov.cn/yjgl/2006-03/22/content_233536.htm.

"被收容者孙志刚之死_深度_南都网." 2003. 25 April. http://ndnews.oeeee.com/html/201302/28/26725.html.

赵戎. 2001. "北京丰台将取缔打工子弟小学 这些孩子何去何从？." 北京晨报, 6 September. http://edu.sina.com.cn/l/2001-09-06/15568.html.

长江商报. 2008. "6.7万家中小企业倒闭 发改委拟建中小企业银行." 5 August. http://finance.sina.com.cn/roll/20080805/08372361106.shtml.

饶漱石. 1950. "Fensui diren fengsuo, wei jianshe xin Shanghai er douzheng [Smash the enemy's blockade and struggle for the development of new Shanghai]." In *Shanghai jie fang yi nian: 1949 nein 5 yue zhi 1950 nian 5 yue*, edited by Jie fang ri bao she. Shanghai: Jie fang ri bao she.

INDEX

CPSIA information can be obtained at www.ICGtesting.com
Printed in the USA
BVOW04s0848270315

393602BV00001B/2/P